JESUS CHRIST THE DIVINE MAN:

HIS LIFE AND TIMES.

BY

J. F. VALLINGS, M.A.,

VICAR OF SOPLEY, HON. FELLOW, SOMETIME SUBWARDEN OF ST. AUGUSTINE'S COLLEGE, CANTERBURY.

WIPF & STOCK · Eugene, Oregon

Wipf and Stock Publishers
199 W 8th Ave, Suite 3
Eugene, OR 97401

Jesus Christ the Divine Man
His Life and Times
By Vallings, J. F.
Softcover ISBN-13: 978-1-7252-9771-5
Hardcover ISBN-13: 978-1-7252-9770-8
eBook ISBN-13: 978-1-7252-9772-2
Publication date 1/19/2021
Previously published by
Anson D. F. Randolph and Company, 1889

This edition is a scanned facsimile of
the original edition published in 1889.

PREFACE.

If any apology be needed for adding another to the various lives of Christ already before the public, it may be well to state how far this little book occupies any independent ground of its own. The object of the writer has been to make some small contribution to the moral and spiritual history of the Life of lives, and this in some especial relation to missionary work and the contact of Christianity with non-Christian religions. "The ethical," as Prof Kuenen well says, "is the universal human" Ethical and spiritual sequences of cause and effect have been especially before the writer's mind. The Gospel history is "a history, which in every part of it," as Weiss says, "must be considered in the light of Him who transcends all history" The superhistorical relations of the historical life have been touched upon in some of their bearings upon the past, present, and future of Christianity Even Keim, from whose point of view the present writer wholly differs, while gladly acknowledging his great ability and learning, and not infrequent reverence of tone and enthusiasm of humanity, affirms of Christ's life that it is "bounded at its circumference by the human limitations of His age, in its centre exalted above all." Such language may imply nothing but hero worship, but it is at all events a recognition of the incomparable grandeur of Christ's life and character.

While the moral and spiritual aspects of the Life have been placed in the foreground, every effort has been made to present the physical and social environment briefly, yet accurately, in the light of modern research. In this connection the archæological and geographical labours of the Palestine Exploration Society have been largely drawn upon, and the most recent records of travel, especially those of Captain Conder, Mr Lawrence Oliphant, and Dr. Selah Merrill.

Upon the whole, the greatest obligations are due to Dr. Edersheim. His wealth of Rabbinical lore, his great theological erudition, his deep sympathy with Israel, springing from the strongest of all sources, the fountain of blood relationship, and his true spirituality of touch, place his work, in the writer's estimate, at the head of all the contemporary literature of the subject. Keim's merits are great intellectually, but it is impossible for him to sink the negative critic, and to help rewriting, mutilating, and

PREFACE.

disintegrating the Gospels. Weiss is not free from the same tendency, but in the main is on the positive side. His psychological and critical powers are high.

Mr. Stanton's book on the Jewish and Christian Messiah is one which deserves more than passing notice. It is the outcome of very patient, fair-minded study of the pre-Messianic and the Messianic period In the interests of apology, and from the earnest desire to give the naturalistic school full justice, he seems to err sometimes in the direction of concession. His estimate of the Talmudic evidence tends to excessive minimizing of its value. Dr. Liddon's Bampton Lectures are too well known to need mention, and are beyond praise. Emil Schurer's work on "The Jewish People in the Time of Jesus Christ" is a deep well of erudition, from which all students of the period must draw. The book is, however, indebted to many other writers from very different, and sometimes quite contradictory, theological schools. Direct quotations are acknowledged in the notes.

In regard to the position taken towards naturalistic and negative critics, and in all debateable ground, it may be as well to state that controversial points have not been argumentatively treated. First, because the spiritual unity, and even the dramatic interest, of the Life is encroached upon. Secondly, because the space required would be much greater. There is however no wish to evade difficulties. They are often met indirectly and suggestively. Conclusions are often stated without elaborate proofs, as the result of carefully formulated opinion, and of some labour. Scholars know where to look for the pros and cons of debateable questions. The general reader satisfies himself with the results of technical investigation. The writer cannot pretend to treat the Divinity of Christ as an open question He writes as an humble adorer, and most unworthy disciple. The four Gospels throughout are treated as trustworthy historical documents The question of their origin, their genuineness, and authenticity, is one far too large to be opened here, and may safely be left by all English Christian apologists in the hands of Drs. Westcott, Hort, Salmon, Scrivener, and Sanday.

Jesus Christ, to the writer, is the Ideal Man, the supreme ethical Term and spiritual Superlative, the Representative Man, the Divine Man, God over all, blessed for ever. To treat His earthly life in its organic spiritual unity and moral relations has been in some degree attempted. May the Blessed One bless the attempt !

CONTENTS.

CHAPTER I.

THE DESIRE OF ALL NATIONS 1
PAGE

The life of Jesus the earthly manifestation of the Divine life of Jehovah—Historical character of that life upon the basis of the Four Gospels definitely accepted—The doctrine of development historically applied—The *præparatio Evangelica*—The unsatisfied spiritual desires of nations—The Roman unsatisfied by power, the Greek by thought, the Jew by Rabbinism, the Buddhist by Nirvana—The Desire of all nations the fulfilment of unsatisfied spiritual needs, individual, national, and His religion alone universal—Jesus the Universal Ideal and Example, and the universal and only moral dynamic

CHAPTER II.

THE MESSIANIC HOPE WITHIN THE CANON 9

Divine differentiation selecting from the woman's seed a nation, a tribe—Typical characters and offices foreshadowing different aspects of the Son of Man—Spiritual and devotional preparation —The Ideal of the Prophets—The King—The Suffering Servant of God—Post-exilian hope—The priestly hope—Minor and relative ideals contribute to the fulness of the complete hope—Unique hope in history—The Divine Man a fulfilment of multitudinous foreshadowings.

CHAPTER III.

THE POST-CANONICAL MESSIANIC HOPE 18

Debased period—Hope persistent—In Apocrypha impersonal and national—In the Apocalypses personal and national—In the Talmud—Rabbinism—Christ's work to re-create and transform as well as fulfil the Messianic Ideal—What might have been.

CHAPTER IV.

THE DIVINE BABE 29

The country priest's home—Zacharias in the Temple—The Angel of promise to the priest—The Angel of promise to the Virgin— The meeting of the holy women—The spiritual songs—The journey to Bethlehem—The holy Nativity—The angelic anthem— The visit of the shepherds

CONTENTS.

CHAPTER V.

THE EPIPHANIES OF THE DIVINE INFANT 38

The Epiphany of the Divine Infant in the Temple — The Epiphany of the Divine Infant to the Gentiles—The flight into Egypt—The return.

CHAPTER VI.

THE DIVINE BOY. THE DIVINE YOUTH 44

Nazareth—Physical environment—Home influence and education—Epiphany of the Divine Boy—The Father's house—The tender Plant—The Divine Young Man—The simple home—Experience of men—Communion with nature—God's silences of preparation.

CHAPTER VII.

THE PROPHET BAPTIST. THE DIVINE BAPTISM 58

John in the Wilderness—The Great Renunciation—The Cry of the Kingdom—The Flow of Penitents—Jesus Baptized—Why?

CHAPTER VIII.

THE DIVINE TEMPTATION 66

Personal Tempter, external and real, not an internal process—First offer—Supposed Buddhist resemblance—Second offer—Third offer—Temptations recurrent—Temptation representative.

CHAPTER IX.

THE LAMB OF GOD. THE DIVINE SON OF MAN AT THE SOCIAL FEAST THE DIVINE REFORMER IN THE HOUSE OF GOD. THE DIVINE AND THE HUMAN RABBI 71

The first disciples—Sense of sin supreme factor—The Lamb of God—The Son of Man—The Cana wedding, its promise—First Messianic passover—The Reformer—The Casuist.

CHAPTER X

THE BAPTIST'S FAREWELL TESTIMONY. THE SAVIOUR AND THE SAMARITANESS. THE NAZARENE 80

Jesus on the Baptist's ground—The Prophet's last testimony—Jesus in Samaria—The Well of Jacob—In Galilee again—In Nazareth again.

CONTENTS.   vii

CHAPTER XI.

THE DIVINE GALILEAN 90

Capernaum—The unknown feast at Jerusalem—Galilee in Christ's time and now—Galilean labours.

CHAPTER XII.

THE DIVINE APOSTLE. THE DIVINE MORALIST 96

The selection of the Twelve—Organization of the Divine society—Organization of the life—Code of the New Kingdom in its past, present, and future relations.

CHAPTER XIII.

THE DIVINE ART TEACHER. THE DIVINE NATURE-WORKER. THE DIVINE MISSIONARY 106

Capernaum—Nain—The Baptist in Machærus—The Saviour and the lost woman—Divine self-assertion—Spiritual industry—Parables of Divine art interpret Nature—Miracle of power over Nature—Demonism—Incessant labours — Mission tours — The martyr of Machærus—The Feeding of the Five Thousand—The Bread of Life—The stormy lake—The contradiction of sinners—Passover retreat—Back to work.

CHAPTER XIV.

THE DIVINE TRANSFIGURATION 123

On the way to Cæsarea Philippi—The Petrine confession—The Rock—The Divine sign—The excellent glory—The descent—The return—The predictions.

CHAPTER XV.

THE ASCENSION JOURNEY. THE DIVINE MISSIONARY IN PERÆA. 131

The days of going up—Peremptory claims--The Feast of Tabernacles—The adulteress—The Light of the World—The Shepherd of Israel—*Pastor pastorum*—Peræan Mission—The seventy missionaries—The Good Samaritan—The devout home scene—The prayer of prayers—Peræan work resumed—The Feast of Dedication— Return to Peræa —Incarnate energy—Missionary Parables—Parables of the Unseen World.

CHAPTER XVI.

GATHERING SHADOWS 148

The resurrection of Lazarus—Back to Peræa—Divorce and marriage—The rights of woman—The rights of children—Behold, we go up to Jerusalem !—Jericho—Zacchæus and the service of man—The blind healed—The pilgrims in debate—The Sabbath rest and unction.

CONTENTS.

CHAPTER XVII.

THE MESSIANIC ENTRY. THE CONTRADICTION OF SINNERS . 160

The Triumphal Entry—The Devil's stand—The Second Temple cleansing—The barren figtree—The "Day of Questions"—The Divine Controversialist—The Divine Apocalypse—Jewish Eschatology.

CHAPTER XVIII.

THE DIVINE SACRIFICE 172

Judas traitor—Wednesday in retreat—The Last Supper—Gethsemane—The arrest—The Divine Prisoner before Annas, before Caiaphas, before Pilate, before Herod—Judas's end—Before Pilate again—Ecce Homo!—Round the Cross—The Seven Words—The Atonement.

CHAPTER XIX.

THE DIVINE SABBATH 187

The marred Body—The Soul free among the dead—Easter Eve.

CHAPTER XX.

THE RESURRECTION AND THE FORTY DAYS 190

The Resurrection—*Magdalena dolorosa*—The Resurrection unexpected, a Divine must be—Emmaus—Appearance to the eleven apostles and other brethren—Differentiation of offices—Doubter Thomas — Messianic critical difficulties — Celsus's objection — Vision hypothesis—Galilee again—The fishers on the sea again—All authority—Undetailed appearances—The great Forty Days—Divine organization—Development of order—Development of faith—Continuity, both of soul and body—The four distinct Evangelic reports.

CHAPTER XXI.

THE ASCENSION AND AFTER 210

CHAPTER XXII.

THE CHARACTER OF CHRIST. CHRIST AS A MORAL AND SPIRITUAL WORKER 214

Miracles morally conditioned—Jesus Christ a spiritual miracle—Strength of right will—His originality, negative and positive—Authoritativeness—Placed humanity upon the throne of the cosmos, and made moral and spiritual interests supreme—Gave a moral ideal, and a moral dynamic—Individualism—Universalism—Women—Children—Practical every-day morality—Consistency — New virtues and graces — Faith — Hope — Love — Humility—Truth—Religion of the Body—Unification of religion and morality—Prayerfulness—Self-assertion of sinlessness.

CHAPTER I.

THE DESIRE OF ALL NATIONS.

"Thirst came upon the worshipper, though he stood in the midst of the waters" (Rig-Veda vii. 89. 4)

Πάσης δὲ τῆς οἰκουμένης ἦσαν (οἱ προφῆται) διδασκάλιον ἱερὸν τῆς περὶ Θεοῦ γνώσεως, καὶ τῆς κατὰ ψυχὴν πολιτείας (ATHANASIUS, "De Incarnatione," xii.).

The life of Jesus the earthly manifestation of the Divine life of Jehovah—Historical character of that life upon the basis of the Four Gospels definitely accepted—The doctrine of development historically applied—The *præparatio Evangelica*—The unsatisfied spiritual desires of nations—The Roman unsatisfied by power, the Greek by thought, the Jew by Rabbinism, the Buddhist by Nirvana—The Desire of all nations the fulfilment of unsatisfied spiritual needs, individual, national , and His religion alone universal—Jesus the Universal Ideal and Example, and the universal and only moral dynamic.

JESUS CHRIST is God over all, Blessed for ever. The earthly life of Jesus was the manifestation in a single province of God's universe of that Divine life which was, and is, and is to be, above and beyond, before and after all the universe, the same yesterday, to-day, and for ever. The life of Jesus Christ is a fragment of a great whole. That whole is the Divine life. eternal, which was seen by men's eyes, heard by men's ears, handled by men's hands for one-third of a century. The study of the earthly life of Christ is the divinely revealed mode of approach to the knowledge, and, through the knowledge, to the possession of the Divine life In the work and teaching of Jesus Christ, the Divine work and teaching were exhibited under the limited conditions of earthly life. The Divine character was translated into earthly forms to be seen and read of all men.

The appearance of Christ amongst men was the greatest event in human history; the relations of God to man and of man to God and of man to man underwent a change. This change was not due to any alterations in the unchangeable character of God, but was the effect of a new approach, long foreshadowed and prefigured on God's side to man. The incarnation of the Son of God introduced to man a new character, a new force, a new example. That character, that force, that example, were the revelation of the Divine under all the varying conditions of human life. The Divine Life stooped down from heaven, humbled itself to the level of its own creatures, submitted to death for its own high purposes. Nature is not conquered but by obedience. The self-humiliation of God is another illustration of the truth of the Baconian epigram. To conquer human nature, to lead it in a willing triumph, the Word became flesh. As the old Fathers have loved again and again to express it, God became man that man might become God. The Divine became human and emptied itself of its glory that the human might be glorified into the Divine.

Reader and writer alike of the life of Jesus Christ do well to remember that every deed and word and thought recorded in the memoirs of Jesus Christ are God's. The contemplation of Christ's life is an act of worship. Worship is the only possible attitude of the soul as it stands before the mystery of the revelation of the eternal God. Here, the absolute and the relative, the infinite and the finite, the unseen and the seen touch hands. The creature can only apprehend and understand the Creator under its own conditions. God has made Himself knowable, intelligible, loveable, by the works of His hands. To impart that knowledge to the creature which is eternal life, to make the children of men children of God. the Son of God became, and continues for ever, the Son of Man. To increase the knowableness of God, Christ manifested Him under directly and immediately knowable conditions

The idea of development is the most important intellectual discovery of nineteenth-century thought. Under the dominion, and sometimes the exclusive tyranny, of this thought, all our historic investigations have been reconsidered. The application of these principles to every department of life and thought is an intellectual necessity. And the Christian welcomes the scientific revelations, wherever and however misunderstood or perverted, as an inspiration from the God of truth.

Read in this light the life of Jesus Christ becomes full of manifold Divine light. All pre-Christian history is seen to be marching from stage to stage to this consummation. All Christian history is seen to be the gradual development of the work of Jesus Christ. The life of Christ is recognized as absolute and unique in itself, but in strict relation to the whole chain of God's eternal purpose. What led up to, and what followed, that life may be regarded as the natural movements of Divine causation, supernaturally born in the bosom of God's thought, and supernaturally conditioned by His will. Then the manifestation of the Christ is viewed as the personal entry of the Divine Being upon a scene long prepared and having before it a long, but unknown, future.

The coming of the Son of Man was not an absolutely isolated event in the history of mankind. There was a long preparation, a continuous development, a gradual differentiation through the ages. Prince after prince, ruler after ruler, prophet after prophet, man of God after man of God, were sent. They were forerunners: they were types: they were links in the chain. They all pointed onwards and prepared the way for the coming Prince, Ruler, Prophet, the Man of God. The gifts, the powers, the excellencies, the glories of all, were to be combined in one. He was to be Crown and Flower as He had been the root of all. All the events in all the ages were marching forward to this culmination. Conscious and unconscious prophecy reached its fulfilment; its partial fulfilment as the earnest of the higher fulfilments to be.

Roman, Greek, and Jewish worlds lay in the shadow of death. The old order was everywhere changing; the birth of the new creation was at hand; the world was sick and weary. Nothing in life could give satisfaction to the human spirit. The cry of the child of Vedic India, "Which of all these gods will hear our cry, and be favourable unto us? Who will come down and deliver us?"[1] was the reverberated wail, or the unexpressed sigh, of an infinite wilderness of hearts.

The Roman conquest had brought into the field of religion a number of competitors, none able to hold the sceptre of

[1] Rig-Veda x. 64 1, quoted by De Pressensé, "The Ancient World and Christianity," p 187.

the strongest. The conquest resulted in a fusion of national gods and religions, a synthesis, not unlike that seen in some of the developments of the Indian Brahmo Samaj. All religions were thus put upon an equally relative footing; and none could claim an absolute sanction. Religions which may be equally true will be equally false, and to such a position thought was actually drifting. The attempt to enforce religion by State policy inevitably tended to destroy any claim to higher than human sanction. "Honour the gods," said the Roman statesman Mæcenas, "according to national custom; and compel others to honour them likewise."[1]

The only god possible to humanity, when all divinities were dethroned, was some anthropomorphic attribute, or combination of attributes. The god of the Roman world was power—his impersonation the Cæsar. He was power and human self-worship incarnate. His name was deified. His apotheosis began to take place in his lifetime. But "permanent and habitual admiration" (according to a modern, but wholly inadequate definition of worship) of embodied power could not satisfy the cravings of the human heart for anything but hero-worship, Still the conception of a Divine Cæsar might have assisted some minds in the Roman world to admit into the shrine of their hearts a Divine man, who claimed to be the incarnation, not of political power only, but of moral and spiritual power, of power over Nature, of power over the heart and conscience, over the temporal destinies of nations, and the eternal destinies of men; and not of power only, which may be worshipped and dreaded, but not loved; but of love, holiness, wisdom, righteousness, which constitute what is loveable as well as what is admirable. A true Roman was prepared to admire Order and Law Incarnate. And the works of Supernatural Order, Law, Power, were just those which were set in the Roman Gospel of Mark for his instruction. The impersonation of Law, Order, Power set upon a new basis, robed in a different uniform, the Imperial purple of His own blood, and wearing a Crown but of thorns, and breathing the new and wholly strange atmosphere of unspeakable love and infinite humility, was the new Divinity who claimed whatever of loyalty, of adoration, of reverence, was left in the debased religion, whose gods were humanised and whose human beings were deified. Here, as

[1] Quoted by Pressensé from Boissier.

always and everywhere, Christ came to recognize, transform, and elevate all pre-existent good, as well as to crush and destroy all pre-existent evil. The disintegration of national divinities resulted in the integration of Cæsar-worship, the actual religion of the Roman world when Christ came to institute a new religion.

The Greeks of the day were merged in the Roman world. The worship of the Greek had been anthropomorphic. Plato indeed had theistic moments. Aristotle had theistic moments. But for both God was a bare abstraction. God was the Thought of Thought, but out of relation, not in relation, to the object of thought. Κινεῖ ὡς ἐρώμενον, not κινεῖ ὡς ἐρῶν ; *i.e.*, He moves the universe as an object of love, not as loving it, as transcending it and out of relation to it. Such a God could only be, and was, to the popular mind a negative quantity, similar to the Brahma of Hinduism.

The real divinity of Greeks was Thought, in its various incarnations of philosophy, art, literature. But even intellectual salvation and mental satisfaction had not been reached, and one inadequate system gave way to another, and left humanity with the whole head sick and the whole heart faint.

On the moral side, Socrates and the Socratic school had created a desire for moral ideals, and so far as ethical systems could gratify the appetite had provided the best of fare. But talking about virtue could never manufacture it. The moral dynamic was wanting, and the concrete impersonation of abstract moralities. Socrates was the nearest approach to the latter. A remarkable passage in the Symposium of Plato indicates that his personality had upon some of his disciples the effect of creating moral self-dissatisfaction, distinct from the mere jealousy of moral or intellectual inferiority. "When we hear any other speaker, even a very good one, his words produce absolutely no effect in comparison. . . . And if I were not afraid that you would think me drunk, I would have sworn as well as spoken to the influence which they have always had and still have over me. . . . I have heard Pericles and other great orators, but this Marsyas has often brought me to such a pass, that I have felt as if I could hardly endure the life which I am leading. . . . For he makes me confess that I ought not to live as I do, neglecting the wants of my own soul, and busying myself with the concerns of the Athenians ; therefore

I hold my ears and tear myself away from him. And he is the only person who ever made me ashamed, which you might think not to be in my nature, and there is no one else who does the same."[1]

If any of the Socratic school did as much as this they did a great deal; they created such a thirst as prompted the question of certain Greeks, " Sir, we would see Jesus," and paved the way for those conversions of proselytes to the Israelites, especially in the dispersion, in the search after a real and righteous God, or from the synagogue of Israel to the Christian Hellenist.

The Jewish world was self-limited, self-centred, and self-absorbed. It was, too, in a state of subjection. How could political degradation but affect the nation, and nullify any extra-national prestige and influence, even if it were claimed? And it was claimed but partially. "Be of the disciples of Aaron (the peaceful); loving peace and pursuing peace; loving the creatures and bringing them nigh to the Thorah"[2]—beautiful words of Hillel's, as Kuenen justly remarks; "but," as he asks rightly, "how, when the theory has to be put into practice, and it appears that this 'Thorah,' with its 'hedge' raised by the Sopherim, and made yet stronger and higher in accordance with the seven rules drawn up by Hillel himself, is inaccessible to the 'creatures' who are to be brought to it?"[3] No, Pharisaism itself, which was the Jewish religion of the day when Christ came. as one says who has done it at least justice (if not, much more than justice), at "its own most flourishing period, proclaims loudly and unmistakably enough its own insufficiency. Within, and still more around it, in the life of the Jewish people, all manner of phenomena might be noted which, to any one capable of observing and fathoming them, could admit of no other interpretation than this."[4]

Judaism left to itself could never ascend to an international, to an universal religion. The best proof of which may be found in modern Judaism, which is the natural development of unchristianized Judaism. Modern Judaism never extends its borders, never makes converts, or tries to.

---

[1] Symposium, 215, 216, Professor Jowett's translation; cf. Trench, "Hulsean Lectures," p. 251.

[2] Pirke Aboth. i. 13.

[3] Kuenen, "National Religions and Universal Religions," Hibbert Lectures, 1882, p 214.   [4] Ibid p. 211.

If neither Greek, nor Roman, nor Jew, could provide an universal, a satisfying religion, we need hardly pursue our investigation far into the Oriental religions. No civilized nation has ever adopted any of these religions, nor could any without denationalizing itself. Whatever truths were in them they had neither vitality nor force to preserve their own believers from falling into the rear of nations. Nor would it require much demonstration to prove that all of them, without exception, had long been on the path of deterioration and decay, even within the limits of their own obedience.[1] One great Oriental religion, that of Islam, destined to play a great part in the world, had not yet appeared in the stream of competition ; and when it did appear, it was " as a side branch of Christianity, or, better still, of Judaism."[2]

Buddhism will be noticed at various points later on. But, as a satisfaction of the desire of all nations, it pronounces its own hopelessness by turning away from the world instead of redeeming it, by expelling desire instead of satisfying it, by pointing to nothingness as the crown of existence, and the consummation of developments. Confucianism again has little room for a doctrine of God. "Whatever of this kind is found in these (*i.e.*, the Shû and the Shîh) exists only in shreds and patches" ;[3] and its worship is carried on representatively only by the Head of the State, unshared by the multitudes of the people.

All religions, all teachers had failed, had vanished in turn. The Roman, the Greek, the Jew, the Oriental, had made their several contributions, positive and negative, to the development of a new faith. The time was come for an universal religion and an universal Person. An Ideal Man was the secret answer to spoken and unspoken needs ; an Ideal Man who should take up, consecrate, and complete all previous moral ideals ; an Ideal Man who should be universal, not fashioned after particularist national idiosyncrasies, who was not a Roman, a Greek, a Jew, an Oriental. He must be a Son of Man.

Nor was an Ideal Man sufficient. He would satisfy the craving for a moral ideal ; but the standard would be as unattainable as ever. Example would be a source and centre of

---

[1] Tàoism is an example after the death of Confucius. Legge, "Religions of China," p. 179.   [2] Kuenen, p. 53.
[3] Legge, "Religions of China," p. 248.

moral attractiveness. But example in itself had been again and again tried and found wanting; and even examples such as Abraham, Moses, Joshua, Buddha, had never raised others to their own level after the image of their life had faded into the dark silence. Power of imitation was required as well as an object to imitate. And this could only be given by one who could communicate the power. Jesus Christ claimed to be the ideal Son of Man, and claimed to give the power to His spiritual children to become the sons of God, His brothers in work, in life, in character, in glory. Jesus claimed to supply moral dynamic; to heal the inveterate, chronic, universal disease of enfeebled will, as well as to supply an absolute and universal standard of character and life.

The Desire of all nations came then to fulfil that desire. He came to raise mankind to the levels of their own ideals, as well as first to transform their ideals. He came, the Son of God, in the uniform language of the Fathers, to make men the sons of God. He came to spiritualize, to divinize, to deify; and so to give the true expression, and the higher conservation, even the infinite promotion, to all the works and workers of righteousness, truth, holiness in all the kingdoms and sub-kingdoms of thought and life. He came to make men feel they were loved by the Supreme Love, and must love the Supreme Beloved.

And the earthly scene chosen for the theatre of Divine manifestation fulfilled the long-ripening process of God which had differentiated one people and country for Divine purpose. It was well fitted, too, apart from antecedent preparation, being the meeting-place of East and West, of many nations, cultures, civilizations, faiths.

CHAPTER II.

THE MESSIANIC HOPE WITHIN THE CANON.

*" E'n now the shadows break, and gleams divine
Edge the dim distant line."*
J. H. NEWMAN.

Divine differentiation selecting from the woman's seed a nation, a tribe—
Typical characters and offices foreshadowing different aspects of the
Son of Man—Spiritual and devotional preparation—The Ideal of the
Prophets—The King—The Suffering Servant of God—Post-exilian
hope—The priestly hope — Minor and relative ideals contribute to
the fulness of the complete hope—Unique hope in history—The Divine
Man a fulfilment of multitudinous foreshadowings.

THE beginning of the coming of the Christ must be looked for where there is no beginning, in the eternal thought of the bosom of God. The Lamb was slain, and, if slain, sent, from the foundation of the world. The protevangelium, or primal germinal gospel, is contained in the first word of Divine revelation. The gospel of hope is contained in the promise of the victorious seed of the woman. The gospel of suffering conquest is implicitly foreshadowed in the vision of conflict with the Serpent. From the world-wide family of the woman to the seed of Shem according to the blessing of Noah passes the first Divine specialization, or selection of grace. From the race of Shem the Divine finger points to the family of Abraham, the servant of the Lord. In the father of the faithful a Messianic person as well as a Messianic nation is distinctly foreshadowed.

Abraham's character forms an important stage in the ethical development of the Messianic idea. For his faith became the model of all faith. His character as the servant of God established a spiritual idea. Such a faith could never die out of the world for ever. Abraham was justified by faith. The gospel of justification by faith in Christ underlay, as it preceded, the law, and was never disestablished. The spiritual forward-looking and upward-looking faith of the father of the faithful constituted a moment in the spiritual history of a world, desiring redemption, peace with God, reconciliation internal and external.

Moses is the next link in the chain of purposive selection. The Lawgiver himself is a suggestive type emphasized by his own promise of a greater Prophet than himself. The Mosaic legislation is a new departure in the Messianic development. Floods of light converge upon the Promise of the ages. The laws, the worship, the institutions of Israel moved towards one central hope, the Ideal Servant of the Lord,[1] the ideal sacrifice, the ideal priest, the ideal teacher and lawgiver. However imperfectly realized the Ideal Sufferer was with graduated distinctness typefied. Judges and rulers paved the way for a single ruler, and suggested the heroism, the manliness, the conquering majesty, which should be finally embodied in the fulness of the Divine formula, the Son of Man.

Great characters, great national movements, evoke and interpret great ideas. As the fortunes and dignities of Israel rose the ideals of Israel ascended.

From the house of Israel the differentiating energy of the Lord selects the tribe of Judah, and from the tribe of Judah the family of David. The prophecy of Nathan is the next landmark in Messianic development. The hope of Israel is a royal hope. The person of the Messiah is brightening into a clearer splendour. The anointed of the Eternal wears a Davidic crown. The servant of the Lord is a sovereign of man. The Messianic idea and the Messianic ideal step by step, subject to relapse and retrogression, become fuller, more definite, more concrete; not shadowy abstractions, nor hazy poet dreams. From first to last the personal and impersonal elements are interwoven; the Messiah and the nation blend in though and feeling never wholly distinguishable. All Israel is ideally a kingdom of priests, a holy nation, a Messianic body; and remains so to the last breath of prophecy and to the post-canonical vaticinations.

[1] Cf. Edersheim, "Prophecy and History in relation to the Messiah" (p. 187) on "The Ideal Destiny of Israel."

THE MESSIANIC HOPE WITHIN THE CANON.

God uses every national development to advance spiritual development. Slowly, but surely, the links in the chain of the Divine philosophy of history unwind. The spirit of the age is moulded to His own uses by the activities of the Spirit of God. The monarchy embodies and accentuates the monarchical aspect of the Messianic hope. An ideal king, an ideal kingdom, point the golden stream. Often the kingdom is expected in the near future, and the kingdom is only a magnified edition of known kingdoms. Wave after wave of disappointment do not submerge, but tend to unsecularize the Messianic loyalty. Psalm rolls to psalm its welcoming "God save the king" to the music of a royal march. Deeper down in the heart of the people sinks and waits the royal hope. Even if the psalms of the directly Messianic royal hope be reduced to but ten or eleven, there are many latent aspirations and inexpressive heart vaticinations feeling towards this centre. Unquestionably the royal portrait of the Messiah was the most popular one to the end. The higher, the deeper, sacrificial beauties of life, of work, of character, appealed to the higher and deeper natures taught of God in the school of devotion and sacrifice. Power and glory are always worshipped in the world. Habitual veneration for power and domination is a notable characteristic of Orientalism. To this day the not real, but superficial, absence of power in the ethical portrait of Jesus constitutes a barrier to His acceptance by the Indian mind.

The devotional wealth and pathos of Psalms, un-Messianic or unconsciously Messianic, must have gradually uplifted the consciences of worshippers. Much of spiritual, as of all education, comes from unnoticed surrounding and secret impalpable forces. Worship, rightly used, is a supreme spiritual educator. The Temple feasts, the private sacrifices, the secret prayers of such as the seven thousand in Israel who bowed not to Baal, the rich incense of family devotions, kept alive among the purer the fire of spiritual worship. The sense of worship reacted upon the conscience, and all the moral life, filling hearts with awe and the consciousness of responsibility, the sense of sin and the need of expiation, to which sacrifices gave the deepest expression.

The monarchical ideal remained an unfulfilled hope, a chronic disappointment, but an unappeasable undying desire. Prophecy sustained the royal hope through evil report and through good report. "Afterward shall the children of Israel return, and seek the Lord their God, and David their king,[1] and shall come with fear unto the Lord and to His goodness in the latter days" (iii. 4, 5, R.V.), says Hosea, after affirming that "the children of Israel shall abide many days without king, and without prince" (i. 10 ; ii. 23), and he promises ingathering mercy to the Gentiles. "Behold the days come," said Jeremiah, "saith the Lord, that I will raise unto David a righteous Branch, and he shall reign as king and deal wisely, and shall execute judgment and justice in the land. . . . And this is his name whereby he shall be called, The Lord is our righteousness" (xxiii. 5, 6, cf. ; xxx. 9). Ezekiel sung the same song of hope : "And I the Lord will be their God, and my servant David prince among them, I the Lord have spoken it" (xxxiv. 24) ; again, "and David my servant shall be their prince for ever" (xxxvii. 25). And whatever date be assigned to the remarkable apocalypse of Daniel the figure of the Prince Messiah is clearly projected.

Even in prophecies less directly Messianic, glowing hopes and longings find expression, or were characteristic of some whom the prophet knew. "The day of Jehovah" as early as the time of Amos had become a definite goal of aspiration. Such language would take shape and colour in more definite outlines as the connection of the future age with a single Personality became more clearly understood, and would contribute to bathe His coming with associations of glory and awe.

But a new and more momentous contribution was made by prophecy to the conception of the Messianic Hope in its portraiture of the suffering Servant of God. The idea of the Servant of God, like that of the kingdom of God, pervades the whole Old Testament. Israel as a people, Israel's rulers, kings, prophets, priests, were ideally servants of the Lord. But it was reserved for prophecy to fill in the colours, and fit on the framework, to preliminary sketches. The prophets had admittedly contemporaneous relations, and a historical basis. But the portrait of the Suffering Servant finds no original before the time of its fulfilment. The germs of the idea are to be found in the Passion Psalms, such as the twenty-second. The Psalmist may have, at times, idealized his own sufferings, but he spake in the Spirit, and his winged words went

[1] "The older Jews, of every school, Talmudic, mystical, Biblical, grammatical, explained this prophecy of Christ" (Pusey, *s.l*).

THE MESSIANIC HOPE WITHIN THE CANON.

farther than his own horizon, and consciously travelled to infinite goals. The sufferings of psalmists and prophets, the sufferings of Israel gave additional intensity of feeling and vividness of realization to a conception already foreshadowed in the primal promise, and in the intimation of the Egyptian bondage of his seed to Abraham, and in that bondage itself, and in all the pre-Messianic sufferings of the servants of God.

Isaiah [1] is the richest treasury of Messianic prophecy, and the largest contributor both to the joys and sorrows of the predicted Messianic life. Isaiah's prophecy of the Servant of God is complete in its wealth of pathetic detail too familiar to need illustration. It is an "archetypal Sorrow," an impersonated Anguish, which appears before him. Yet his "internal programme" is gorgeous with triumph, and radiant with victorious hope. And he sees more clearly than any what Psalmists at times apprehend, the universal relations of His royalty. "He will be the rallying point of the world's hopes, the true centre of its government" (xi. 10).[2] The conceptions of Isaiah foreshadow a superhuman being. His language attributes Divinity to Messiah. He is to Isaiah, however far his vision soared beyond the flights of ordinary contemporaneous aspiration, "The Mighty God" (ix. 6), as Jeremiah in the passage already quoted identifies Him with Jehovah (xxiii. 5, 6).

The chastisement of the Captivity touched with a new pathos the traditional hope And "while the Messianic ideas were growing in spirituality, they were also increasing in influence. This is the most characteristic note of the new age. The Messianic ideas were popularized. Hitherto they were the hopes of the prophets ; now they became the hopes of the people."[3] Haggai contributed to the Messianic hope the remarkable prophecy " of the latter glory of this house " (ii. 6-9). Zechariah announces definitely : "And many nations shall join themselves to the Lord in that day, and shall be My people " (ii. 11) ; and identifies the One " whom they have pierced " with Jehovah Himself. Malachi closes the Canon with mingled promises and

---

[1] The question of a second Isaiah, or Great Unknown, need not here be discussed. The outlines of the Messianic portrait remain the same, however many hands may (or may not) have held the brush.

[2] H. P. Liddon, Bampton, p. 84

[3] W. F. Adeney, "The Hebrew Utopia," p 295

warnings clustering round the rising of the Sun of righteousness, and the mission of Elijah the prophet (iv. 1–end).

The monarch, the prophet, brought various lights, and embodiments of attributes, to the fulness of the Messianic conception. Had the priesthood of Israel no relation to the blessed Hope? Indirectly, or directly, we can trace a priestly element in the Messianic ideal. Indirectly in the stamp of holiness. To adopt Kuenen's words,[1] without his conclusions. "'Be holy, for I, Yahweh, am holy' (Lev. xix. 2 ; xx. 7, 26, cf. 24 ; xxi. 8, 15, 23 ; xxii. 9, 16, 32 ; xl. 44, 45 ; Numb. xv. 40, 41). In these words the priestly thorah itself sums up its conception of religion. It is with this demand that it comes to the whole people and to every several Israelite. . . . The centre of gravity for him lies elsewhere than for the prophet ; it lies in man's attitude not towards his fellow-man, but towards God ; not in his social, but in his personal life." A second mark of the priestly ideal "may be found in the assumption of worship amongst the duties of the people consecrated to Yahweh, and of every Israelite in particular." Such a deeply-rooted feeling could not be satisfied with anything short of a Priest, as well as a Prophet, Messiah. But the conception of His priesthood was latent rather than explicit. The One Hundred and Tenth Psalm, a Messianic Psalm of David, to which Christ Himself referred His objectors, declares—

> "The Lord hath sworn, and will not repent,
> Thou art a priest for ever
> After the order of Melchizedek."

In Psalm cxxxii. the anointed, the Heir of David, the Lord's Servant, "wears not the kingly crown (*átarah*), but the priestly (*nezer*), with its golden plate or flower (*tsits*)."[2] Zechariah predicts the Lord's Servant, the Branch, who "shall sit and rule upon his throne and be a priest upon his throne."

Such conceptions must have prepared the way for the full Christian doctrine of the Priesthood of Messiah unfolded in the Epistle to the Hebrews. Nor can there have been wholly wanting in Israel men like Zacharias, the spiritual forefathers of the great company of the priests who became obedient to the faith,

[1] Hibbert Lectures, p 160 foll.
[2] 'Church Quarterly Review," No. 51, p. 112.

THE MESSIANIC HOPE WITHIN THE CANON.

men who had risen in some degree to the purpose of the Divine election, and were recognizably in life and heart as well as external communion with God, those " whom He hath chosen," those "who are His," who are "holy," whom He " will cause to come near unto Him " (Num. xvi. 5). Such men could not but raise the standards of holiness. Such men could not but suggest an ideal Holy Priest, who should show forth their holiness, while He transcended and ennobled it. And so the stock of Aaron would prepare for the Priest not of their order, but of Melchizedek's. In the wonderful Messianic chapter of Jeremiah predicting the Branch of righteousness, the prophet connects the promise of a perpetual priesthood with that of a perpetual throne. Both are put on the same level ; and the former, the covenant of priesthood is repeated several times. Jeremiah does not suggest that " David My servant " would also be " David My priest." But his words must have gone far towards universalizing the conception of the priesthood, and extending its functions into the infinite distance.

Ezekiel the priest in his apocalypse of the glorified temple and service shows the priestly bias and prepares the way for an ideal worship and priesthood.

The place of worship in the devotional preparation of the people and in the moral education of the conscience has been alluded to already. And we may add, in connection with the development of the priestly aspect of the Messianic ideal, that "we find from beginning to end the deep impress of a sacrificial system which must have been unmeaning and self-imposed, and is consequently an unexplained phenomenon in history if it did not lead upward and point onward to the perfect priesthood and sacrifice of One "[1] " who hath been made, not after the law of a carnal commandment, but after the power of an endless life" (Heb. vii. 16) That these sacrifices led up to, and were fulfilled in, the sacrifice of Christ, seems to the Christian as undeniable as the historic fact that since that one Sacrifice for sins for ever " the blood of bulls and goats " has ceased to flow.

To the eye of Christian faith the stream of Messianic prophecy deepened and widened through the ages. Many conceptions, primary and secondary, direct and typical, poured

[1] Professor Leathes' " Religion of the Christ," p. 92.

into the quickening waters their various and enriching deposits. The figure of the Christ becomes more concrete, more definite. The Ideal takes up within Himself all the ideals of prophet and priest and king. Every relative revelation contributed its subscription to the sum total. The temperaments of the prophets, the spiritual characteristics of psalmists, the surrounding conditions of the social and religious atmosphere bathed the coming age and man in a thousand lights, many coloured, and variable from age to age, and from mind to mind. "But on the whole there is a wonderful continuity and persistence in the stream of prophecy which flows down the ages,"[1] and an internal consistency. The various elements harmonize in a most complex and intricate concord of Divine music. Even a modern Jewish Rabbi[2] affirms that "the doctrine of the coming of a personal Messiah is the purple thread that runs through the writing of our prophets and historians." And "one of the thirteen fundamental articles of faith, which every Israelite is enjoined to rehearse daily, is, 'I believe with a perfect heart that the Messiah will come; and although His coming be delayed, I will wait patiently for His speedy appearance.'"[3] The very possession of this splendid hope is an unique fact in the history and literature of nations. Its vitality, its colour, its imperishable interest, its indestructibility, are evidenced through all the rises and falls, changes and chances, which embarrassed or assisted its fulfilment.

And so the Ideal Divine Man was foreshadowed. And the prayers of the righteous were a factor in the Divine development no one can recover from the higher side of history, that of the unseen. "Each victory, each deliverance, prefigured Messiah's work; each saint, each hero foreshadowed some separate ray of His personal glory; each disaster gave strength to the mighty cry for His intervention; He was the true soul of the history, as well as of the poetry and prophecy of Israel."[4] And the ideals, dimmer, but indestructible, outside the chosen people shed their lustre, or moved moral desire, onward and upward. Using "sculptors" and "painters" in the sense of

[1] W. F. Adeney.
[2] Adler's "Course of Sermons," pp 125, 126, quoted by Gloag, "Messianic Prophecy," p 81.   [3] Gloag, s. l.
[4] Dr. Liddon, Bampton Lectures, p. 92

moral and spiritual art workers, we may adopt the noble lines of a modern poet :

> " All partial beauty was a pledge
> Of beauty in its plenitude . . .
> The one form with its single act,
> Which sculptors laboured to abstract,
> The one face, painters tried to draw,
> With its one look, from throngs they saw.
> And that perfection in their soul,
> These only hinted at ? The whole,
> They were but parts of ?" [1]

---

[1] R. B. Browning, "Christmas Eve and Easter Day.'

CHAPTER III.

THE POST-CANONICAL MESSIANIC HOPE.

"Blessed art Thou, O Lord our God and the God of our fathers, the God of Abraham, the God of Isaac, and the God of Jacob, the God great and powerful and terrible, God Most High, who bestowest Thy benefits graciously, the Possessor of the universe, who rememberest the good deeds of the fathers and sendest a Redeemer unto their sons' sons for Thy Name's sake in love. Our King, our Helper, and Saviour and Shield, blessed art Thou, O Lord, the Shield of Abraham" (Tephillah, "The Prayer," the first of the Eighteen Benedictions, translated by Bishop LIGHTFOOT, "Clem. Rom." p. 462).

Debased period—Hope persistent—In Apocrypha impersonal and national—In the Apocalypses personal and national—In the Talmud—Rabbinism—Christ's work to re-create and transform as well as fulfil the Messianic Ideal—What might have been

WE enter now upon a different phase of the Messianic development. It is in some respects retrogressive. The debased period of Messianic architecture has arrived. But we have the clearest historic evidence that the hope of hopes had not withered away. Indeed if it had, we should have found ourselves, first, in absolute collision with the Gospels and Josephus and secular historians, which show a very vivid and widely existing working of the hope in all classes, and beyond Palestine ; and secondly, in absolute collision with all doctrines of development which look for great effects in the operation of an antecedent concourse of progressive causes ; so that Christ and His disciples would have first had to manufacture a Messianic idea and permeate the nation with it, and then claim to satisfy it. Adequate data are preserved to indicate, not as fully and clearly as would be desirable, but with sufficient fulness for historical

THE POST-CANONICAL MESSIANIC HOPE. 19

requirements, the persistence of the Messianic hope outside the limits of canonical history. The age of the Apocalypses succeeds the age of the prophets. The disintegration of the historical life of the nation encouraged supra-historical tendencies. The imagination ran after ideals when the school of reality shut so many doors to hope. In a similar way peoples who have enjoyed a very small measure of political freedom have sometimes shown an extraordinary tendency to free speculation and audacities of mental venture.

We come first, for convenience of arrangement, in contact with the Apocryphal books, Palestinian and Grecian, which are of very various dates. It is in vain here that we look for a personal Messiah. Messianic hopes are vague and impersonal. There is, however, nothing irreconcilable with a personal Messianic hope. Indeed the Messianic times and a Judaic kingdom are the undercurrent of all Apocryphal aspiration. And there are various elements which survive of the older hope, but narrowed, nationalized, and distorted. The oldest of the Palestinian books is the Wisdom of Jesus ben Sirach, or Ecclesiasticus. Here we find glimpses of an everlasting priesthood, "Moses consecrated him" (Aaron), and anointed him with holy oil; this was appointed unto him by an everlasting covenant, and to his seed, so long as the heavens should remain," &c. (xlv. 15). So again of "an holy temple to the Lord which was prepared for everlasting glory" (xlix. 12).

In the Book of Tobit (xiii. 16, 18) we hear of a Jerusalem rebuilt with sapphires, and emeralds, and precious stone," all whose "streets shall say Alleluia," and that "all nations shall turn, and fear the Lord God truly, and shall bury their idols. So shall all nations praise the Lord," &c. (xiv. 6, 7). In the beautiful Book of Wisdom placed by some at about 150 B.C., which however may be of Christian date, we read of the righteous—"they shall judge the nations, and have dominion over the people, and their Lord shall reign for ever." In 1 Maccabees hints appear of a coming "faithful prophet" (iv. 46; xiv. 41). In 2 Maccabees the dim but remarkable hope that God, "as He promised in the law, will shortly have mercy upon us, and gather us together out of every land under heaven into the holy place" (ii. 18). In Baruch the burden is "Take a good heart, O Jerusalem" (iv. 30). Alike in Ecclesiasticus (xxxvi. 1-17), in Baruch (iv.), and in Tobit (xiii. 14), national prospects, national exaltation, and Gentile depression, are the prominent landmarks in the far, or near, distances.

But we have other documents of the post-canonical period which are much richer in Messianic colouring. The Apocalypses distinctly pre-intimate a personal Messiah.

In the most ancient pre-Christian fragment of the Jewish Sibylline verses, a famous passage speaks of the coming of a king from the sun,[1] ἀπ' ἠελίοιο:

"Then shall God send a king from the Sun, who shall cause the whole earth to cease from wicked war, when he has slain some and exacted faithful oaths from others. Neither shall he do all these things of his own counsel, but in obedience to the beneficent decrees of the Most High."[2]

And again in the later, but pre-Christian fragment :

"But when Rome shall rule over Egypt also, uniting it under one yoke, then indeed the supreme kingdom of the King Immortal shall appear among men. And there shall come a pure king to hold the sceptres of the whole earth for ever and ever as time rolls on."[3]

In the pre-Christian portion of the Book of Enoch (here, as before, we refer to the critical editors for the chronological and textual questions, and adopt only probable conclusions), we find most important Messianic contributions. Here there is the remarkable apocalypse of the white bullock :

"And I saw that a white ox was born, having great horns, and all the beasts of the field and all birds of the air feared him and prayed to him continually."

In the Book of the Three Parables the Messiah is repeatedly called the "Son of Man;" but the expression sounds like a Jewish Christian insertion.

The Fourth Book of Esdras is supposed by some to be preChristian, but more probably dates from the reign of Domitian. The Apocalypse of Baruch is also too late to be pre-Christian.

But in the beautiful, so-called Psalter of Solomon we are in

[1] Better than as Schurer, "from the East."
[2] Stanton, p 114.
[3] Ibid., p. 117.

THE POST-CANONICAL MESSIANIC HOPE.

the presence of undoubted pre-Christian documentary evidence to the Messianic Hope.

The desolation of Jerusalem, the dispersion of the "holy people," and God's encouraging promises to them form the subject of a book, which both in its loftiness of moral beauty and literary skill "has remarkably caught the tone of some of the noblest prophecies of the Old Testament."[1] The date is probably the time of Pompey's capture of Jerusalem. The great Messianic passage is fiom xvii. 23 to xviii. fin. ; and herein is found the specific use, some consider the first, of the term Christ as the title of One to come. A fragment only may here be briefly rendered from Hilgenfeld's text :

"Behold, Lord, and raise up unto them their king, the son of David, in the time which Thou, God, knowest, to reign over Thy servant Israel. . . . And he shall gather together an holy people, whom he shall lead in righteousness, and shall judge the tribes of the people sanctified by the Lord their God. . . . And there is no unrighteousness in his days in their midst, for all are holy, and their King is the Lord Christ. . . . And he is pure from sin, to rule a great people, rebuke rulers, and destroy sinners in strength of word. . . . Shepherding the flock of the Lord in faith and righteousness, and he shall not suffer them to be weak in their pasture. . . . Under the rod of chastening of the Lord Christ . . ."

The Assumption of Moses, and the Book of Jubilees, of doubtful date, the former placed by Schurer at the beginning of the Christian era, contain no Messianic King but general outlines of a blessed future.

In the great Hellenised thinker, Philo, we seem to find no prominent traces of a Messianic King—a possible suppression of conviction upon political grounds—but a God-sent warlike hero does appear, though the Messianic hopes find expression more in a picture of a national restoration of glory and greatness.

Josephus, like Philo, is of the first century A.D. He so far apostatized from the national hope as to apply Messianic prophecies to Vespasian. But his pages overflow with testimony to the presence and intensity of the hope amongst the people, and its influence upon the rebellion against Rome.

[1] Stanton, p 77.

Jewish works written after the Christian era are coloured by the violence of the anti-Christian controversy. But they clearly represent Jewish traditional views, however modified by the impact with Christian thought. Mr. Stanton seems to unduly minimize the evidential value of Talmudical literature. That literature is so strictly traditional, so substantially self-consistent in spirit, and so clearly a development of the debased Judaism, that it is unhistorical to ignore its evidential validity. Very full treatment of the Rabbinical expectations must be sought in Edersheim's wealth of quotations. These point to the conclusion that the Rabbinical Messiah was a super-human man, hovering between Divinity and humanity, higher than the angels, existing before the world. They indicate also a "character of finality"[1] in His work and office which would assist minds towards a belief in His super-human greatness, in His essential Divinity.

The contrast upon merely literary comparison between the canonical and post-canonical literature is striking. Even Josephus follows "the uniform Jewish tradition to the effect that the prophetic succession ceased with Malachi, and marks the time of Artaxerxes as the limit of the period of inspiration."[2] With the ebb of the prophetic spirit had drifted away the glory and spiritual beauty of the Scriptural Messianic Ideal. From the rich creativeness, both in literary art and spiritual science, of the God-gifted members of the goodly fellowship of the prophets, religious literature sunk for the most part into the hands of the Sopherim, and religious life under the guidance of the late-born sect of the Pharisees.

The great fact in the religious condition of Israel at the time of Messiah's Advent was the dominance of Rabbinism. The religious post-exilian revival lacked the breath and health of inspired movement. Palestinian Judaism sank into narrow legal sectarianism. The letter of the Law became a religious fetish after the spirit had been quenched. Foreign subjugations drove the Palestinian Jews more into themselves religiously. Hellenism, and the intellectual breadth and general culture which accompanied it, exercised the greatest influence upon the Jewish dispersion, who formed the majority of the nation, and especially upon the western diaspora, both negatively and

[1] Stanton, p 148.
[2] "Josephus," in Smith's "Dictionary of Christian Biography," article by Dr. Edersheim

THE POST-CANONICAL MESSIANIC HOPE. 23

positively made important contributions to preparedness for the new revelation. But in Palestine, "the land," as Jewish pride called it, Hellenism, while affecting commercial life and industry among the middle classes, while attracting and often altogether secularizing and half-paganizing rulers of the Herodian School, and the wealthy and powerful Sadducee faction, made no impression upon the dominant and popular religious feeling. Pharisaism, through its organ, the Synagogue, controlled all the religion of the most religious of peoples. The Scribes and Pharisees had succeeded to the spiritual and intellectual supremacy of the prophets. The priests, under such secularized leaders as the tools of the Roman Government, who dishonoured the pontificate and turned it into a source of personal gain and political and social power, had but little religious influence. Their lips had ceased to keep knowledge; and men would not seek the Law at the mouth of the son of Levi, but at the mouth of the Rabbi.

The Sopherim, or Scribes, were the professional doctors of the Law; they held the key of knowledge. The Pharisees were their disciples, "who put their theory into practice. If the Scribes consecrated themselves wholly to the study of the Law and its application to life, or more truly to the subjection of the life of the people in all its branches to the precepts of the Law, the Pharisees are absorbed in its observance and in the realization of righteousness, regarded as conformity to its ordinances."[1] The Scribes sat with the chief priests and elders as judges in the ecclesiastical courts, both in the capital and in the provinces. Even in heaven they claimed posts of supreme honour, the flatteries of the angels, and the eulogies of God. Religion under their influence became a profession; the conduct of life a high art. "To know the six hundred and thirteen commandments of the written Law, the incalculable number of the unwritten,"[2] was the province of the elect.

When we wonder at the subjection of the common people (the Am-ha-arets) to the Rabbis we have to bear in mind that no such thing as individualism could exist, or ever did exist except among the select few, in any ancient people. The sense of individual freedom and independence and moral and intel-

---
[1] Kuenen, p. 208, Hibbert Lectures.
[2] Wellhausen, "History of Israel," p 502

lectual responsibility is of modern and, above all, of Christian extraction and growth. The very word conscience is practically speaking of Christian birth and education; though the moral feeling it certifies and conveys of course is coextensive with human nature down to the most degraded types in some form or other.

Again the material interests of the people followed in the wake of those of the rulers. This is true to some degree, even under modern conditions. And the material power and prosperity of the time lay largely in the hands of the Sadducees and Romanisers, who for religious purposes supported the Rabbinical party in opposing a Messiah who made spiritual claims on spiritual grounds, and exacted a corresponding moral, spiritual allegiance from the heart and life, instead of ceremonial adhesion, or political support. All the material influences of the time worked against Christ. We see it in the extreme sharpness and decisiveness of His own words about the danger of riches, and the hardness with which rich men entered the Kingdom of God. It is not always easy now to be true to Christ, when the kingdoms of trade and industry, the acquisition and distribution of wealth, material prosperity and social comfort, and the forces of politics, have bowed to the sceptre of Christian influence, and always nominally in Christian countries, and, in part actually, acknowledge His lawful control. It must have been as hard then when the sacrifice required was most violent to become a Christian, as it is now for a modern Jew or high caste Hindu.

Nor were the people intellectually qualified for that independence of judgment, which is so characteristic of Western individualism, even without the basis of competent knowledge. They revered the Law, but could not read a word of it in the original Hebrew. The Interpreter must translate the sacred lore from the Hebrew into the vernacular Aramaic. Here he was dependent upon the current interpretation of the Scribes, and they upon the tradition which they had accumulated and formulated with vast labour. So the Mishnah or Second Law, "which intended to explain and supplement the first," superseded and overrode it. "This constituted the only Jewish dogmatics, in the real sense, in the study of which the sage, Rabbi, scholar, scribe, and Darshan, were engaged." The Halachah applied and extinguished while professing to interpret the Old Testament. The Haggadah, or popular exposition, claimed only personal authority. " But all the greater would be its popular influence, and all the more dangerous the doctrinal license which it allowed." [1]

Because religion had sunk into externalism, and moral interests had been crowded out, therefore the Messianic ideal had inevitably fallen with religion. Rabbinism had proclaimed as its watchword devotion to the Thorah. Such an ideal might have been nobly conceived and nobly carried out. Unhappily the Law had ceased to be that of Divine revelation. Traditionalism, while professing to explain, had actually superseded the Law. Obedience to the Law meant external obedience; the righteousness of the Law meant external righteousness. The result of obedience was merit, and the result of merit sonship. The Law had thus lost most of its moral content and force. Legal holiness had degenerated into ceremonial purity, like that of the Brahmin. The ceremonial law was multiplied into an infinity of petty pedantries, pressing upon the minutest details of daily life as an intolerable yoke.

The favoured ideal of the Messiah was now that of a great Rabbi, who should exalt the Law to its utmost bounds, who was also a great conquering king who should impose the Thorah upon the necks of the Gentiles, and the Rabbinical party high enthroned upon the heads of all in material and social supremacy.

Jesus Christ had to chose between the Scriptural and the Rabbinical ideals. They were irreconcilable, they were incapable of mutual concession, of modification, or of transformation. He chose to revert to first principles. He was a restorer of the old. He preserved the Law by casting off the parasitic incubus of traditionalism. He preserved all that was of universal moral validity in the old by transforming it. He did not merely restore, He renewed, re-created.

If Christ had adopted the Rabbinical ideal, He would, undoubtedly, have been accepted as the Jewish Messiah. And the temptation constantly presented itself to Him. As it was, He had to unteach as much as to teach. He had to destroy as much as to build up. He was a destructive critic as well as a constructive founder.

We cannot then admit much force in certain modern

[1] Edersheim, i. 11, 12.

26   JESUS CHRIST.

apologies for Rabbinism. They have, for the most part, naturally emanated from Jewish writers, who have maintained their tradition, and are the modern representatives of the Rabbinical schools. It is to be regretted that so great a scholar as Kuenen,[1] while keenly criticizing some of the more patent defects, should have done Rabbinism what seems something more than justice. Whatever may have been the merits of individual Rabbis, however much better they, or their disciples, may have at times been than their creed, the damning fact remains that they were at the head and front of the anti-Messianic opposition. Although upon the Sadducaic high priests rest the chief guilt of the national apostasy, consummated in the judicial murder of the Messiah, yet it was the Rabbis who were the sleepless opponents, the malignant critics, and false accusers, in their consistent hatred of the Messiah and all His words and works.

The sense of sin, both individual and national, of spiritual failure and shortcoming, which breathes in all the minor keys of the Psalter, had amongst all but, it may be, a small remnant, vanished away. National and individual pride, externalism, exclusiveness, fanaticism, were the dominant features in the character of pre-Christian Israel. Some remnant the chastening fires of discipline, the beatitudes of the school of suffering, had purified and prepared. But they were as invisible in the general mass as the unseen stars in the unapproachable heavens. To such the sacred music of the Psalms still spake in intelligible accents; the words of the prophets searched their hearts; the Temple feasts and sacrifices, and the great fast moved them to penitential tears, or raptures of thanksgiving; the worship of the Synagogue and the home stirred and lifted them to Divine communions, and penetrated with the sense of the unseen Holy One. Some of this type may have originated, or appreciated in an extra legal sense, the saying that "if all Israel would together repent for a whole day, the redemption by Messiah would ensue."

But, taking Israel as a whole, the question referring to the Second Advent might have been applied to the first, when the Son of Man cometh shall He find faith on the earth?

The   hard task that lay before the Christ was then twofold.

---

[1] *Vide* especially, Lecture V., in the Hibbert Lectures.

First, to convince people that He was the Messiah. Secondly, to convince them that He was not the Messiah of their preconceptions, but of Scriptural revelations; to rehabilitate the Messiah of the prophets; to transform their whole Messianic conception. His task was to change and transfigure their whole life, with all its wealth of hope, and love and passionate desire; and to plant in the torn soil of hearts bruised and broken for a new seed a living faith in Himself, as the Messiah and the Son of God. Alas the Messiah was rejected before He came, in His inspirations and prophecies, types and shadows! Had the Divine light been truly reflected, it would not have shone into darkness. Had the level of inspiration found a corresponding height of Messianic belief, height would have answered to height, re-echoing the Divine Voice, and deep to deep.

Through Him and His Israel, as His ministering servants, all nations were called to be servants of God; Israel was to be universalized. All Israel should have been John the Baptists. Israel failed their high mission, but their casting off, because they cast off, did not thwart the plan of God, and involve the Gentiles in their loss. The Greek translation of the Hebrew Scriptures, the dispersion of Jewish thought and morals with the Jews, were Messianic stepping-stones to Gentile hearts. Even now a great future appears to await Israel repentant; and their Divine work of service and place of honour is only half lost and half deferred. Had but Israel known the things that belonged to their peace! Had they but preserved the true tradition of the Messianic prophets, had they but arisen and stood upon their feet, an exceeding great army, when the trumpet call of the prophet of the wilderness sounded—then to a people who had been true to God's call—the Christ would have come. This new demand upon their faith would have been met with the fervour of instant and wholesale acceptance. The Christ of God, acknowledged by His own, would have gone forth at the head of His people, His chosen, and gathered in, without the slow long agonies of patient missionary conquest, the fulness of the Gentiles. On Israel rests the first and heaviest responsibility for what is and what might have been.

> " For of all sad words of tongue or pen
> The saddest are these ' It might have been.' "

But, of Israel too, may it be said—

> "Ah, well ! for us all some sweet hope lies
> Deeply buried from human eyes,
> And, in the hereafter, angels may
> Roll the stone from its grave away."[1]

---

[1] J. G. Whittier, "Maud Muller," fin.

CHAPTER IV.

THE DIVINE BABE.

"For it was no other God whom the Israelite shepherds were glorifying, but Him who was announced by the Law and the Prophets, the Maker of all things, whom also the angels glorified" (IRENÆUS III. x. § 4. translated by Keble).

The country priest's home—Zacharias in the Temple—The Angel of promise to the priest—The Angel of promise to the Virgin—The meeting of the holy women—The spiritual songs—The journey to Bethlehem—The holy Nativity—The angelic anthem—The visit of the shepherds.

THE sacred scene opens in the rural home of a faithful priest of Israel. Most of the priests lived out of Jerusalem; in Nehemiah's time about four-fifths of the whole number.[1] In the hill country of Judæa, probably near[2] the ancient and priestly Hebron, lived a righteous, *i.e.*, pious and dutiful, priest and his wife, Zacharias and Elizabeth. Both were aged, both of Aaron's blood. Zacharias belonged to the eighth of the twenty-four courses, or "divisions," or "families," into which the priesthood had been originally divided in David's time (1 Chron. xxiv. 7–18). Four of these only had returned from exile (Ezra ii. 36–39), and had been redistributed under the old designations. One trouble vexed the godly home, and shaped many prayers. An "heritage of the Lord" (Psa. cxxvii. 3), even the

"dower of blessed children"

had been denied them. Like Sarah, Rebekah, Rachel,

[1] Cf. Nehem. xi. 10–19 with Ezra ii. 36–39 and viii. 2.
[2] Not "in," as Keim, for then Hebron would have been mentioned.

Manoah's wife, Hannah, the most privileged daughters of Israel, like her own people "until the fulness of the Gentiles be come in," Elizabeth was barren.

Emphasizing this fact for its spiritual connection with after events, the sacred narrative bears us from the hill-side home into the Temple. As it was October, it must have been the second time that the course of Abia ministered that year, for to each course a week of duty was assigned. Upon what day Zacharias officiated we are not told. The critical hour of his life had come; the more abundant answer to all who looked for the consolation of Israel. One was waiting to be gracious both to a childless mother's prayer and a Messiahless wistful people. In the chain of Divine preparation two homes formed the last, but not least, links—the home of the country priest, the home of the unwedded maiden.

The great gates of the Holy Place had been opened. The three blasts of the silver trumpet had rung through the city. From before dawn the morning sacrifice had been prepared. For the third time the priests had met in the "Hall of Polished Stones" to draw the third lot, to choose the incensing priest, and the fourth lot,[1] "which designated those who were to lay on the altar the sacrifice and the meat offerings, and to pour out the drink offering" The coals from the altar of burnt-offering had been spread on the golden altar. The assistant priests had withdrawn, and left the celebrant, golden censer in hand, alone in the Holy Place. It was the sacred, the cherished, "enriching," moment in the life of any priest. Erect, before the altar, clad in white linen vestments "for glory and for beauty" (Exod. xxviii. 40), symbolizing purity, turban on head, with feet bare, looking towards the Veil which hung before the Holy of Holies, having the table of shewbread on his right, on his left the sevenfold flame of the golden candlestick, stood Zacharias, waiting the signal of the president to spread the incense upon the altar, and to meet his God (Exod. xxx. 6; xl. 26).

When the time had come the "cloud of odours" rose up to heaven, mingling with the prayers of the people. The whole multitude without, with hands outspread, bowed down in worship, as with the silence of heaven at the opening of the seventh seal. The incense offering was the most solemn phase of the whole sacrificial process, as "gold to stones"[2] compared with

[1] Edersheim, "Temple," p 137, Schurer 1. 294 f. [2] Philo.

THE DIVINE BABE.

the blood offerings. Such was the fittest time for Divine revelation to priests. John Hyrcanus, "alone in the Temple, as high priest, offering incense, heard a voice that his sons had just then overcome Antiochus."[1] Farther back, David had been called and anointed of the prophet at the time of the family sacrifice. Never before, or after, did Zacharias " burn incense before the Lord," and offer therewith the representative intercession of all the farspread sons of Israel. And this was the most august burning in time, in manner, in result, ever offered. For on the right, or auspicious, side of the altar appeared an angel, and announced to the trembling priest the promise of a son—the forerunner of the Messiah. Gabriel, the strong man of God, who had about the time of the evening oblation announced to Daniel the yet distant march of the Prince, had now the mission to report His near approach. The interview must have lasted some minutes, for the multitude waited in wonder. Zacharias came out to "the top of the steps which led from the porch to the Court of the Gentiles." But the multitude left without the triple benediction, gathering from his signs that the dumb-struck priest had seen a vision, and in this way were prepared for further signs to come.

Nine months of speechlessness in the retired rural home gave the priest much time for devout contemplation. Such a shock would leave an indelible impression and quicken the development of Messianic faith. A sudden blaze of light had fallen upon the ancient promises of Divine lore, and the symbolic anticipations of Temple worship. Faith supplied a key better than learning. The whole stream of Divine purpose, obscured, corrupted, and darkened indeed, but less among the Am-ha-aretz than in the city, must have been lighted up with new promise and potency of glory. Such influences at work in the heart of the chosen priest and his wife must have taken effect on the unborn child, and after his birth prepared the way, and in some degree accounted for, the fulness and wealth of his spiritual development, and the depth and maturity of his Messianic conception. What other home in Israel could have been the training ground of the prophet? What more fitting nursery for a personal force, inspired by and steeped in the Scriptures, unindebted and indeed hostile to contemporary urban authority and petrified traditionalism? The prophet did not

[1] Josephus, "Ant." xiii. 10. 3.

owe all his originality and unique moral force to himself. His character owed its primary development to the home of a devout priest, blessed by an immediate Divine revelation, and living in the light of a recognized Divine purpose.

St. Luke, who must have counted among his basal authorities the mother of the Lord, or her family and friends, before bringing together the two holy mothers into the foreground, passes by a rapid stroke from one home-centre of grace to another. While Elizabeth waited in glad expectancy of assured promise, the Angel Gabriel went on his yet greater mission to another highland home. A poor, but royal born, maiden, betrothed to a village carpenter, with the common name of Miriam, or Mary, is greeted by the awful messenger. The record of the Annunciation is as simple and unadorned as a legend of Oriental imagination would have been gorgeous and hyperbolical.[1] The details are as few as possible consistent with the historic preservation of the mystery revealed. Was she rapt in secret devotion at the hour of morning or evening sacrifice? Was she borne on the soaring wings of Messianic desire, and

"Faint for the flaming of His advent feet"?

There must have been some spiritual preparedness and "ripened receptiveness"[2] of the highest order of grace. There is a Divine fitness of time and place about the Epiphanies of the Eternal, Divine self-reverence when He would manifest His mysteries to the meek and pure-hearted. "Hail, favoured," or "graced," one. So was the flower of Israel and humanity approached. The words recalled the Divine message to such as Gideon, "the Lord is with thee," and preface the supreme Annunciation that she is the chosen mother of the Messiah. The question of maidenly simplicity follows. How? And supernatural faith, never so taxed in any earthborn before or after, is rewarded with the promise of the overshadowing Spirit and power of the Highest. The Son of Mary would be the Son of God. An unsought sign is superadded, the sign of Elizabeth, her own kinswoman.

[1] See, *e g*, the legends of Buddha's conception and birth, the white elephant entering into the side of Queen Màyà as she lay on a celestial couch in a golden palace, &c , &c.
[2] Cf. Dorner, "System of Christian Doctrine," iii. 343, E. T.

THE DIVINE BABE.

> "Yes, and to her, the beautiful and lowly,
> Mary, a maiden, separate from men,
> Camest thou nigh and didst possess her wholly,
> Close to thy saints, but thou wast closer then." [1]

"The altar of the Virgin's womb was touched with fire from heaven." [2] "Conceived of the Holy Ghost" is an article of faith on a level with "born of the Virgin Mary." It was the function of the Creative Spirit to form the human nature of Jesus, as by Him "He is always born anew in the hearts of saints." [3] In patristic language, "this ray of God entering into a certain virgin, and in her womb endued with the form of flesh, is born Man joined together with God." [4]

There is a deep touch of nature in the narrative following, which is its own evidence of truthfulness. Burdened with a blessed and awful secret, Mary seeks the home of her who alone can give and exchange with her womanly and spiritual sympathy. Her kinswoman, Elizabeth, can verify the angel's annunciation, and alone in Israel can counsel her with full knowledge of her unique position, added to the weight of her many years of piety and her own share in the Advent glory of the Messiah. The meeting of the two saints, the young maiden, and the aged wife, linked in closer communion than that of their own blood, was one of as pure joy, as when two friends meet in the further light. The mother of the past, and in her the Law and Prophets of whom the unborn babe was the last representative, rendered homage to the mother of the future. Affected by the mother's exultation, the babe leapt in her womb in unconscious homage. Deep emotion, human and Divine, kindled by the breath of the Holy Spirit, broke into the greeting of the elder mother, and the sublime prophetic lyric of the younger. The holy song gathers up the song of Hannah and many prelusive strains of expectant Israel into a new and golden sheaf of praise. Poetic power was, and since has been, a singular gift of the women of Israel. Apart from its rhythmical form, the Magnificat is "a gem of purest ray serene." Not Hebrew, not lyrical only, but all poetry is the utterance of impassioned truth. "Every truth which a human being can enunciate, every thought, even every outward

---
[1] F. W. H. Myers, "Saint Paul."   [2] Bp. Alexander.
[3] Without reference to the Holy Spirit, Ep. to Diognetus xi.
[4] Tertullian, Apol. 1. 21, for copious parallels *vide* notes *s. l* in Oxford translation.

impression, which can enter into his consciousness, may become poetry," J. S. Mill[1] has well said, " when invested with the colouring of joy, or grief, or pity, or affection." "All deep speech is song;"[2] and this ode is deepest song of deepest speech. Triumphant joy is the dominant note of the Hymn of the Virgin Mother. Joy and thanksgiving in the kingdom of God her Saviour—which in the prophetic cast of the singer's vision has already come to the help of Israel, in fulfilment of the promises made to Abraham and the fathers. The exact nature of the incarnate kingdom has not risen into definite proportions. Song and singer alike looked behind and before, and belonged to both dispensations.

After three months this rare communion was broken, Mary returned to her own home, and to Elizabeth came her time of fulfilment. The child was born; mother and kin and neighbours rejoiced together. On the eighth day he was circumcised. Unforgetful of the angel's promise, the father closes the discussion about the name by writing down John (Jochanan), and his long-sealed lips were lit with priestly-prophetic fire. The promised horn of salvation had been raised up in David's house. His new-born son was to be the forerunner of the Saviour. The song strikes the deepest gospel notes—salvation, light, peace to the people of God.

Meantime the condition of his espoused brought painful questions to the mind of Joseph, and suggested to the humble conscientious Tsaddiq of Nazareth a private divorce. His trial of faith ends at the third angelic annunciation, this time in a dream. Each link in the chain of angel ministries completes the one

" Far-off Divine event "

" to which " unconsciously

" The whole creation moves."

Each person within the sacred circle of the two families contributes something to the development of the Divine Advent.

St. Luke connects the journey of Mary and Joseph to Bethlehem with the decree of Augustus. It is incredible that with all the contemporary sources of information open to him he should have blundered as the negative critics aver. He was

[1] "Essay on Poetry." [2] T. Carlyle.

THE DIVINE BABE. 35

aware that a census took place ten years later (Acts v. 37), and could not therefore have confused the two. It has been shown by A. Zumpt that Quirinius was probably Legate of Syria for the first time B.C. 4 to B.C. 1, and that this registration, begun under Herod, was fully effected later during his tenure of office. In obedience to the law, Joseph went up to the city of his forefather David to be enrolled, accompanied, as was natural under her condition, by Mary.

The place is now called Beitlahm, inhabited by five thousand people industrious and well to do. Flocks and herds abound, and the vineyards are good and plentiful. Up the two-terraced limestone hills, girt with figtrees and olives, to the long grey village, now crowded with travellers, the two poor Galileans came, after passing the still existing site of the Tomb of Rachel. Thoughts of the faithful Ruth and the shepherd lad, David, must have crowded upon the mother expectant, flesh of their flesh, promise of their promise, the instrument of fulfilling of David's hope. To any child of David's house Bethlehem was revered and holy ground. To her, if she knew Micah's prophecy and had heard of the coincidental Rabbinical tradition, "little" (v. 2, 4) Bethlehem was the recognized place of sacred travail, and more than mother's joy. The frowning castle of Herod in the north-east, looking over to Machærus across the Dead Sea would pass unheeded or lamented.

The very inn, which may have been Chimham's (Jer. xli. 17) was too crowded to take them. No doors opened to the unborn Saviour. His own received Him not. Here the Divine Babe was born in the stable. After ages have honoured the place, and honour and dishonour it still. The Grotto of the Nativity is now covered by the chancel of the Greek Church, but Mahommedans keep guard. The rock-cut stable where Jesus was born was one of countless such throughout the neighbourhood. The simplicity, the lowliness of the scene in every tone and detail, ran counter to all contemporary Jewish expectation and Oriental pre-conception. The birthplace of the Hero of Christianity is adorned with the unheroic and the commonplace. "Aufer a nobis pannos et dura præsepia" was the exclamation of Marcion. Mythical heroes have very different origins. The birth at the "House of Bread"[1] is typical of Jesus' life and character of

[1] But C. R. Conder, H G. Tomkins interpret Bethlehem, as the House, *i.e.*, Holy Place, of Lakhmu, the Creator, deriving the name from pre-Hebrew

lowliness, simplicity, poverty, humiliation, and of its honour of the poor and ignorant. The cattle gave the Son of Man a shelter. He giveth them food and increase, and counts theirs amongst the groans of created nature. Shall they not partake of His redemptive blessing, and the glorious, more than recovered, liberty of the children of a new earth?

Meantime hard by the Tower, Migdal Eder, now said to be marked by the ruins of a church built by Empress Helena, the shepherds were keeping night watch over the flocks intended for the Temple sacrifices. A sweet heavenly joyance of song burst over the silent hills. It was the first Christmas greeting of glad tidings, as of a chime of heaven's own bells, announced by an angel of the Lord, confirmed in responsive chorus by a multitude of the heavenly host.

> "Glory to God in the highest
> And on earth peace among men in whom He is well pleased." [1]

> "Sweetly over all,
> Dropping the ladder of their hymn of praise
> From heaven to earth, in silver rounds of song,
> They heard the blessed angels sing of peace,
> Goodwill to man and glory to the Lord." [2]

It was a hymn of praise which has been appropriated into the thanksgivings of all Eucharistic liturgies.

Surely unknown of the shepherds the songster angels accompanied their hurried steps, and did homage before the face of their Incarnate Lord. All the wondering words of the shepherds, and those to whom they spake, Mary stored up in her heart—a psychological touch characteristic at once of the mother and of the historian. One cannot but wonder whether any of the shepherds lived to hear the Baptist's preaching. Hebron lay but a few miles farther south. The devout shepherds may well have been known to the family circle of Zacharias, or have heard of the happy birth which was noised about, and set pious country folks thinking of a coming Sign. And with

Semitic pagan inhabitants —"Syrian Stone Lore," p. 33, and Palestine Exploration Society Reports, 1885, p. 112

[1] εὐδοκίας, R V., Tischendorf, Westcott and Hort, &c.

[2] J. G. Whittier, "The Dream of Pio Nono," changing "he" to "they"

THE DIVINE BABE.

the sacrificial flocks they must have often gone the short six-mile journey to Jerusalem. Some may have witnessed the Temple cleansings. St. Luke is so careful an historian that he may have sought information on the spot. But without such local investigations the memory of the Virgin would have preserved all, and much more than all, the details he has handed down.

CHAPTER V.

THE EPIPHANIES OF THE DIVINE INFANT.

" May to Him the spirit's kings
Yield their choicest offerings."
ARCHBISHOP TRENCH, "Silvio Pellico."

The Epiphany of the Divine Infant in the Temple—The Epiphany of the Divine Infant to the Gentiles—The flight into Egypt—The return.

THE Circumcision of the Infant Christ took place on the eighth day. He came to fulfil all the righteousness of a true child of Abraham. The name assigned by the angel, Jesus (Jeshua), was given to the child apparently in privacy, without the congratulations of relatives and friends. After the Circumcision the Child must have been at least forty-one days' old when the mother went up to the Temple for her own purification and the redemption of her firstborn (Lev. xii.; Numb. xviii. 16). It was the first visit of the Infant Saviour to His Father's house. The Child was presented to the priest, representatively, that is, to the Lord; the redemption money was paid, five shekels of the sanctuary (Numb. *l. c.*), of Tyrian weight, according to Rabbinic requirements, about ten to twelve shillings in value.

And now the maiden-mother stood at the top of the steps which led up from the Court of the Women at the great gate of Nicanor. She had already dropped the price of the turtle doves, "the poor's offering," into the third of the trumpets, or the trumpet-shaped chests; and as the incense rose in her sight from the golden altar, such a prayer as only a mother can offer accompanied it. The Christian "Churching of Women" is

THE DIVINE INFANT.

rather a thanksgiving, but the older name was the "ordo ad purificandam mulierem post partum ante ostium ecclesiæ," and all the spiritual significance of the Jewish service passes into the richer breath of the Christian.

Perhaps at this moment one who had been waiting for the Menachem, the consolation of Israel, received the reward of patient waiting. Extremes met and blended. The aged saint, the young mother, the unconscious Babe.

With the Divine Infant in his arms Simeon had reached the crown of his life. Before the wondering parents he poured out to the Lord his dismissal hymn of thanksgiving—a life's evensong to many watchers for the dawn. The rapt vision of the inspired singer extended to far shores and lofty heights of Messianic expectation. The long musings of silent prayer, bosomed on Messianic hope, found voice in divided accents, boding both light to all nations, and strife to Israel breaking in twain,[1] some to rise and some to fall.

> " Its voice the wise have understood;
> They cry, ' Thy servants hear , '
> While some shrink farther from their good,
> Because it comes so near " [1]

His own saddened experience of life in the harlot city, his ripe insight into the unfruitfulness and decay of leaders and people, his knowledge of contemporary Messianic political religion, formed the material which caught the spark of the spirit of prophecy as he spake of a divided Israel, and prepared Mary for the future of the *Mater dolorosa*. Such a painful forewarning of disappointment may have jarred upon a soul unriven with the reproach of which the Cross was the full and final agony. But after shepherd acclaims and angel carols it may not have been unnecessary Mary must have been like all of her time, imperceptive of a suffering Messiah.

There is a dim resemblance to this incident in the life of Gautama in the visit of the old sage, who after his birth predicted that he would be a Buddha, and rejoiced to have seen him.[2]

---

[1] W. Bright, D.D.

[2] Bishop Copleston on Buddhism in *The Nineteenth Century*, July, 1888, and Professor Kellogg, "The Light of Asia and the Light of the World," p 71.

Another sympathetic saint joined the group. Widow Anna, the aged daughter of Phanuel, a member of an unreturned tribe, long faithful to human love, yet among those

> " Thrice blest, whose lives are faithful prayers,
> Whose love in higher loves endure."

She almost lived in the Temple. The burden of her unceasing prayer redemption.

Two aged men, one a country priest, the other a dying saint in Jerusalem ; two aged women, and a poor provincial maiden ; all obscure in life, in station, things that are not—such are the *dramatis personæ* when the Divine scene opens. Nothing could be more out of keeping with the current of contemporary Messianic expectation, nothing less suggestive of the advent of a superhuman Being, nothing more natural after the spiritual order, nothing more flagrantly opposed to the surroundings of a mythical or legendary prince !

Three circles are now formed as Messianic nuclei. The circle of the Baptist's parents and friends, a priestly group ; the circle of Bethlehemite shepherds, a rural group ; the circle of elect in Jerusalem waiting under the shadow of the temple for redemption, a Zion group.

After the presentation of the Infant to God in descending order comes His presentation to the world. The spiritual fitness alone would go far to determine the question of the priority of the former to the Epiphany. In contrast with the consciously expectant watchers of devout Jerusalem, the representatives of the unconscious desires of all nations approach the Infant King. From what province of the East the Magians came is undetermined by the sacred narrative and subsequent research. The name connects them with the priestly caste of Persia, who were spread widely over the East. In them not the kings of Sheba and Seba only offer gifts (Psa. lxxii. 10), but heathen religions which felt after God, seekers after truth in " the far countries," and workers of righteousness in every nation. If they were Persians they came of a gentle race, and one which had often shown favour to their Israelite subjects, as the Books of Ezra, Nehemiah, and Esther show.

Was the star which led the Magians on a long and perilous journey natural or supernatural? Was it a special providence

THE DIVINE INFANT.

or a miracle which lightened their way to the Light of all? Was their interest founded upon a scientific or a religious basis? The last question may be confidently answered—upon the double basis of earthly and spiritual science. The former question is still *sub judice*, and invites further scientific investigation. The journey altogether took about two years. The birth of Christ took place December, 5 B.C. Two years before, the famous conjunction, discovered by Kepler, of the planets Jupiter and Saturn in the constellation Pisces took place three times. When a similar conjunction took place in 1603-4 a bright evanescent star appeared between Jupiter and Saturn. Such may have been the star of the Epiphany. Modern believing thought entirely accepts the principle of economizing miracles. On *a priori* grounds the Christian prefers the natural without giving up a supernatural explanation. That signs in heaven, however, naturally accompanied the first, as they will the second, Advent of the Lord of heaven and earth is true in the spiritual order, whether those signs were ordinary cosmical, but specially timed, or wholly supernatural.

The Magi were Eastern men of science, in whose minds, as in much later days, astronomy and astrology were not as yet distinct. Their religious interest in the star is partly explained by that mental confusion, and partly by the spread of Jewish belief. Jewish prophecy and tradition also, as seen in the Talmud, connected the appearance of a star with that of Messiah. They were virtual, or perhaps actual proselytes of the Jewish faith. The first question asked by the Eastern pilgrims in the Jewish capital, was—Where is He that is born King of the Jews? The question creates a stir throughout Jerusalem, and Herod the king jealous of any possible rival, summons a special council, and submits to it in general terms the question of Messiah's birthplace.[1] Scripture and tradition left no doubt as to the answer. The decisive text of Micah is *Targumed*, or interpreted, by St. Matthew, according to his practice in referring to Old Testament prophecies, in the light of complete fulfilment. "Such *Targuming* of the Old Testament was entirely in accordance with the then universal method of setting Holy Scripture before a popular audience."[2]

[1] γεννᾶται indefinite present.
[2] Edersheim, i. 206, u. v, and "Prophecy and History in Relation to the Messiah," p. 116.

After his public inquiry, Herod holds a private interview with the Magians with the secret intention of learning the exact age of the Child, and any other identifying particulars which would assist him to its destruction. Once more the bright pioneer "magnifica lingua cœli,"[1] shone in silent eloquence before the rejoicing travellers, not to indicate a well-known way, but to reward those who by faith saw the invisible and obtained promises.

The Holy Family had now found the shelter of a house. The humble roof is the first Palace of the royal Infant, the Eastern savants are the first courtiers, and the gold and frankincense and myrrh (comp. Isa. lx. 6) the choice products of their own East, the royal coronation homage. Those who have seen Holman Hunt's "Shadow of Death" will remember the use made by the artist of the holy offerings.

Warned by a dream not to return to their false and crafty friend Herod, the firstfruits of the Gentiles returned to their own East. The Divine Epiphany had taken place. The Divine rejection had already begun.

Joseph's hasty night flight into Egypt follows in obedience to angelic warning. A very large number of Jewish colonists resided in Egypt, enjoying the rights of citizenship. In the north-eastern part of Alexandria a quarter was assigned to them "that they might lead a purer life, by mingling less with foreigners;"[2] and they had scattered their homes and houses of prayer in all parts of the city. Among the million Jewish inhabitants Joseph and Mary would easily find friends, and deposit a germ of Messianic faith which should bear fruit after many days. Out of Egypt God's Son, first His people, and then their Representative who identified Himself with them, and spake long after of His Exodus (Luke ix. 31), was called in due time.

The innocents at Bethlehem are privileged to die for the Innocent, foremost of the white-robed army. Some score or more in a small town were sacrificed to Herod's jealous wrath, unrecorded amidst bloodier massacres on the page of Josephus, but recalling to the mind of the sacred historian, the lamentation of Rachel, comfortless mother in Israel, over exiled and slaughtered children.

Divine retribution swiftly follows. The blood of thirty-seven

---

[1] St. Augustine.   [2] Josephus, "Bell Jud." ii 18. 7.

THE DIVINE INFANT.

years' reign of murder and crime called for vengeance. Herod died at Jericho, almost within hearing of the rejoicings of the people.

Another angelic intimation turns Joseph's steps homewards. Archelaus, the elder brother of Herod Antipas, the nominee of Herod's fourth will, had been proclaimed king by the army, and his accession under the title of Ethnarch had already been, or was afterwards, confirmed by Augustus. Joseph intending probably to live at Bethlehem is by another angelic warning directed to Galilee.

CHAPTER VI.

THE DIVINE BOY. THE DIVINE YOUTH.

> "Love had he found in huts where poor men lie;
>   His daily teachers had been woods and rills,
>   The silence that is in the starry sky,
>   The sleep that is among the lonely hills."
> WORDSWORTH, "Song at the Feast of Brougham Castle."

Nazareth — Physical environment — Home influence and education — Epiphany of the Divine Boy—The Father's house—The tender Plant—The Divine Young Man—The simple home—Experience of men—Communion with nature—God's silences of preparation.

NAZARETH, the "watcheress" or "protectress," lay white on the bosom of the surrounding hills. The horizon of the town is limited to the smooth bare limestone hill-tops. But from the summit of the hill above the eye swept over a wide, a varied, and a stirring scene of beauty. To the north rose, tier above tier, the mountains of Upper Galilee, the three-peaked Hermon's hoary crown; closer, gleaming Sepphoris, now Seffurieh, some four miles off, "the city set on a hill," made by Herod Antipas the capital of Galilee; and many of the towns of populous Galilee, stretching to "the hollow bay of Acre with its white circle of surf." Hard by in the east the cone of Tabor round which the many coloured caravans would wind; afar the long rough ridges of the Bashan mountains and the Jordan valley; westward, but twelve miles, the long-wooded reach of Carmel's prophetic hill, "as seen through a pure atmosphere, almost within touch,"[1] away over its ridges to the south-west the far flash of "the great sea" dinted with sails; southward the rich

[1] A. Henderson.

THE DIVINE BOY.

historic plain of Esdraelon, field of many battles, to the mountains of Gilboa on the east, and the hills of Samaria on the north.

Modern Nazareth lies "as in a hollow cup,"[1] lower down upon the hill, as is indicated by the position " of the old cisterns and tombs."[2] It is a flourishing town, and most of its six thousand inhabitants are Christian. The Virgin's Fount, then, as now, a favourite resort of the youth, is the one hallowed spot. The fair beauty of the women, the bright coloured dresses of the inhabitants are traits which may be a pre-Christian survival ; the quarrelsome violence, which is still a Nazarene characteristic, may have prompted the olden question of Nathanael. But of buildings nothing remains of our Lord's time.

Nazareth was a town, not a village. Its population numbered, probably, at least ten thousand.[3] From Ptolemais, the port of communication with Rome, the distance was six hours ; from the Sea of Galilee, five ; from Sepphoris, the capital of Galilee, till Tiberias rose into greater importance, one hour and a half. Nazareth was near several caravan commercial routes, one of the three which led from Acco to Damascus passed through it. Merchants and travellers to and from Damascus, the Mediterranean, the Sea of Galilee, Scythopolis, must have passed along its terraced way or within easy distance. From Jerusalem the journey was but three days.

While it was not a mere highland village, neither was it a great commercial or social centre. It must have escaped the paganizing civilization of Herod. No theatres, baths, temples, were there. The atmosphere was Jewish; the hereditary influences were all Jewish. Under a purely Jewish and Galilean environment Jesus was brought up. His breeding was uncontaminated by Greek elements and unwarped by the dominant Pharisaism of Judæa.

The natural surroundings must have asserted their influence upon the natural development of the Divine Child. Children have little conscious sense of the beauties of form and colour, of light and shade in scenery, little of historic imagination in places of national interest. But they artlessly delight in the

[1] "Cruise of the Bacchante," ii 675.
[2] Conder, "Tent Life," i. 138 foll.
[3] Merrill, fifteen or twenty thousand.

flowered meadows, and the verdurous hills, and their lively fancy weaves a hundred tales from nature's picture-book. The charismata of the "living garment of God" can never have been lost on the sensitive spirit, the observant eye, the dutiful heart of the Child. How many walks upon the Nazarene hillsides must have gladdened the young heart! The bright spring flowers picked, the red anenomes, the pink phlox, the rock roses among the commonest, who could count? Many pages of Jewish history lay an open self-explaining Bible on the surrounding plains and hills. An intelligent, a patriotic mother in Israel, like the singer of the Magnificat, could never have forgotten for herself, or for her child pupil, the histories writ large upon the neighbouring battlefields. The names of Gideon, of Deborah and Barak, of Saul and Samuel and Jonathan, of Elijah, of Jehu, whispered from the very ground. Childhood drinks in the sunshine of life, but the dark shadows are hidden from unsuspecting innocence protected by parental care.

Of all the early factors in His human development the home influence must have been supreme. The homes of Israel were the brightest spot, the love of children the tenderest chord, the respect for women a most honourable mark of Jewish life. This is abundantly provable from the Talmud.[1] "All the verses of Scripture that spoke of flowers and gardens were applied to children and schools. 'Do not touch Mine anointed ones, and do My prophets no harm.' 'Mine anointed' were school children, and 'My prophets' their teachers. The highest and most exalted title which they bestowed in their most poetical flights upon God Himself was that of Pedagogue of Man." So in regard to women. "It is woman alone through whom God's blessings are vouchsafed to a house. She teaches the children, speeds the husband to the place of worship and instruction, welcomes him when he returns, keeps the house godly and pure.[2] 'A good wife,' says the son of Sirach, 'is a great gift of God to him that fears God is she given'" (Ecclus. xxvi. 1–4).[3]

[1] E. Deutsch, "Remains," p. 147.
[2] Cf. Saadi, the popular Persian poet, translated by Col. W. Mackinnon—
[3] E. Deutsch, "Remains," p. 54.

> "A handsome, loving, chaste, obedient wife,
>   Maketh a man a king, though poor in life; . . .
> Surely God's favour is on him bestowed
>   Whose wife makes glad and prospers his abode."

THE DIVINE BOY.

The love of children breaks through the arid technicalities of the Talmud like a strain of sweet music. The mother is the household queen. The reign of motherhood was more sacred under the Law than elsewhere. Under the old covenant there were Sarahs and Rachels, Hannahs and Susannas. The word-portrait of King Lemuel (Prov. xxxi.) cannot wholly have been an ideal one. The Gospels and Acts are still richer in examples and types of holy womanhood. Whatever of tenderness and moral beauty and devout faith there was among the chosen daughters of Israel must have signalized the mother of the Lord. Whatever of motherhood that is most human yet most Divine Christian homes have known, must have been present in the first and best Christian home. The influence of mother over child, the responsive love, inexpressible, between the bearer and the born, must here have attained its full perfection.

Nor must we forget the father, whose especial duty it was to teach his child the Law, and whose humility and conscientiousness are apparent under and by reason of the gospel silence, and whose title to sainthood has been acknowledged by grateful Christendom. Modern ethical thought assigns a supreme place to reverence. " Reverence towards goodness, which . . proves to be identical with devotion to God."[1] "This apex and crown of human goodness"[2] cannot have failed to mark the character of the thoughtful son of the house of David and the nursing father of Messiah. Believers in the unbroken virginity of the maiden mother have always seen in the faithful Joseph an example of purity. Graces so fragrant as these may well have been privileged to assist in the nurture and teaching of the holy Boy. The sacredness and the beauty of family life has never been realized as fully as in the present day. The family circle at Nazareth at once suggests and sanctions the highest family ideals. Family love formed a very important factor in the expansion of the faith, as the family of the faithful spread from one domestic centre to another, federating all in one family of God.

That Christ was taught by His mother the Shema, or elementary Jewish creed, as soon as He could speak, that the Psalms were His child's hymn-book, the Law, the Torah, the object of

[1] J. Martineau, "Types of Ethical Theory," ii. p 206.   [2] Ibid.

His sacred study from five or six years of age, is beyond doubt; for such was the education of every Jewish child of dutiful parents. From first to last it was religious. The Jewish child lived and moved and had his being in a religious environment. Till ten years of age Jesus must have studied the Bible. That He passed on according to the usual course to the study of the Mishnah may be doubted. His knowledge of the traditions of the elders may have come only from the experience of its application to every day and every hour of Jewish life. We may be permitted to doubt whether the pure fountains of revealed truth were ever sullied by Mishnic admixture in the early home teachings and self-instructions of the Forerunner or the Messiah.

Whatever intellectual education the Boy Jesus received, His spiritual training must have been the first care. The Bible cannot have been a mere lesson-book. "From His intimate familiarity with Holy Scripture" (and that in the original Hebrew) "in its every detail, we may be allowed to infer that the home of Nazareth, however humble, possessed a precious copy of the sacred volume in its entirety."[1] The services in the synagogue upon the Sabbath day, and perhaps on the week-days, the family worship, the private prayer, were absolutely real to the Holy Family. The inward history of that soul, the functions of the unseen life within, the communion with the Father—these are subjects past the thought of sinners! In all these ways known and unknown, the Divine Child increased with the increase of God.

The higher intellectual and moral currents of the time can hardly have left Nazareth uninfluenced. The tide of human thought and national feeling sweeps into the most secluded regions.

But whether Joseph was a cultivated man there is no evidence of judging. Culture to a Palestinian Jew consisted entirely in the knowledge of the Law. If he had any acquaintance with the later Jewish literature, their study began, continued, and ended in the glorification of the Law. This is true of the native history, such as 1 Maccabees; of the later Psalms, such as the Maccabean (Psa. lxxiv., lxxix, cxlix.; perhaps lxxxiii. and lxxxiv.), the literature already noticed in chapter

[1] Edersheim, i. 234.

THE DIVINE BOY.

iii. From these he would have learned and taught first and last, in every tone of the moral scale, the fear of God. The love of God was an idea fully developed only in the teaching of Christ. The spirit breathed in all these writings is pure, genuine Pharisaic Judaism. It is clear that if Christ imbibed any such teaching from Joseph or other Nazarene elders, all that was partial, all that was typically Pharisaic, was rejected by the pure and healthy mind, while what was true and spiritual, what was scriptural and universal, was appropriated and assimilated.

That Jesus was a solitary Child seems unnatural to suppose. Compulsory education was the law of the land. If the law was in force in Galilee, He must have attended the national synagogue school, and formed one of a circle round the Chazzan, or minister, of the synagogue. As there was no pride, singularity, or exclusiveness about Him whose delight it was to be with the sons of men, He must have joined in childish sports with His schoolfellows and neighbours and foster-brothers,[1] as well as in childish lessons. That He showed unselfishness and conscientiousness, a bright and loving spirit, an open heart at home and out of doors, that He honoured His adopted father and His mother, that He actively assisted them in the simple duties of the household, as age and strength permitted, goes without saying; that He throughout His life enjoyed good health and bodily strength seems implied in the sacred memoirs.

Christ passed through all the stages of life to redeem and consecrate all. He was a real Child as well as a real Man. He spake as a child, thought as a child, understood as a child. The history of the Divine Childhood is summed up in the words of St. Luke (ii. 40, 52). There was a natural development of body, soul, and spirit. None of the Nazarene townsfolks remembered or recorded any extraordinary feats of mind or body on His part. As upon Samuel, the grace of God was upon Him. It was a permanent, not a special or official, endowment. The attractiveness of transparent innocence, the beauty of ideal holiness, drew ever the increasing favour of men. The Divineness of child-life and of the "eternal childhood," which, with all other perfections, "exists in God,"[2] was here exhibited. The Epiphany of the Divine Boyhood follows in nature and in

[1] *I e.*, Joseph's sons by a former wife.
[2] Rev. H. N. Grimley.

spirit the Epiphany of the Divine Infancy. The darkness lifts for a moment, and the light breaks upon a boyish figure and character. He is seen in His Father's house. The act is typical. It is the Epiphany of the Divine Boyhood.

At the time when Jesus went up to the feast, Quirinius was Legate, or governor, of the Roman province of Syria; Archelaus was in banishment in Gaul under Roman displeasure. Coponius, the first of the Roman procurators, was there. There, too, at his official duties, must have been Ananos, the son of Seth, the high priest Annas. It was the spring of A D. 9. Joseph, as a conscientious Jew, and Mary, out of self-imposed obligation or from the example set by those women of Hillel's school who went up once a year, were in the habit [1] of going up to the holy city. For the first time the Child accompanied them. He was not yet son of the Torah, legally of age, but wanting a year only, according to the custom of the time, and perhaps with other boys of His age or kin He went. If His mother had never gone before, she would not have left Him to go without her

The songs of Zion must have cheered the pilgrim march, most of all the Psalms of Ascent, such as

> "I was glad when they said unto me,
> 'Let us go to the house of Jehovah.'
> Our feet stand at last
> Within thy gates, O Jerusalem." [2]

Many children entering their teens are vividly sensitive to religious ideas. The first journey to the city where God had set His Name, where all Jewish worship and life and history had centred for generations, must have been an epoch in the life of any young Israelite. Add to that the sacred purpose, the Divine and national feast, the holy place, the house of Jehovah—above all, the Personality of the Child-pilgrim, Son of God and Son of David—and the lingering in the Father's house, the naive question of the conscious Son of the Highest seems strictly natural. Looking back through the after-lights, we ask, not—could it have been? but could it not have been?

Some have supposed that at this visit He first realized His Divine Sonship . the profound Dorner,[3] *e.g.*, "it flashed upon

---

[1] ἀναβαινόντων tense. [2] Psa. cxxii. (Cheyne).
[3] "System of Christian Doctrine," iii 365.

Him in the holy city, in the midst of types of Him, He knew it also to be His mission, to be about what was His Father's. God is to Him Father in a special sense; therefore He also knew Himself in a special sense to be His Son. And to assert and carry through this consciousness He knew to be His mission. He, this man, must remain in the Divine home." It may be so. The occasion was fitting. But considering the reality and rapidity of religious conviction in children of pious parents and devout environment, it seems not unnatural to suppose that His consciousness of His Divine Nature had begun as early as His intelligent and self-intelligible conscious-ness of God. Once knowing God as a Father, could He have failed to know God as His Father in an unique sense?

But we are here on the edge of mysteries. The sources of knowledge are in any case mysterious; and in the case of Christ most mysterious. But against the supposition that He only used this language in the sense that any child of Israel could have used it, and that He did not arrive at His Divine con-sciousness till His baptism, we enter every protest, theological and psychological.

It was the third day of the feast, and the two following ones, that the Child Jesus was at once a pupil and a teacher of the Rabbis. On the first two days attendance at the Temple was compulsory. The Paschal meal had been eaten, the *Chagigah* offered, and "the first ripe barley reaped and brought to the Temple, and waved as the Omer of first flour before the Lord." [1] Joseph and Mary had begun their homeward journey. They rested, according to tradition, at Beeroth (*Bireh*), nine miles north of Jerusalem, spent the second day on the return, and the third in finding Him. In some part or other of the vast precinct of the Temple, perhaps on the Chel, or Terrace, where the Temple Sanhedrin on feast days gave popular instruction, amongst the Rabbis, sat the young questioner. There was nothing very unusual in the fact, for the precocious Josephus at the age of fourteen was consulted by the high priests and principal men. But there was everything extraordinary about His intelligence. He was at home. He spake of His own, as the great thinker of Alexandria said, himself a boy of most rare promise, " Interrogabat magistros, et quia respondere non-poterant, ipse his, de quibus interrogaverat, respondebat. . . .

[1] Edersheim, i 246.

Interrogabat, inquam, magistros, non ut aliquid disceret, sed ut interrogans erudiret."[1] But it was impossible for the Messiah to remain in Jerusalem. Rabbinism would have choked Him. The inevitable breach would have come earlier. Obedient at any sacrifice He returned to the simple home and parental supervision. The light of the evangel is turned off. Silence falls round the Divine home; the figure of the Messiah is hidden for eighteen years. One welcome word tells us of natural, intellectual, spiritual growth (Luke ii. 52).

He grew up as a tender plant on a wholly Jewish soil, with nothing between Him and the pure air and light of heavenly grace but the better native surroundings of the day. His mental and spiritual development was natural, not artificial; healthy, not forced. Of His loving fidelity to Nature, His keenness of observation, His scientific accuracy of description, sufficient evidence is supplied by His parables and allegories. The freshness and originality of His mind from a human point of view sprang from the immediate perfection of His realization of fact in all departments, and the absence of the technical lore and pedantic traditionalism of the schools. Whatever "bias," in Spencerian language, He had, whatever hereditary predispositions played upon Him, were conceived and born in Jewish thought, in Jewish devotion, in Jewish Scripture, in Jewish family love and honour, in Jewish Messianic expectation nursed through long years of suffering and decay, sweetened and purified by trial and discipline, and lighted up with secret, undying hope.

Neither was Nazareth a secluded town, nor the life of Jesus a secluded life. Life in the East is always and altogether public. He increased in favour with men, and cannot, therefore, have isolated Himself from the townspeople. Simple and reverent, honest and laborious, loving and faithful, true and just, of transparent innocency and guilelessness, He did not fail to win affection and respect. Into all that was honest, pure, lovely, and of good report, He would enter freely and heartily. From all that was the contrary He would shrink. His education for affairs was derived from His experience of men and things. The realities of life are as appreciable on a small as on a large scale. His pure spirit was sensitive to the touch of truth as the leaves to the breath of spring, wherever it was met. His

[1] Origen, in Luc., Hom. xviii xix (954, 955).

THE DIVINE YOUTH.

perfect insight into the ways of men's hearts, and the springs of human conduct, was brought on its human side by the suffering shocks of contact with pure evil, or mixed good, and by the joyous sympathy which flows from love of all that is right. The Christ in youth was sober-minded, strong in grace. He fled youthful lusts, He followed righteousness. He was irreproachable in conduct. Not even calumny and the fierce light of after-criticism could rake up any ashes of scandal from the pure fire of that white young life. More pious and devout and simple than a Samuel, fairer and braver than a David, purer and fuller of the milk of human kindness than a Joseph, He was at all times and in all companies the pattern youthful Israelite, the Ideal Young Man. At home, eating and drinking, working at the carpenter's bench, worshipping on the housetop or in the synagogue, keeping feast and fast, with the maidens as sisters, with the young men as brothers, Jesus Christ was the same in character, as in after-days of public ministry, as He is now, to-day, and for ever.

The outward circumstances of His Nazarene life may be briefly noticed. The kind of house in which He lived is still found in a perfect state. "They are generally square, of different sizes, the largest, however, not thirty feet square, and have one or two columns down the centre to support the roof, which appears to have been flat as in the modern Arab houses. The walls are about two feet thick, built of masonry or of loose blocks of basalt. There is a low doorway in the centre of one of the walls, and each house has windows twelve inches high and six wide."[1] Sometimes "the house was divided into four chambers."

Daily food and clothing were simple and sufficient. He wore in manhood the national turban, probably white; and tunic of one piece, and therefore valuable; over that the talith ($\iota\mu\acute{\alpha}\tau\iota o\nu$), loose and flowing, whether white, or the common blue, or white with brown stripes, with the *Tsitsith* blue or white fringes at the four corners.[2]

The political movements of the day in a people so intensely national as the Jews, in whose eyes patriotism was a religion,

[1] L. Oliphant, "Haifa," p 231.

[2] Stapfer, ch. x p 100, but the white of the Transfiguration was the whiteness of intense colour, and does not imply that His garment was not white before.

and whose politics were summed up in the one word, the Messiah, cannot have failed to excite the interest of Nazarenes. How seriously, how intently, the political horizon must have been watched by parents who shared in some degree the ideas of the time respecting the political character and national mission of the Messiah and kept to themselves the tremendous secret! Christ Himself may have thought out some of the political problems of the day, as travelling merchant from the west or returning priest from Jerusalem brought in news. Such questions as afterwards confronted Him, as the moral obligations of taxation, the respective duties to the Roman government and its representatives, and to the national government and its representatives, were settled in the court of His private life and conscience, before He was publicly required to state His principles. His kingdom was not of this world, but this world was of His kingdom and of His love.

Years brought experience of men; increasing knowledge increasing sorrow, increasing desire to take away the evil. As lives and characters were gauged by Him, as hollowness and unreality, corruption and hypocrisy, dropped their disguise before His open gaze, as wickedness and vice and all the wrongful dealing of men burned like fire against the spotless white of His soul, as hearts lay open before Him, if He willed, He took the measure of men, of His own people, of His own generation. If His voluntary exinanition limited Him to the ordinary media of human knowledge there is a moral insight, peculiar to holiness of a high order, exemplified in the history of saints, which even upon a purely human basis must have distinguished Him above all His holy offspring, which must have vibrated to every breath of good, and jarred at every shock of evil. Nor is life on a large scale, in populous centres, amongst seas of human activity, necessary to breadth of view and intensity of perception. On the contrary, individuals, where fewer, offer more points for attraction or repulsion. The microscopic view of life becomes possible. Characters, individual forces, are more easily measurable. The village Hampden or the village tyrant are more appreciable by their nearness. In the thriving country town Jesus saw types of every contemporary class and interest. The after experiences of life do not seem to have stirred many surprises in Him. He knew what was in man from the intuitive insight of perfection.

THE DIVINE YOUTH. 55

He knew what was in man from the accumulated experience of pain, and the intensified sympathy of an irrepressible stream of love. If any ambitions presented themselves to Him from without—from within they never could come—from flattering friends or home Messianic misapprehensions, they made no mark upon a heart cased in the panoply of God. Experience and observation formed the ethical sources of His inductive knowledge of men. The mysterious powers which were involved in His Divine nature are unknowable in their intrinsic energies.

Friends cannot have been wanting to the family circle. The town may have had its Simeon and Anna, its holy and humble of heart, its righteous according to the law without self-righteousness ; but we know of no Nazarene apostles, or even disciples, except His long unbelieving " brethren." Such an absence is conspicuous.

During these silent years He may have been shaping His life plan ; if the comparison may be made without irreverence, like Milton, "late choosing and beginning late," with conscious self-education. But it seems more becoming to think that He lived faithful to the simple light of everyday duty, turning every detail to heavenly account, waiting patiently for the Divine summons to wider fields of action and higher " vocation and ministry."

Upon Jesus Christ's youthful high communings with Nature it is needless to dwell. It has ceased to be the monopoly of artists, poets, physicists to taste the sacramental gifts of Nature. That it has so ceased is due to Him who opened the book of the Gospel of Nature. Nature to Him spoke in most melodious tones of the fair beauty of the Lord ; His righteousness, His all-providential care, His wisdom, His power in the things that were made were read as in an open book. In St. Paul we see a man of culture and city tastes who found in nature a gospel which supplied his new faith with the lofty analogies of the resurrection body and the starlike in glory—a gospel muffled to his unconverted ears. In Christ we have One whose eyes nor ears required opening to a Presence in the summer hills and flowers or the wintry frosts and snows. The Old Testament is full of Nature's worship. The Psalms, which were Christ's special manual of devotions, in every cadence spoke of and from the works of His hands to the Maker. To Christ is due as discoverer the first revelation of the truth of the unity of Nature in God, the community of Nature and human nature, their interdependence, their common dependence upon the Personal God. To Him, then, the meanest flower that blows upon the Nazarene hillsides brought thoughts not only too deep for tears, but passing human understanding—thoughts of His Father's love and power and wisdom, thoughts of man's unlove, impotence, folly, misery,[1] sin, which Nature as truly mirrors, and as pathetically expresses with her thousand shadows as with her ten thousand lights she proclaims the Light of the world.

The silences of God are not the silences of inactivity, of indifference, of oblivion. They are the silence of infinite preparative industry, of the march of myriad evolutions, slow and sure and invisible. There was the silence before the call of Abraham; there was the silence of heavens as brass during the travail of Egyptian bondage; there was the silence as of the coldness and disappointment of an outraged friend before the call of Samuel; there was the long pre-Messianic silence after the last of the prophets had lifted up his voice in promise of the messenger, Elijah the prophet, before the great and terrible day of the Lord; there was the silence of the prophet-priest in the solitudes of the deserts, before he put the trumpet to his lips and sounded the alarm; there was the silence of the Messiah Himself, gathering up the forces of His soul for the day of battle, storing the spiritual sinews of war for the superhuman strife, awaiting the Divine mandate and the trumpet ring of His human forerunner; there was the mysterious and most forbearing silence of God while the Son of Man waged His single-handed warfare with all the accumulated heritages of lies, the armed fortresses of evil, the concentrated organized hosts of the prince and potentate of ill. And the wondering, scarcely broken silence of the angels! And the Divine silence still remains in the majesty of self-reserve till it is burst by the trump of the angel.

But these silences of ages have been the preludes to utterance. There has been neither speech, nor language, till the fulness of

[1] Cf. J S Mill's hard reading of Nature in the famous passage in The Three Essays on Religion, but it is only of one side of Nature, and to a Christian suggests the redemption and resurrection of Nature implied in that of human nature through Christ.

THE DIVINE YOUTH.

each time—till God spake and it was done. Busy, working lives of men, ye need the golden silences of patient, teachable prayer and preparatory suffering devotion above all needs of this work-a-day world if ye would find out God's purpose, fulfil His ends, and do His work !

Years passed by over an uneventful life and a silent heaven. The people called Him by their wants and miseries, the family of sinners called Him by their sins, the prayers and desires of thousands who had gone to Sheol disappointed called Him, the spiritual Messianic watchers for their satisfaction, the deluded and debased for their correction called Him, " the world with all its ideals called Him ;"[1] but His Heavenly Father called Him not, and He waited His hour. By such a discipline of waiting and patient endurance God had tried Abraham, had tried His people Israel, tries His faithful for their hour and His.

How the Christ prayed in flawless prayer, how His human spirit held communion with the Divine, is unwritable in any gospel, and unthinkable but on the knees. The patience and faith of the saints had been tried, had been tasked ; and the Saint Himself of saints revealed more than all, and bore much more than He revealed.

But it may be without presumption inferred that He prayed the customary prayer of the adult Israelite. Morning and evening He would have recited the Shema, or devotional creed, derived from Deut. vi. 4-9, xi. 13-21, and Numb. xv. 37-41. Morning, afternoon, at the time of the Minchah offering, and evening, even in childhood, the Shemoneh Esreh, "the prayer" consisting of eighteen, and in its final shape of nineteen, Berachahs or benedictions. The latter form indicates how large a place thanksgiving filled in pure Jewish devotion. The duty so often insisted upon by St. Paul was doubtless an improved survival of his Jewish days, and must have been perfectly fulfilled by the perfect Son of Abraham. The usual grace (Berachoth), too, would be said before and after meals from childhood without attention to the petty and complex regulations of Rabbis, such as—" If the blessing has been pronounced over a side dish before the meal, the side dish after the meal is exempt."

[1] Lange in a different context.

CHAPTER VII.

THE PROPHET BAPTIST. THE DIVINE BAPTISM.

"The brave strong spirit of the man supports him. So mighty is the source of strength within him, that, as the prospects of the present darken, the prophecy of the future grows more splendid in his soul ; as earth sinks into shadow heaven grows more radiant around him" (J. A. SYMONDS, "Dante in Exile").

John in the Wilderness—The Great Renunciation—The Cry of the Kingdom—The Flow of Penitents—Jesus Baptized—Why?

THE things that Jesus learned, the things that He suffered especially, in the country town, with all its narrowness, folly, sin, were the school for the Messianic venture into the public field. That venture of faith was now at hand.

The silence of Israel was broken by a voice as startling as if one of the old prophets had risen again trumpet-tongued. It was the cry in the wilderness of the new prophet. His life, like Christ's, had been a hidden fire. He had retired to the desert at the imperious bidding of the Voice within, even in boyhood, when strong surrenders and great renunciations are by rare spirits only, and then but seldom made. Spiritual strength was his great mark.

The forerunner had retired into the desert in boyhood. But the child life must have begun to take shape before he left the priestly home. Perhaps the death of his aged parents was the immediate cause of his going into the wilderness, which lay south of Jericho and the Jordan fords. There he abode like other solitaries in outward life, but in the secret burden and glory of his soul alone and unapproachable. The principal factor in his home and desert education was the study of the

THE PROPHET BAPTIST.

prophets. If a child can be brought up in a pious home for a missionary career, if a prince's son can be trained for high station, if a philosopher's child may be steeped with learning, like John Stuart Mill from infancy, the son of the Jewish priest could be prepared by holy discipline and many-fountained prayer to full consciousness of his Divine mission and venture. Deliberate preparation for a special purpose constitutes a technical education. A technically prophetic education in the lives and words of Israel's prophets would stamp into the sensitive heart of the child of Aaron an intensity of conviction, an absorption of desire, an openness to the fires of inspiration, an irrefragable independence of extra Scriptural authorities and worldly ranks, which should characterize a shaft polished for Divine aim (Isa. xlix. 2, 3), a mouth like a sharp sword, a life long hidden in the shadow of His hand, a servant of the Lord in whom He would be glorified.

He was an ascetic, but neither in dress, nor food, nor rule, still less in spirit or in teaching, was he an Essene. He belonged to no religious school. But he had made the great renunciation demanded of founders of schools in the East and Reformers. In the wild steppes of the desert nothing came between his soul and God. To a purely spiritual atmosphere he was acclimatized by a long specialization to prophetic work, resulting in a character altogether unworldly. To every local or national interest he was dead save one. To every movement from or towards a spiritual direction he was as tremulously sensitive as a ministering spirit. Asceticism hardens and ossifies some natures, but others it intensifies for spiritual impact or impression. Such a man as the priestly son of Zacharias, trained in a long course of spiritual self-discipline, whose meat and drink had been the words of the prophets and the promises of God, was a fully adjusted organ for Divine communications, and one who corresponded with popular ideals, not in Judæa only, but all over the East. Had he willed the prophet John might have been numbered among the Gautamas, the Confuciuses of the world. He might have been a false Messiah, and a "lost leader."

No mere force of genius, spiritual or intellectual, nor any fulfilment of popular ideals, can account for the depth of the impression made by the Baptist. The Acts (xviii. 25 ; xix. 3) show that his influence, in the course of a quarter of a century, spread as far as remote proconsular Asia. And his name became even a "watchword of direct antagonism" and rival Messiahship.[1] And Josephus, with his anti-Messianic bias, himself is a witness to the popular influence he wielded.

Two facts account for the Baptist's success. First, his personality. Secondly, his opportunity. The man himself was "a spiritual splendour,"[2] a moral force of extraordinary momentum. The ante-natal prayers, the long discipline of waiting, the vivid realization of his prophetic vocation growing with his growth, the stream of self-consecrating prayer which bore him on the tide of God's undisappointed will, had borne their proper fruit. He was the one man of his time who could stand upon the naked truth of the Bible, and knew that he was of the spiritual lineage of the Samuels and the Elijahs. Such a power within him, such memories behind him, such a special assurance and conviction, stamped him as a strong man of God, a prophet, and more than a prophet.

But great characters may tower in unrecognized oblivion. Great men require great circumstances. Had not the times been ripe the Baptist might have been a volcano in the desert. But it was the time of times for making an impression. The cry of the kingdom of God went to the breathing heart of the people. What was this kingdom of God but the ruling idea of the old covenant, the beginning, the middle, the end of its rites, institutions, laws; the promise to the fathers, the passionate dream of the prophets, the unsatisfied desire of a people whom past sufferings and exiles, whom present subjection, never crushed out of their pride as the people of God? Everywhere the political and religious atmosphere was charged with the idea, actual or latent. Consciously or unconsciously, directly or indirectly, men were looking for, or groping after a Divine kingdom. Pharisees and Essenes were discussing it in their schools. The Book of Enoch most, and the other apocalypses expressed and encouraged the same aspiration. St. John took up the conception, but in a different sense. He had derived his thought from the Messianic prophets. He was driven by the Spirit of prophecy into the wilderness. He brooded over his Isaiah till substance and spirit, tone and temper, passed into him. But for Stephen there had not been a Paul. But for an Isaiah there had not been a John the Baptist. Although he

[1] Bp. Lightfoot, "Colossians," p. 403. [2] Dante.

THE PROPHET BAPTIST. 61

was distinctly affirmed by Christ to be the second Elias predicted by Malachi (iv. 5) he did not admit the title himself. Perhaps he did not think he had risen to the spirit and power of that prophet, and had fallen short of his high vocation. True greatness, true holiness, are humble and self-depreciative. In this, as in all respects, John contrasted with the Hillels and Shammais of the time, and of the time to come.

> "Still, some few
> Have grace to see Thy purpose, strength to mar
> Thy work by no admixture of their own,
> Limn truth not falsehood, bid us love alone,
> Thy type untampered with, the naked star!"[1]

He alone then saw that the kingdom of God was a moral and spiritual fabric, and that moral and spiritual, not political, reconstruction was its necessary presupposition. He alone left theories and formulæ and stepped forward into action. And he, in the teeth of current opinion, directed the sword of Jehovah, not against the Gentiles, but "towards Israel itself."[2] He began the transformation which Christ completed. He was His intellectual as well as spiritual forerunner.

All sorts and conditions of men, high and low, from city and country, came down to the Jordan. The movement spread from Judæa to Galilee. A national regeneration seemed at hand; a religious reform to have taken root. A stream of inquirers came down to the river, like Hindus to the sacred Ganges, to wash and be clean, but with moral rather than ceremonial intention. The religious revival of the second Elias was repeating that of the first.[3]

As the kingdom the Baptist proclaimed was a new and yet old kingdom, so the typical initiatory rite he required was new and yet old. Old for "proselytes of righteousness" (*Gerey hatst-sedeq*) submitted to baptism (*Tebhilah*) in order to be "born anew," in Rabbinical language, as children of the covenant; old because water was familiar as an instrument of outward and a symbol of spiritual cleansing, both in Scripture and earlier or later tradition.[4] Rabbi Akiva says, "Blessed are ye, O Israel! Before whom are ye cleansed? and who is he that cleanseth you?

---
[1] R. Browning, "Francis Furini"   [2] Hausrath, p. 103.
[3] Cf. Milligan, "Elijah," in Men of the Bible Series.
[4] Hershon, "Treasures of the Talmud," pp 99, 112, 140.

even your Father which is in heaven;" for it is said (Ezek. xxxvi. 25), "I will sprinkle clean water upon you, and ye shall be clean." And again it is said (Jer. xvii. 13), "The ablutionary bath of Israel is the Lord. As the ablutionary bath cleanses the unclean, so does the Holy One—blessed be He!—cleanse Israel." To this day a Jew bathes on the eve of the day of atonement, to wash away his sins. But it was also new.

By submitting to this washing in Jordan the penitents expressed their personal sense of sin, and need of reconciliation to God, disclaimed the imputation of the "merits of the Fathers" to Abraham's children, and entered into a new covenant relation with God. Such a baptism, like the Law itself, of which St. John was, so to speak, the personal embodiment, and last representative, could only create, or deepen, without satisfying the consciousness of sin. The Baptism of Christ was as much above the Baptism of John as the Gospel was above the Law, the master the servant. The Baptism of John led to that remission of sins which the Lamb of God brought into the world. The penitential element remains in Christian Baptism. The simple wooden cross often set up by the banks of flowing rivers in heathen lands, signifies to the converts who partake of the bath of regeneration a baptism of repentance whereby they forsake sin, and a remission upon entrance into a new covenant of life.

How exactly the kingdom of God was coming, what shape it would take, lay outside the prophet's immediate perception. As his life was as eminently practical as his teaching, his penitents appear to have been organized into the germ of a Messianic community. It was a kingdom as yet kingless. Its members were under training for a higher Presence and kingdom, were being led from a Baptism of hope to a Baptism of life and pardon. As John followed the winding course of the Jordan from Judæa to Decapolis, increasing multitudes, enjoying the holiday of a Sabbatic year, came from various motives to see him, and some to remain with him.

The date of his appearance is carefully fixed in St. Luke's account. The third Evangelist often shows that he has Gentile and cultivated readers in view, who looked for scientific method in history and chronological data. How long he had been preaching before Jesus came to him we are not told.

What particular impulse drew Jesus to John's baptism is not

THE DIVINE BAPTISM.

revealed. Whether He was conscious that His pre-official life was at an end, whether He had inward Divine intimation, or whether He went as a son of Israel in response to the Divine appeal by the prophet, in unconsciousness of Messianic inauguration, we cannot say. Certainly in the perfection of His human sympathy, in the desire of His soul "to devote Himself to the kingdom of God,"[1] He went as a runner to the mark. And the Baptism itself was Godward, an expression of His self-consecration to the service of the kingdom. And His prayer awakes the Divine assurance of His accepted surrender as well as manward laying "the foundation of all future baptisms."[2]

It may have been at 'Abârah,[3] the recently recovered probable site of Bethany, or Bethabara, that the great event in the Baptist's life took place. It was "in winter, according to the unanimous tradition of the early Church,"[4] and possibly on January 6 or 10 (B C. 4), according to the Basilidean tradition, that the Messiah stood unrecognized on the bank. He was last of a crowd. The prophet recognized Him.

" Tantum egregio decus enitet ore "[5]

The moral majesty and unearthly grace of rapt unconscious beauty could not fail to impress the one man most sensitive to a breath from heaven. The power wielded by unfallen Innocence and transparent holiness was as that of an incarnate infallible Conscience.[6] The spiritual sympathy of St. John would have felt some of this even if he had never heard the name of Jesus mentioned in his home life. He tried to escape his official duty, and become the penitent of Jesus.

" How didst thou start, Thou Holy Baptist, bid
To pour repentance on the Sinless Brow ! "[7]

St. Luke characteristically mentions that Jesus was praying when the sign was given of the rending heavens and the de-

---
[1] Dorner, "System," &c , III. pp 377, 378.   [2] Ibid.
"Twenty-one Years' Work in the Holy Land," p. 94 foll.
[4] Bp. Ellicott, p. 105.   [5] Virg , "Æn ," IV. 150.
Dr Wace, "Christianity and Morality," p 247 f , in a different context "Conceive yourselves in the presence of a Conscience Incarnate, and then try to realize the awful homage which would be extorted from your souls."
[7] J. H Newman.

scending dove, and the confirming word of the Father uttered itself.

Why the Christ sought to be baptized is a question which was first raised by His baptizer, and it has been variously answered.

Some have seen in Jesus the Representative Penitent ; others view the Baptism as the inauguration of His ministerial life ; others as the last act of the private life of the Perfect Ideal Israelite, going to the Baptism of St. John, because it was from heaven, and of His Father, without ulterior motive. In the fulness of the words "fulfil all righteousness," in regard to the past, the present, and the future, every partial interpretation expresses but one aspect. It was the righteousness of the perfect Israelite acknowledging the obligation of obedience to the prophet of Israel imposing a rite from heaven, and attesting his Divine mission. It was the righteousness of the Son of Man, the Representative of humanity, inaugurating a new relation with the Father of all. It was the righteousness of the Apostle of God devoting Himself to a life of perfect fulfilment of His will.

Nor did the long-withheld Divine response delay. The sundering heavens, the descending dove, the articulate voice were the outward and visible signs of the descending Spirit. The Baptism of the Spirit completed the Baptism of the Divine Penitent. The reward of self humiliation was given in Divine exaltation. The Christ was anointed as Prophet, Priest, King, of the new Israel, the new Church, the new kingdom, consecrated to His triple office and work by the washing of water and the unction of the Spirit, even as the high priests were consecrated by the washing of water and the affusion of "the anointing oil" (Exod. xxix. 4, 7 ; Lev. viii. 6, 12). It was the anointing, too, which fulfilled Messianic prefigurements and types—the anointing of the promised sanctuary of the great Messianic eighth chapter of Isaiah (viii. 14 ; cf. Ezek. xi. 16) ; the anointing of the Most Holy after sixty weeks of Daniel's vision.

As the Baptism of the Messiah fulfilled prophecy, so was it itself a prophecy of the "mystical washing away of sin," and all the other blessings connected with His own Baptism of the future. This prospective and retrospective character belongs essentially to all the work of the Divine Man. His life cannot be considered in a purely historical context ; nor could it, had He been only a human being of extraordinary power and beauty of nature. For "before" and "after" belong to every human

THE DIVINE BAPTISM. 65

life which but faintly ripples over the ocean of time ; how much more to that which has relations to all time?

The Divine Messiah had waited for the Divine Investiture. And now His official life was to begin. It was as a second birth to a new life. In the language of the Church of old, " His second nativity."[1] The Voice from heaven spake in the Messianic language of the Second Psalm and the forty-second chapter of Isaiah, accrediting to the Baptist, who, as he saw the Spirit descending as a dove, in his own words, can hardly have failed to share alone with Christ the hearing of the Voice, the man Jesus, as the beloved Son of God.

To Jesus it was the seal of Divine authentication. It was the Fatherly recognition. It was the first break in the silence and loneliness of thirty years. It was, so to speak, a breath from Home. If the occasion was marked by the first visible and audible Divine intervention, it must have been one which called for it. God's acts are not arbitrary, but according to law. It was the meeting-point of the private and public life Divine, of the unasserted and the asserted Messiahship, of the old and the new kingdom, of the old and the new covenant, and of the old and the new righteousness.

As the Nazarene life of obscure devotion, so the public Baptism and the descent of the Dove, were contrary to all Rabbinical Messianic preconceptions. Jesus, as decidedly as John, broke with the current Messianic idea at once. This cannot have been done in ignorance. From a purely human point of view He could not have lived till thirty in populous Galilee without hearing the current versions of the Messianic hope. Alike the Baptist and the Baptized had waited for a sign, waited for God to declare Himself, prisoners of hope.

[1] Abp. Trench, "Studies," p. 3.

CHAPTER VIII.

THE DIVINE TEMPTATION.

> "Some bodily form of ill
>   Floats on the wind, with many a loathsome curse
>   Tainting the hallowed air, and laughs, and flaps
>   Its hideous wings."
>   J. H. NEWMAN, "The Dream of Gerontius."

Personal Tempter, external and real, not an internal process—First offer—Supposed Buddhist resemblance—Second offer—Third offer—Temptations recurrent—Temptation representative.

WITH the rapture of His Father's greeting in His ears, and the exultation of the Spirit within, Jesus stepped out of the decisive baptismal waters like a young soldier into the *gaudia certaminis*. He was strong in the Lord. The joy of the Lord was His strength. Even His bodily energy was at full tide. So strengthened, "He found and felt no need"[1] of food for all the forty days of strife.

There is a Divine fitness in the Temptation. The second Adam suffered this humiliation that all Adam's sons might share in the victory. The tempter came. An external[2] coming alone satisfies the conditions of the narrative. The history must be accepted as authentic, or relegated to the region of myth. To regard the Temptation as an inner process in the mind of Jesus is to destroy the historical value of the sacred records not in this place only, but in all. The presence of Satan may, or may not, have been visible. The supreme master of the science of evil knew the outward life of Jesus, and all that had been

---

[1] Abp Trench, "Studies," p. 13.
[2] Against Weiss's, &c., &c., "inner process."

THE DIVINE TEMPTATION.

said of Him. He knew His claim to be the Messiah. How far a hostile spirit, without the internal conditions of faith and spiritual sympathy, could penetrate, *ab extra*, into His Being and Nature, can only be known to purely spiritual beings. It is a remarkable fact that the demonized recognized Christ, though with horror and fear.

Christ was led, driven. An unseen Personal Force bore Him —a certain violence is implied in the words. Necessity was laid upon Him. The Temptation was not self-sought. It was an act of obedience. The constraining power of duty, even in the Christian, may be at times consciously felt like the pressure of an Invisible Hand.

How the impeccable Son of God could suffer temptation is a mystery. That the Temptation was real is expressly asserted in Scripture. The reality of it stands or falls with the reality of the Human Nature assumed by the Divine Word. The point of attack throughout is the Man Jesus' sense of duty to God. God or self were the alternatives, stripped from disguise, set before His human spirit. A moment's consent to the mental picture would have been a declaration of victory to the world and its prince.

If the demoniacal hierarchy knew Him, who He was, it is difficult to suppose their Head and Prince was not a partner in their belief and in their trembling, perhaps as the result of his discomfiture. The first Temptation was directed not only to the outward senses, but to the inner spirit. Its attractiveness, "its subtlety, lay in its very simplicity."[1] The arguments in its favour sounded irresistible. To make the stones bread would preserve a life in danger, and that life the most precious of all, and would preserve it without injury to any one or anything The end was good, but the means bad. The method was not the one appointed by God. By making stones bread Christ would have violated the conditions of His submission to human limitations. He would have broken the laws of Nature, which are the laws of God. He would have fallen into independence of God and distrust in His earthly providence, would have wrought a work for His own individual glory and comfort. He would have ceased to be a true Son of Man, for His Humanity would have been unreal. With His real Humanity would have gone His

---

[1] Bishop John Wordsworth, "University Sermons," p 87.

Mediation. And whatever the result, the object was to be attained at the bidding of the adversary.

By way of contrast the Buddhist legend of Gautama's temptation may be compared. In the latter case the austerities during which Mâra, the destroyer, stood behind him, watching his opportunity, remonstrating with him for his self-destruction, were the instrument of self-mortification; they began and ended in self, and had no external relation to God and man. In Christ's case the asceticism was incidental to the Temptation, not an end in itself. There are other decisive points of contrast. Gautama's first temptation was to *attavâd*, the first of the Buddhists' Ten Sins, *i.e.*, the assertion of a self or individuality; in fact, to believe that he had a soul. Gautama was also tempted to *arùparagà*, the seventh of the Ten Sins, or "desire to live in some one of the formless heavens."[1]

In the second Temptation, the scene is changed from the lonely wilderness to the crowded city. The particles, "then," and "again," present in St. Matthew's report only (vers. 5, 8), indicate the historical order. St. Luke prefers the psychological classification, and presents the Temptations in order of their appeal to body, soul, and spirit. Foiled in awaking the lust of the flesh, the Tempter invokes the lust of the eye. The former temptation had been to hopelessness. The second temptation is to over hopefulness. "The Spirit of God had driven Jesus into the wilderness; the spirit of the devil now carried Him into Jerusalem. Jesus stands on the lofty pinnacle of the tower, or of the Temple porch, presumably that on which every day a priest was stationed to watch, as the pale morning light passed over the hills of Judea far off to Hebron, to announce it as the signal for offering the morning sacrifice."[2] Shall not the Messiah cast Himself down, borne angel-like and by angels, into His Father's house below, where priest and people thronged the courts for worship, ready to receive the Divinely-attested sign from Heaven? Would not a Father's love, and a Son's trust, be proved and certified? But Christ's answer unmasked the lie. He would use, not abuse, His filial relation. He would not vindicate His own Divinity at the expense of His own Humanity. He would not please Himself.

---

[1] Professor Kellogg, "The Light of Asia and the Light of the World," p. 141 foll., *u.v* on Mr Edwin Arnold's perverse misinterpretations in "The Light of Asia"   [2] Edersheim, i. 303.

He would not become Supreme Head of the Church by the assertion of mere power. " Never might the hour of Christ the King be anticipated in order to accomplish more speedily or more easily the work of Christ the Priest and of Christ the Prophet."[1] The victory of grace, the Headship of the Church, was to be won by suffering. Christianity minus the Cross was a forbidden fruit. This Temptation was essentially religious.

The scene changes from the Temple height to a very high mountain. Ecclesiastical supremacy has been offered, imperial earthly dominion is now held out, a Messianic empire and dominion of which Cæsar's would be an item. All the kingdoms of the world could be seen, not arithmetically but representatively. from one of the heights, where the second Moses, as from a Pisgah, could behold a land of promise— eastward and westward, stretching to the blue distances of the Euphrates, and the sheen of the Mediterranean flecked with cloudlike sails. The character of the Temptation suggests one of the heights of Abarim ; Nebo itself, commanding a view of the whole of Western Palestine, might have been the very place. Certainly the sharp hill of Quarantania, of Crusading tradition, could not be the mountain emphasized in the first Gospel as exceeding high. But the spot must be left, like the burial place of Moses, in its sublime secresy.

As the first assault had been delivered upon the body, the second upon the human spirit, the third tries the human soul of Christ. It was the largest bid the Prince of this world could offer. The second place in the kingdom was offered Him. "What Satan sought was, 'My kingdom come,' a Satanic Messianic time, a Satanic Messiah ; the final realization of an empire of which his present possession was only temporary, caused by the alienation of man from God"[2] The height and depth of Satanic usurpation was here nakedly disclosed. The arch rebel shows his colours. His despair of success breathes in the unspeakable audacity of the offer. It is the gambler's last stake, all that he has.

The first Temptation had been personal, the second ecclesiastical, the third specially Messianic. The first attacked His Manhood, the second His Priesthood and His Prophetic office, the third His Royalty. All three involved a denial of

[1] Bp. Magee. [2] Edersheim, 1. 305.

His Messiahship, of His character and office as the Servant as well as the Son of God, of His true Manhood. In the last analysis, the essential principle in each case amounted to, Deny God,

"Evil, be thou my good." [1]

The last Temptation closes with the address of Satan by name. The issue had never been in doubt. The defeated assailant flies from the field. The Second Adam, and in Him humanity, have more than retrieved the Fall. The place left vacant by the fallen angel is filled by those who had been watching, it may be, hard by, spectators of the lists (cf. 1 Cor. iv. 9). Man did eat angels' food in angels' society. It is a foretaste of the triumphal march through Paradise, of the Royal Coronation at the Victor's return home.

The Tempter left for a season only. The Temptations recur under various forms and forces. One of the titles to office and work in His Name was based upon the fact of having been with Him therein (Luke xxii. 28, 29). The Temptation was not, then, an isolated incident; it was intermittent, if not chronic. It was an haunting pain, a dogging mystery, a dark presence,

"Teucris addita Juno."

"His last word, 'I have overcome the world,' tells how sharp the strife had been, which is remembered even in heaven, as He speaks to His militant Church, and tells them that they shall overcome, even as I also overcame." [2]

The Temptation in the wilderness stands out above the others in its solitariness as the Temptation of temptations. The edge of the Tempter's sword was broken. The end was as the beginning, the victory of suffering and faith. The Temptation was not the victory of one man, but of the race of the Second Adam. The Temptation was typical. The Temptation was sacrificial. The Temptation was mediatorial. The Temptation was redemptive.

[1] Milton.
[2] W. Robertson Nicoll, "The Incarnate Saviour," p. 88.

CHAPTER IX.

THE LAMB OF GOD. THE DIVINE SON OF MAN AT THE SOCIAL FEAST. THE DIVINE REFORMER IN THE HOUSE OF GOD. THE DIVINE AND THE HUMAN RABBI.

"Who for His immense love's sake was made that which we are, in orde that He might perfect us to be what He is" (IRENÆUS v., preface, translated by Keble).

The first disciples—Sense of sin supreme factor—The Lamb of God—The Son of Man—The Cana wedding, its promise—First Messianic passover—The Reformer—The Casuist.

WHILE Jesus was in the wilderness His servant John was ripening to spiritual maturity. He had reached the full height of Messianic faith; and now crowned his self-devotion by the free surrender of the flower of His disciples. Jesus was returning, and passing Bethany. or Bethabara. The morning before the Baptist declared he himself was neither the Messiah nor Elijah, nor the prophet of Moses' promise; nothing but an impersonal voice. The next day (John i. 29)—could the writer fail to remember the minute incidents of his spiritual birthday? —John stood with the Baptist John and Andrew, and saw their master's look upon Jesus, and heard his confession of the Lamb of God, which taketh away the sin of the world. As St. Augustine eloqently paraphrases it, "digito demonstrans ait, 'Ecce Agnus Dei, ecce qui tollit peccatum mundi: tanquam dicens, Quem multi justi videre concupierunt, in quem venturum ab ipsius humani generis initio crediderunt, de quo Abrahæ dictæ sunt promissiones, de quo scripsit Moyses, de quo Lex et prophetæ sunt testes."[1]

[1] Con. duas Ep. Pel iii. iv 11

The words show how the strongest force which impelled the Johannine disciples to Christ was a personal sense of sin. They were such as could use the beautiful confession of Augustine, "I perceived myself to be far off from Thee, in the region of unlikeness."[1] It was the sense of sin which the Law had fostered but not been able to remove. It was the glory of the Law that it could reach so far. Non-Christian religions lack this largely, or altogether; even when equivalent terms are used the meaning is wholly different. A Chinese Buddhist, for instance, would consider it *tsiu*, or sin, for which he suffered, if he had done "some improper act unconsciously, or in childhood, as treading on an insect, wasting rice-crumbs, &c."[2] So again in Confucianism, the restriction of the worship of God to the sovereign "has prevented the growth and wide development among the Chinese of a sense of sin. Their moral shortcomings, when brought home to them, may produce a feeling of shame, but hardly a conviction of guilt."[3] "So Hinduism does not ignore man's sinfulness altogether, but it explains it away or palliates it." The populace make God the author of sin; others, a man's misfortune rather than his fault as the result of former births; others, that sin, like the world, is "a mere illusion." "In Hinduism, considered as a religion, moral teaching finds no place."[4] Where there is no sense of moral evil in religion, the sense of sin has no religious existence, and tends to depart from any moral connection into a ceremonial one, or to disappear altogether. In Mohammedanism again orthodoxy covers a multitude of sins. Sin and wrong seem to the Mohammedans, says one who speaks from long practical as well as literary experience, "things that can be wiped out by a word, and they must be very grievous indeed if an orthodox profession does not win them forgiveness. They have never learnt that all forgiveness implies sacrifice."[5]

The modern eclectic Theists of the Brahmo Samaj similarly regard "sin as only a natural evil requiring remedial treatment,

---

[1] Conf. vii 10.
[2] Dr. Edkins, "Chinese Buddhism," p. 193, in Dr. Kellogg; and cf. Hardwick, "Christ and other Masters," p. 160.
[3] Prof Legge, p 296.
[4] Bp. Caldwell, "Christianity and Hinduism," pp, 29-50.
[5] Bp. Steere, Croydon Church Congress Report, in *The Guardian* 1877, p 1386.

THE LAMB OF GOD.

and not as a moral evil deserving punishment."[1] The presence of Christ always and everywhere, acted as a consuming fire. The sense of sin would be increased, or created, when a seed-word or look dropped upon unhardened soil. Contrition would sometimes have brought the weary and heavy-laden to Him, and sometimes followed upon discipleship. It is so still. "I read them," said a Tâoist dignitary who had for fifty years studied and tried to reach the ideal of Lâo-tsze; "I read them," said this Chinese Simeon, referring to some Christian tracts, "and it was as if scales fell from my eyes."[2] John himself could instil contrition, but he pointed to the Lamb of God to supply its satisfaction.

The words show, too, the greatness of the Baptist's faith. No other man could have made that confession, and condensed into an epigram of the soul the whole prospective teaching of the Law, the Prophets, and the worship. "Behold the Lamb of God which taketh away the sins of the world!" It was more than a stroke of spiritual genius, it was a coruscation of the Spirit of God who spake to and by the prophets, breaking in light upon the Paschal Lamb, the daily offering, the figure of the Atoning Sufferer, in Isaiah liii., and the "still sad music" of sin and salvation which underlay the chants of psalmists, the burdens of prophets, the sacrifices of priests, the prayers of the God-fearing. It was a decisive speech for Christendom, a birth moment.

Such a venture of faith was the consummate result of ages of spiritual development, refined and specialized in the disciplined patience and heart-whole devotion of the chosen prophet-priest. The Messianic confession takes immediate effect upon the not unprepared Andrew and John.

"'Tis the taught already that profits by teaching."[3]

The Rabbinic answer of Jesus, "Come, and ye shall see," to the question (John i. 39), "Rabbi, where abidest Thou?" is a formal invitation to discipleship. He appeals to personal experience. Experience is a test as valid in things spiritual as physical.

---

[1] Canon Churton, from Rev. N. Goreh, "The Brahmos; their Idea of Sin and its Punishment," *Mission Life*, October, 1883.
[2] Legge, p. 297
[3] R. Browning.

Andrew, the first Christian, findeth his brother Simon, and with the most momentous words a son of Israel could hear, " we have found the Messiah," leadeth the son of John to Jesus. This family forms the germ of the Church. The Church develops by families. The family is the primitive unit of Church life and propagation. The house of Andrew foreruns the house of Zebedee, the house of Zebedee the churches in the house of Prisca and Aquila, of Philemon, of Nymphas and his friends. of the " collegium quod est indomo Sergiæ Paulinæ."[1]

On the morrow, minutely remembered, Philip of Bethsaida, a fellow townsman, and doubtless friend of Andrew and Simon, is found of Christ, and himself finds Nathanael. By a Divine thought-reading Jesus works instantaneous conviction in the heart of the guileless Israelite. Spiritual affinities flash into contact. Nathanael saw in Jesus the Son of God and the King of Israel ; the very thought of his thoughts as he mused under the shadow of his fig-tree.[2] Jesus revealed Himself to him as the Son of Man.

The Cana miracle explains the title in action. How far the title was new to Jewish experience is a critical question. Daniel's vision of a Son of Man seems far too distinctly personal to be dreamed into an idealized nation. Enoch, in the Book of the Three Parables, frequently uses the title, but this portion of his Apocalypse is probably of Christian origin. In Rabbinic literature the name, Son of Man, is not used of the Messiah.[3] The name, then, seems to have been unknown as a Messianic title to the Jews of our Lord's time. Here we have, then, a title due to the creative mind of Jesus Himself, or drawn out from unsuspected germs. The fulness of meaning germinant in the term remains for all the centuries of Christian life to develop.

If Conder's identification of Bethabara, or Bethany, with the ford of 'Abârah, near Beisan, as the place of Christ's Baptism be accepted, it was but a day's journey distant from

[1] Col iv 15, and Bp Lightfoot, *s. l*

[2] As a sacred fig-tree is mentioned in the case of the Buddha, as the place of the first conversions to his religion, and of his entrance on his ministry, Professor Seydel grounds upon this, in connection with four other alleged but illusive coincidences, the inference that the gospel is more or less dependent upon and derivable from the Buddhist legend *Vide* Kellogg, p 85 foll , Kuenen, lecture v and note xiii for a complete refutation.

[3] Stanton, confirmed by Dr Schiller Szinessy.

THE DIVINE SON OF MAN AT THE SOCIAL FEAST.

Cana or Nazareth. 'Abârah is the principal ford of the Jordan,[1] north of Beisân,[2] and is "about twenty-two miles in a line from Kefr Kenna." The variant and preferable reading, Bethania, is probably only Beth-Oniyah,[3] the house of shipping, and another appellation for Beth-Abara, the "house of passage," or "of shipping." This identification invalidates the objections of Schenkel, and the author of "Supernatural Religion," to the geographical accuracy of the fourth Evangelist, and the assumptions built thereupon.

Kefr Kenna, the traditional Cana, is now a large village, lying on the southern slope of the plain of the fertile "Golden Plain," or plain of Toran. The balance of authority strongly supports it in preference to Khurbet Kâna.

The distance from Nazareth is but five miles. The proximity suggests that the bridegroom or bride of the marriage feast were friends of the family of Mary or Joseph. At the south of the village is still found "a copious fountain of excellent water," which may have supplied the waterpots. The village of Christ's day appears to have been "at least thrice as large as now." Cana is still the "reedy," as its name suggests.

Here, probably Wednesday, Jesus and His mother and His disciples came as guests to a wedding feast. Jesus had consecrated home life at Nazareth. The highest and holiest point of home life He consecrates at Cana. The Divine origin and character and meaning of marriage He reaffirms most fitly where Scripture and Rabbinical tradition alike would hallow the mystery. The presence of His mother appears to have occasioned the invitation to Jesus and His disciples. The unlooked-for addition possibly caused the insufficiency of wine. Galilean simplicity and kindness ruled the day.

When the wine fails the mother turns naturally to Jesus, as in any need of the Nazarene household. But "the hour", the time for Messianic revelation—and Mary could not have been a stranger to all that had happened in the last forty and more days, and the confessions of faith—lay not with her, but with God. Having vindicated His Messianic independence, the

---

[1] For a picture of a Jordan ford see Warren, "Recovery of Jerusalem," p. 335.
[2] "Survey," p. 131 f.; "Twenty-One Years," p. 96; Conder, "Tent Life," ii. 65 f.
[3] Edersheim, i. 278.

Son of Mary grants her indirect prayer. The water which filled the six waterpots, perhaps drawn from the existing fountain, variously estimated at from 63 to 153 gallons according to the measure of the metretes (Hebrew bath), became wine.

The Messianic effect of the first miracle is specially noted by St. John. His and his fellow-disciples' faith was confirmed.

Christian thought has seen much more than a wedding gift in the boon of Jesus. The first supper points on to the last, and both to the marriage-supper of the Lamb. The Cana wedding looks back to the marriage between Jehovah and His people, ratified and renewed betwixt Christ and His Church. The transmutation of water into wine suggests the final transformation and glorification of Nature, the consecration of matter under ennobled forms. The Christ blessing of the wedding party shows that "all life is potentially divine,"[1] and that all social relations are transformable into a communion of saints.

Again, the miracle deserves all the emphasis of its first place. For it is typical. "As the first act of the new creation, it shows what the nature of that creation is to be."[2] "As the first leaf which the plant produces is the type upon which the whole plant is constructed; and foliage, flower, and fruit are but modifications of the primordial leaf;" so the first Divine work is "a key to the character of the whole series." It is Eucharistic. The gospel is joy. The Christ came from joy to bring to joy, from glory to glorify.

Family ties were breaking, but not yet sundered. The Holy Family and the disciples went down to Capernaum, thenceforward the head quarters of Messianic work.

As the Cana sign was typical of the Divine power of benedictory joy entering into a joyless world; so the Temple-cleansing which soon followed was typical of Divine wrath. It was the same character under opposite conditions. As a Messianic sign the former was to bless, the latter to ban. The one as much as the other was an assertion of the Messianic claim. The Divine Man to nature, to society, to religion, was uttering Himself. On either occasion, time and place are fit-

---

[1] H. Macmillan, "The Marriage in Cana," p. 16.
[2] Ibid., p. 224.

THE DIVINE REFORMER IN THE HOUSE OF GOD. 77

test scenes for Divine drama, the wedding feast, the national Temple, the home of man, the house of God.

The first Messianic passover was now nigh at hand. All over the country preparations were going on. Over flower-lit plains and hills, along repaired roads, by cleansed streams, by tombs freshly whitened, pilgrims poured from all parts of Jewry. The far-shining marble walls and golden roof of the Temple was their goal. All this preparatory purification was an unconscious prophecy of the Messianic work of purifying which would begin with the House of God. From the 15th Adar the money changers' stalls rang in every town. The statutable Temple tribute must be paid in the half-shekel, and the charge of qolbon [1] must be met for the change.

What a scene of noise and confusion opened upon the eyes of the Messiah as He made His first entrance as the Son of Man into His Father's house. What disappointment to a mind filled with preparatory awe in approaching the greatest feast of the Church! The lowing of the sacrificial oxen, the bleating of the sacrificial sheep, the moan of the sacrificial doves, the jingling of coins, the hubbub of barter, had turned the court where Gentiles worshipped the Father of all into a Babel market. The shock was too great to be borne. The evil must be met full face at once. If any ordinary Jew, Phinehas-like, might champion God's honour against illegal authorized desecration, much more should the Messiah vindicate God's exclusive claim to the place where He had put His Name. Casting out all the lawbreakers, Jesus in one judicial moment stood upon the platform of the prophet and the reformer. The boldness and success of the stroke was a miracle of moral force. It was a direct challenge to the priestly faction, who were the chief shareholders in this Vanity Fair. The Temple market was probably the "Bazaars of the sons of Annas," the covetous oppressor (Chanuyoth beney Chanan). The Temple was profaned by its own highest officers. The unpopularity of the traffic may have given negative support to Christ's action. The effect upon the priest party was to awake a rancour which never forgot. The effect upon the disciples was naturally to deepen their convictions, and likewise to increase their number. Such a temper was pre-eminently

[1] 1½d to 2d., hence κόλλυβος, κολλυβιστής.

Messianic. A Messianic Psalm had foreshadowed the devouring zeal shown by the Lord. And other signs followed.

This act was critical and formed two parties. The "sign" was spoken for and against. The disciples formed the nucleus of the Messianic party, the Jews, as St. John terms the hostile faction, the anti-Christian. The latter demand a sign, the invariable reply to any Messianic assertion. The answer was mystical. The Temple of His Body, which was now the true Temple into which all the meaning and worship of the latter was passing, let them destroy it, He would raise it again in three days. This intimation in His first official Messianic work shows that the end was full in view. Sacrifice, Death, Resurrection—the end was before the beginning. Nor were the words forgotten by His enemies.

The sharp turns in the Johannine narrative may be of set purpose. Scene in the life contrasts with scene; and cross lights converge upon the one character. From the crowded Temple the disciple carries us to the silent room (John iii). From the public clamour to the darkness and the solitary thinker. From a descriptive picture to a character sketch. The writer's object is not to give an encyclopædic history, but a vivid personal memorial. He selects typical scenes. The fourth Gospel is the most individual and the most universal. The light, the truth, the Word, absolute, very God. The light, the truth, the Word in contact with individuals, faith or unbelief the necessary answer. Nicodemus (Naqdimon) was a representative man. A Sanhedrist, a cultivated gentleman, an intellectual inquirer, a seeker after truth. Like many of the nation he was spiritually awake. The miracles of the Passover week had arrested his attention. Miracles had done for him all they can do, they had brought him questioning, seeking, to the Royal Presence. The obstinate questions which importuned an answer must be brought to Him who raised them. The "how" of Nicodemus exactly reflects his character and point of view. Christ throughout replies to his latent as well as expressed thought. There is no concession to the social position, educational prejudices, or intellectual prepossessions of the master in Israel The master must learn to be a disciple, the teacher to be taught of God. The kingdom of God, the substance and desire of all Jewish thought, was come and in His own Person. The laws of that kingdom were after a

THE DIVINE AND THE HUMAN RABBI.

heavenly and spiritual order. A second birth and spiritual childhood were required to enter into it. The night wind that swept past the aliyah along the dark and narrow street was an "apt figure of a self-determining invisible force"[1]—that force the action of the Divine Spirit. Jesus not only lays down the law of Christian Baptism as the initial Sacrament of the Kingdom, but also determines the rightful temper of the mind towards the mysteries of the Kingdom. The "how" is knowable to faith alone. The child years, or the child heart, accept the personal word of Christ as credible upon its own merits.

The conversation moves on from mystery to mystery. To a mind so thorough and so well furnished as Nicodemus', at all events in the Law, the only culture of the Palestinian Jew, one question suggests another. St. John has doubtless given but a fragmentary outline. The new teaching and the demand it made raised the question of its authorization. Christ speaks openly of His pre-existence, and of the coming shadow of His death, in fulfilment of the type of the brazen serpent.

The death to which He had obscurely alluded in the Temple is still in His mind. This truth sunk deep into Nicodemus' mind. It bore fruit. The Cross is always the turning point. Under the Cross the victory of conviction was complete, and he stepped forward to honour the forsaken Body.

Nicodemus, the Jewish savant, honestly yielding to the pressure of evidence, as to an imperious spiritual and intellectual necessity, is a speaking likeness of many moderns. Among the higher class of cultivated heathen there are not a few in whom the prejudice of society and the pride of secular culture are breaking up. But with them conviction may be slowly wrought. And the distance between conviction and action—*e.g.*, in the case of the native Indian half-Christian—is as great as Oriental irresolution can make it. And within the Christian circle, too, there are many who are asking the inexorable how, in every tense of the interrogative mood ; and many too impatient to wait for an answer "a little while."

[1] H. P. Liddon, "University Sermons," ii. 80.

CHAPTER X.

THE BAPTIST'S FAREWELL TESTIMONY. THE SAVIOUR AND THE SAMARITANESS. THE NAZARENE.

> "Life. I repeat, is energy of love
> Divine or human, exercised in pain,
> In strife, in tribulation, and ordained,
> If so approved and sanctified, to pass,
> Through shades and silent rest to endless joy."
> WORDSWORTH, "Excursion," Book V.

Jesus on the Baptist's ground—The Prophet's last testimony—Jesus in Samaria—The Well of Jacob—In Galilee again—In Nazareth again.

JESUS now left the City for Judæa. His disciples administered a symbolical preparatory baptism, empty as yet of the Spirit. The work of the Baptist was carried on. But it is possible that he had never been as far south. The traditional site of his baptizing in Judæa would then have to be given up. The Gospels only mention Bethabara and Ænon, both north of Judæa. But as the people of Jerusalem and all Judæa are specially mentioned as coming to his baptism, and as he would be more likely to begin in the south and move northward, it is more likely that he had been in the very places, and left among those who dwelt in the neighbourhood of Jordan souls maturing for the advent of the King (Matt. iii. 5). "At this point, then, the work of Christ and of His Forerunner met. Christ had not been acknowledged as King in the chief seat of the theocracy, therefore He began His work afresh in a new field and in a new character."[1]

[1] Dr. Westcott.

THE BAPTIST'S FAREWELL TESTIMONY.

As Jesus passed northward His disciples and John's would meet and intermingle. The stronger force overbore the weaker. Perhaps in jealousy the disciples of the Baptist upon the occasion of a controversy with a Jew upon one of the numerous current questions connected with purification bring him the tidings of Jesus' greater success, and of what might appear to them as the defection of his own partisans to another. The answer of the forerunner was as noble as characteristic, "He must increase, but I must decrease." Nothing equal to it had been said before him, except Moses' "Enviest thou for m y sake?"

It was a fitting peroration to his life's testimony. He had borne the prophet's cross without of malice, and calumny, misrepresentation—of fighting as God's standard-bearer against a rebellious house. He had borne the prophet's cross within of failure, self-distrust, and the coming short of high ideals. He now bore the rising tide of loss in personal disciples and personal influence, the diminution of the faithful remnant, not with equanimity, but with joyous joy.[1]

Whilst Jesus' disciples were baptizing in Judæa, John seems to have followed the course of the Jordan southward from Bethabara. This may have been partly to avoid the growing ferocity of Pharisaic antagonism, partly to prepare the way of Christ at a central situation, convenient both for the north, for Samaria, and for the main road from the south. For Ænon near to Salim is by Conder and others identified with 'Ainûn, at the head of the Wâdy Fâr-ah, "which is the great highway up from the Damieh ford for those coming from the east by way of Peniel and Succoth;" Salim being seven miles northward, perhaps the Shalem of Gen. xxxiii. 18. The Wâdy Fâr-ah, starting at Shechem, formed the north boundary of Judæa; and the open ground there is just the place for crowds to assemble. Here, too, is the "much water," or many springs, indicated by the name.

The objection, however, that Ænon and Salim would both then be in Samaria has great force. And the old tradition, mentioned by Jerome, placing it eight miles south of Beisan (Scythopolis), apparently "at the opening of the Wâdy Khusneh into the Ghôr,"[2] on the border of Samaria and Galilee, "has this in its favour—that it locates the scene of John's last public work close to the seat of Herod Antipas,

[1] χαρᾷ χαίρει (John iii. 29).   [2] Caspari.

into whose power the Baptist was so soon to be delivered."[1] It is also nearer 'Abârah where John was last heard of. In any case there is not the slightest indication, but every probability to the contrary, that Jesus and John met again after the Baptism.

The Baptist's martyrdom of life was now drawing to an end. Herod was a suspicious coward like Tiberius himself, and according to Josephus, "fearing lest such influence of his over the people might lead to some rebellion, for they seemed ready to do anything by his counsel,"[2] resolved upon his arrest and death.

"Calm 's not life's crown;"[3]

this life's crown was very storm. His capture, of which we should have been glad of particulars, for we might have found some of the indignities of Herod's soldiers to the Master anticipated upon the servant, took place about this time. The Synoptists ignore the ostensible, and disclose another and weightier, reason which actuated Herod; for personal offence is a deeper spring of hatred than political antipathy, and would be keenest of edge in such a mean, sensual, nature as Herod's. His outspoken rebuke of his incestuous connection with Herodias stung him too sharply for pardon. When he was in his power the king paid him the tribute of attentive listening. He was interested. He had, if no religious scruples, religious curiosity and sensibility. He could be moved in his feelings to anything but repentance and heart change. Like the guilty, conscience-stricken king in Hamlet, he would like to

" Be pardon'd, and retain the offence."

The capture of the Baptist endangered Christ. The Pharisaic party, with the sharpsightedness of hate, must have already seen that the cause of the two was identical. They would take the one life on their way to the other. Had not the Lord kept out of danger He could easily have been arrested on such a false accusation as He afterwards was. He could have been imprisoned in Machærus. The Forerunner and the Messiah would have been executed together, and the blood of the world's ransom been shed in a rocky cell. So would Scripture

---

[1] Edersheim, i. 393.   [2] "Ant" xviii. 5. 2   [3] M Arnold.

THE BAPTIST'S FAREWELL TESTIMONY.

have been unfulfilled, and the agony and Cross spared to the Saviour, and lost to the children of His salvation. The life of the Son of Man was too precious to be thrown away. Our Lord was courage itself, but not presumption or rashness. Persecuted from one city, He would on occasion flee to another. Endangered in one place, He would seek safety of His life, and His kingdom, and His teaching, and all that depended upon them, without hurrying to fatal issues, or hastening by one moment the movement of Scriptural fulfilments, and the season of Divine appointment.

To reach Galilee the natural road lay through Samaria. This was taken by the Lord. One Samaritan incident is graven in the memory of the fourth Evangelist. Perhaps for personal reasons. He may, as some think, have been the solitary witness ; and the account bears the marks of an eye-witness in such incidental pictorial details as "sat thus," and the woman "left her waterpot." And the Samaritan episode as a whole formed a most encouraging contrast to the Judæan experience. The Messiah was well received. The conversion of the unnamed woman was fruitful in a harvest of ingathering. Samaria was, too, the scene of St. John's own apostolic labours when he and St. Peter went down from Jerusalem to lay their hands upon those who had been taught and baptized by Philip the Evangelist. Personal associations are so impressing a factor in memories of time and place that some of the above-named reasons would account for the minuteness and freshness of personal portraiture and local colouring shown in the account.

While Jesus sat in the weariness of a real humanity at the sixth, or evening, hour,[1] let us pause to reflect upon the associations of the scene, and its present condition to-day. It was the Well of Jacob—the laborious work of "a stranger in the land" where surface springs were abundant, who was confident of its tenure by his prosperity, according to Divine promise. It was a monument to the industry and faith of Jacob, and bears his name, honoured by Jew, Samaritan, Moslem, and Christian to this day. Joseph, too, had his memorial hard by, less than half a mile, on the north. The Tomb of Joseph occupies the accepted authentic site, and is now a square, roofless, white-walled enclosure, resembling most of the Moslem cenotaphs.

[1] Westcott and Maclellan have settled the question of the Johannine reckoning of hours quite conclusively.

On the south towered the rough, rocky slopes of Gerizim "about 1000 feet above the valley east of Shechem, 2848 feet above the sea," the mountain of the Old Beatitudes, the "holy mountain" of Samaritan faith. On the west the olives, vineyards, and varied foliage of the many-watered Vale of Shechem, most fertile of valleys, Ebal rising behind, mountain of curses and Joshua's altar of unhewn stones. On Ebal's slope the town of Sychar, now the mud huts of 'Askar, about half a mile off; coming from which to the well the Samaritans would have been in the Lord's sight. The site, too, of the Tomb of the "Holy King Joshua," as the Samaritans call him, appears to be rightly identified as but nine miles south of the present Nablûs. On the north-east the neighbourhood of Shalem, but two miles distant, with its memory of Jacob's tents, at Shechem, a mile and a half distant, Abraham had made his first encampment, and built the altar on the ground which Jacob had afterwards purchased. Here, too, "by the oak of the pillar that was in Shechem" (Judg. ix. 6), Abimelech had been made the first king. Hither had come Rehoboam, "for all Israel were come to Shechem to make him king" (1 Kings xii. 1); and here Jeroboam set up his rival kingdom.

However weary the Lord was, such a speaking scene could not have been mute to the Son of Israel. The spot where He rested, being so certainly identified, is all but the most worshipful in the Holy Land. The well is now covered with a ruined vault, which may "possibly be the crypt of the church built over the well about the fourth century."[1] The well is now generally dry. Originally it must have been of great depth, for in 1838 it was 105 feet deep, according to Robinson; in 1866 the accumulation of *débris* had reduced it to 75 feet; in 1875 it remained the same. The groove in the stone made by the ropes which drew up the waterpot may still be felt.[2]

While Jesus rested the disciples went to buy food, allowably purchasable of the Samaritans then, but not later. If John did not stay with Him—as would be the most natural negative inference from the twenty-seventh verse, and the omission of any mention of another witness, the absence of a third person may have not been fortuitous in the Saviour's solemnity and delicacy of contact with the fallen daughter of Samaria. In

---

[1] "Survey," ii p. 177, Barclay, 1881.
[2] "Twenty-One Years," p. 194, and illustration.

THE SAVIOUR AND THE SAMARITANESS.

that case the narrative may well have come from the thankful lips of a convert, at the time, or at St. John's after-visit.

It is another contrast which now fills the Johannine canvas, a contrast of scene, society, and character. The dialogue with the Samaritan woman follows close upon that with Nicodemus. The scene is very fully given. Doubtless St. John's apostolic visitation of Samaria was one of the later fruits of this Samaritan episode. Christ's spiritual treatment of the doubly outcast Cuthite is the opposite of His treatment of the Jerusalem Sanhedrist. In the latter He repels; in the former He attracts. In the latter He is sought; in the former He seeks. In the latter His speech has the ring of authority; in the former He stoops to conquer. The spiritual meeting-point between the Divine and the earthly Rabbi was found in the signs of Divine power. The spiritual touch between the Saviour and the sinner in her consciousness of sin.

Nicodemus and the Samaritaness agreed in a Messianic hope of some sort. But the former started from the full Scripture canon and the post-canonical literature; the latter from the Mosaic books only, in a tampered and falsified text. The former from the Law, of which he was a master; the latter from the inferiority and ignorance of a degraded womanhood. The former from orthodoxy; the latter from heresy and schism. The former from social honour; the latter from shame. The venture of faith was as slow in the former as rapid in the other. The "personal equation" made the difference, and unknown developments of inward history. No one else in the world could have united in a common interest, preparatory to a common brotherhood, two such opposites as the proud Sanhedrist, and the low Samaritaness.

As the Lord sat by the well in restful silence, the woman of Sychar came there, as she may have come hundreds of times before. Evening is still called in that changeless East "the time that women go out to draw water."[1] She was indeed an unconscious type and representative of the thousands upon thousands of the then and still degraded, downtrodden daughters of Eastern lands, whom nothing but the strong arm of Christian faith can raise, and the power of Christian civilization elevate to their true place and function in the kingdom of a world-winning Christ. It is not likely that the women of half-heathen Samaria

[1] Rev. J. Neil, "Palestine Explored," p. 19.

occupied as honourable a position as those in Israel, and the
higher-class women of Israel fell far below the standard of
respect, of chivalry, of importance, of influence, of work
accorded to them in Christian societies and civilizations.

In defiance of conventional manners and proprieties the Lord
spoke first. The dialogue is deeply instructive as showing more
clearly than any other on record how the Lord dealt with those
He sought to salvation. There is the quick play of conscience
alarmed, but evasive ; the rapid thrust which wounds in order to
heal ; the courtesy, the respect to a woman, a Samaritaness, and
a bad character ; the change of front by wounded self-love to a
controversial subject ; the wonderful and profound revelations
of Christ. of His Father, and of the worship of His Father,
undisclosed to Jewish ears.

The earthly water our Lord graciously asked for suggested
the spiritual. The local reference to Jacob on the woman's
part, the well whereof he drank, his children, and his cattle, was
as natural as that to this mountain—her religious world. This
leads to further explanation of the water of eternal life. The Lord's
manner was something no gospel, however faithful, could reproduce ; we can only know that it must have added to His simplest
words that impression of power, of love, of holiness, which He
left whenever and wherever His fulness of grace and truth
uttered itself. Manner and tone must be superadded to words
in themselves such as never man spake, and the home thrust at
the guilty life follows. It was a personal attack, and the woman
would parry it by shifting her defence to the question of
questions between Jew and Samaritan. The absence of falsehood, the implied confession, leave an opening for the Spirit of
truth to enter. After the memorable words which have been
a foundation-stone of the charter of the faith (John iv. 24), the
controversial decision, the judicial affirmation, that salvation
was not of the Samaritans, but of the Jews, suggested without
mentioning the Messiah. The woman follows the lead ; and
the first open declaration of Messiahship immediately follows :
" I am, I that speak unto thee."

The Samaritan conception of the Messiah was that of a prophet or teacher. When Messiah cometh, He will announce to
us all things, the woman said. His teaching would be final and
absolute. He was the *Hashab*, the Converter, and *Hathab*, the
Guide, now *El Muhdy* in the Samaritan vocabulary. As such

THE SAVIOUR AND THE SAMARITANESS. 87

the Cuthite accepted Him. Faith with the Samaritans was a plant of quick growth. Before the Lord had departed they not only believed in Him as the Hashab, but arrived at the certitude of knowledge that He was the Saviour of the world. The Messianic seed had fallen on favourable ground. The un-Jewish friendliness of Master and disciple may have more than disarmed prejudice, and converted it into goodwill. This episode must have been a sort of holiday, a time of refreshing, among the months of disappointed labour.

Just as Jesus announced Himself the Messiah, the disciples came up and marvelled at His breach of etiquette. An incidental touch reveals the eye-witness. " She left the water-pot" (John iv. 28). It was filled but forgotten, for other water had been tasted. The rapid faith of the woman bore rapid fruit. As the whitening ears, so the ripening harvest of the Samaritans spread out before them. Some, perhaps, were actually approaching the well. The Messianic evidence which convinced the Samaritans was the Messiah Himself.

If the Messianic purification of the Temple be regarded as only an indirect confession of Messiahship, the first direct declaration was this. It seems better to seek the fitness in spiritual causation than in prudential policy, as some have done. The Samaritans were strangers to the political Messianic hope, and may have been riper on this ground for spiritual development. But the success which attended Christ's personal ministry continued to attend upon that of His servants a few years later. The memory of the Messiah kept alive, and the shame of the Cross He suffered at Jewish hands would have been a lesser barrier to Samaritan belief.

After "the two days of" Samaritan work (John iv. 43), perhaps passing through Herod's magnificent Sebaste, once Samaria, now *Sebustieh*, where remains of Archelaus' temple to Augustus still are found, Jesus came across the plain of " El Buttauf" into Galilee. His fame had already preceded Him. The eye-witnesses of His works at Jerusalem spread it abroad. Perhaps there was some touch of provincial pride in welcoming the distinguished Galilean Prophet whom " His own " Judæa had rejected. Cana is the scene of a second miracle. Possibly the son of Chuza, Herod's court official, is the restored sufferer. The Galilean ministry, which follows,[1] is briefly summed up in

---
[1] *Vide* Edersheim against Tischendorf, &c

Mark i. 15 (Matt. iv. 17; Luke iv. 15). The cry of the Baptist is resumed, but with the addition, "believe in the gospel." Many must have heard the former appeal, and were ready for its fulfilment. Later, if not sooner, these, or some of them, recruited the ranks of the Christian brotherhood, and may have been some amongst the five hundred and more who beheld the risen Christ, and among others who spread northward to Antioch and Damascus.

The next scene opens at Nazareth. Jesus has returned to His own Galileans. Jesus had declared Himself in the Temple, the one centre of Jewish worship. He now declares Himself in the other centre, the Synagogue. He came as was His Sabbath wont. He is invited to act as the *Sheliach Tsibbur*. Facing the sanctuary, with His back to the people, He leads their devotions. After introductory prayers the Shema, or "Hear," is recited. The form of prayer follows (Tephillah), *i.e*, the Eighteen Eulogies, or Benedictions (Shemoneh Esreh). Of the present nineteen, some, notably the three first and three last, are of great antiquity. As these have left a marked, but as yet unexplored,[1] influence upon Christian devotion, and as we may so catch some echo of the public devotions of Christ upon this occasion, the first and second only may be quoted[2] for fear of length, and a fragment of the eighteenth.

1. "Blessed art Thou O Lord our God, and the God of our fathers, the God of Abraham, the God of Isaac, and the God of Jacob, the God great and powerful and terrible, God most High, who bestowest Thy benefits graciously, the Possessor of the Universe, who rememberest the good deeds of the fathers and sendest a redeemer unto their sons' sons for Thy Name's sake in love. Our King, our Helper and Saviour and Shield, blessed art Thou, O Lord, the Shield of Abraham."

2. "Thou art Mighty for ever, O Lord; Thou bringest the dead to life, Thou art mighty to save. Thou sustainest the living by Thy mercy, Thou bringest the dead to life by Thy great compassion, Thou supportest them that fall, and healest

---

[1] The relation of Synagogue prayers to early liturgies awaits inquiry. The development of early liturgies from various germs is a subject requiring the attention of liturgiologists, and as a basis the examination of MSS. and the continuation of Canon Swainson's labours.

[2] Bishop Lightfoot, "Clemens Romanus," ii 461. "Dictionary of Christian Antiquities," i p. 1022, and Schurer, ii 85.

the sick, and loosest them that are in bonds, and makest good Thy faithfulness to them that sleep in the dust. Who is like unto Thee, O Lord of might? and who can be compared unto Thee, O King, who killest and makest alive, and causest salvation to shoot forth? And Thou art faithful to bring the dead to life, Blessed art Thou, O Lord, who bringest the dead to life" ;—and the last clause of the eighteenth Benediction, so suggestively pathetic to a Messiahless people—

"And may it seem good in Thy sight to bless Thy people Israel at all times and at every moment with Thy peace. Blessed art Thou, O Lord, who blessest Thy people Israel with peace."

And so patient are the words of Christian adoption and adaptation that we are not surprised to find traces of them in the long liturgical prayer at the end of St. Clement's Epistle to the Romans, and possibly in the Greek Liturgy of St. Mark, and the "introductory part of the present Greek Office is a Christianized epitome of the first eight."[1]

After the seventeenth followed the threefold blessing pronounced by the priests, or offered as a prayer in their absence. The congregation said Amen. They had prayed standing. They now sit to hear the first lesson, from the *Thorah*, on Sabbath mornings ; and the second from the Prophets, the *Haphtarah*. The *Methurgeman* stands by the reader to translate the Biblical Hebrew into the current Aramaic. The sermon (*Derashah*) follows. This was the form which the teaching in the synagogues so often mentioned in the New Testament and in Philo took, and which in Apostolic Missions supplied the basis for the new Evangel.

Jesus stood to read the lection from the Prophets : Himself targumed it ; and sat down to deliver His first Nazareth sermon. It was a personal claim to be the Hope of Israel. But words of light and power were insufficient to change obstinate prejudices. The claim was too absolute for local bias and narrow hearts, unconvicted of sin sickness.

"Without the city wall,"

as later, the rebellious answer is given. The site of precipitation is still seen on the hill above the Maronite Church, where they would have pushed Him down (Luke iv. 29). It is a sharp descent of forty feet.

[1] Freeman, "Divine Service," 1 p 64

CHAPTER XI.

THE DIVINE GALILEAN.

"I shut my door against my Saviour, but, lo, He stands before me day and night as a prisoner, whom His own mighty love hath enchained in the house of His beloved child" (An Indian poet of "The New Dispensation ").

Capernaum—The unknown feast at Jerusalem—Galilee in Christ's time and now—Galilean labours.

NAZARETH is left to its darkness. Capernaum becomes the Christian mission centre. The Light shines upon the land of Zabulon, the way of the sea becomes the way of the King (Matt. iv. 15). What better centre of the new spiritual industry could be found than busy thriving Capernaum? Capernaum was a fishing, an agricultural, and a mercantile centre. Fishermen, shipbuilders, dyers, weavers, stonecutters, jostled with the caravans from Egypt and the sea-coast, backwards and forwards to Damascus and the East.

The controversy respecting the site of Capernaum is as yet unclosed. Tell Hum and Khan Minyeh are the rival claimants; but as they are within two and a half miles of one another neither can be far wrong. Tell Hum is supported by the balance of authority, and the suggestion that Bethsaida was the fishing suburb of Capernaum seems a very likely one.

The return visit of Jesus to an unnamed feast at Jerusalem is recorded with much detail by the fourth Evangelist (John v. 1–47). The feast, *a* feast merely according to the better reading,[1] appears to have been that of Trumpets,[2] the new moon of

---

[1] Westcott and Hort, Tregelles, and R.V. omit ἡ, but Tischendorf and Gebhardt retain it. [2] Westcott, u. v.

September, shortly before the Day of Atonement. The Messianic crisis centred in the feast. The great question became more urgent. Upon this visit Jesus directly formulates His Messianic claim,[1] and His equality with God. This had been implied in the Temple cleansing. His works are the evidence which accredits Him. As so often, the increasing contradiction of sinners called out the clearer statement of truth. Christ on His defence must vindicate His authority. His own cause and work He identified with John's; but as the greater contains the less, the perfect flower, the spring bud. His works in the present must be considered in the light of the immediate past of the Johannine work, and the historic testimony of their acknowledged Scriptures. Christ, then, appealed to history like Christianity; and like Christianity to the inward light of the human heart. Whoso had the Divine in him would recognize the Divine in Himself. The Messianic conflict had not now begun, as some say, but it had deepened. The Jews, *i.e.*, the Sanhedrist party, are standing in sharp outlines on a hostile horizon. The whole controversy took occasion, but not cause, from three several festal healings—this at Bethesda of the impotent man; the second of the man born blind at Jerusalem; the third, and most victorious, and unpardonable, the resurrection of Lazarus.

A decisive step had been taken. No disciples appear to have attended Him. The final call had not as yet separated them for His work. The brief ministry in Galilee had been the first effort. The great Galilean ministry in its full sweep now begins, the final call to the fishers of men. Consider the scene of the Divine Galilean's work.

Galilee in the time of Christ was densely peopled. Josephus estimated the number of cities and villages, the smallest of which numbered above fifteen thousand inhabitants, at two hundred and four. His estimate has usually been rejected as an absurd exaggeration. But it must be remembered that as military governor of that province he had unusual facilities for gauging its resources; that he raised without difficulty an army there of above one hundred thousand young men; and that a gross misstatement would have been easily detected. We are inclined, therefore, to agree with Dr. Selah Merrill[2] in attaching more credit to his testimony. In any case Galilee must

[1] Stanton, p. 276, hardly does justice to this.
[2] "Galilee in the Time of Christ" (R.T.S.), p. 63 foll. and p. 19

have presented to the eye, from outlying heights, the spectacle of a sea of habitations, an unbroken sheet of towns, " a land of brooks of water, of fountains" (Deut. viii. 7), having in its two thousand square miles a possible population of three millions.

The fertility and beauty of the country at the time are well known. It was the "garden of God." It was a "watered garden," and the splendid wealth of the soil was turned to the best account by the industry and enterprise of a vigorous and intelligent agricultural population.

"All the trees and fruits of Palestine flourished here to perfection." To quote again one[1] who has the technical knowledge of years of special study on the spot; " forests, in many cases, covered its mountains and hills, while its uplands, gentle slopes, and broader valleys were rich in pastures, meadows, cultivated fields, vineyards, olive-groves, and fruit trees of every kind. Here, in this garden 'that has no end,' flourished the vine, the olive, and the fig; the oak, the hardy walnut, the terebinth, and the hot-blooded palm; the cedar, cypress, and balsam; the fir-tree, the pine, and sycamore; the bay-tree, the myrtle, the almond, the pomegranate, the citron, and the beautiful oleander. These, with still many other forest, fruit, and flowering trees, and shrubs, and aromatic plants, together with grains and fruits, to which should be added an infinite profusion of flowers, made up that wonderful variety of natural productions," which smiled in undefiled beauty round the houses of Jesus' Galilean work.

The products of the province were fish, wine, wheat, and oil, flax, all in great abundance. The port of Tyre connected the Galilean market with consumers from the far West to the far East. The lake cities were centres of the fishing industry; Tarichæa seems to have been specially famous for its fish factories, and had about forty thousand inhabitants.

Nor was art very far behind Nature. Architecture was not an indigenous Jewish product. The Jews were not great builders. But modern critical research and exploration have shown how widely Hellenizing influences had spread, and many magnificent buildings, temples, theatres, palaces, chiefly under the inspiration of Herodian taste, covered the land with Græco-Roman monuments. Even the Temple at Jerusalem showed abundant traces of the influence of the Grecian style; just as in Solomon's

[1] Dr. S. Merrill.

THE DIVINE GALILEAN. 93

time Memphis, and possibly Nineveh, supplied suggestions,[1] and Tyre, masons and skilled artificers. Synagogues, too, were often handsome edifices, with ornate mouldings. "But the Jewish ordinary architecture was, on the whole," probably "much what is now the natural style of the country," and "the buildings were neither large nor solidly constructed."[2]

The Sea of Galilee has little in common to-day with the bright, busy populous lake of Christ's time. The purple blush of the oleander still fringes its shore. The green or brown hills still "stand about" it. The turf is still starred with myriad wild flowers varied and lustrous. The waves still beat their monotonous music upon the white shingle. Hermon's snowy dome still shines afar. But all else is changed. Where hundreds of sail winged their whiteness over the sparkling water, where Herod, Josephus, or Titus could easily collect fleets of from three hundred to five hundred vessels, where numbers of fisher-folks plied their nightly craft to furnish the numerous markets of a densely-crowded neighbourhood, where the magnificent Tiberias, lately built by Herod the Great, and named after the Roman Emperor, lined the lake-shore for nearly three miles with handsome public buildings, temples, the palace of the Tetrarch, and fashionable residences, "all built in the sumptuous style of Græco-Roman art, with their spacious courts, surrounded by marble columns, adorned with elaborately carved designs, the whole embosomed in palm groves, and gay with gardens of tropical luxuriance;"[3] where the Plain of Gennesareth spread out its fruit orchards and gardens ; now is the plain all but uncultivated, now is a squalid town, now are some rows of columns lately discovered by Mr. Schumacher, representing Tiberias, now are half-a-dozen miserable villages, the black tents and the cattle of the Bedouin on the hillsides, a few small dilapidated fishing-boats resting on the banks, or moving languidly over the waters, the only signs of human life.[4]

"On the shores of this lake might be seen temple after temple rearing their vast colonnades of graceful columns, their courts ornamented with faultlessly carved statues to the deities of a

[1] Cf. C. R. Conder, "Syrian Stone Lore," p. 122.
[2] C. R Conder in "Survey," iii p. 441 f.   [3] L Oliphant.
[4] S Manning's, "Those Holy Fields," pp. 196, 202, Selah Merrill, "East of the Jordan," p. 461, L. Oliphant, "Sea of Galilee," *English Illustrated*, December, 1887.

heathen cult. Here were the palaces of the Roman high functionaries, the tastefully decorated villas of rich citizens, with semi-tropical gardens irrigated by the copious streams which have their sources in the Plain of Gennesareth and the neighbouring hills. Here were broad avenues and populous thoroughfares, thronged with the motley concourse which so much wealth and magnificence had attracted—rich merchants from Antioch, then the most gorgeous city of the East, and from the Greek islands, traders and visitors from Damascus, Palmyra, and the rich cities of the Decapolis; caravans from Egypt and Persia, Jewish Rabbis jostling priests of the worship of the Sun, and Roman soldiers swaggering across the market-places, where the peasantry were exposing the produce of their fields and gardens for sale!"[1]

In such a hive of half-Hellenized civilization, Oriental commercial industries, and mixed cultures and faiths, did the little body of Christ's workers set to leaven the whole mass. The nearest modern parallels are still to be found in the East rather than the West. In Calcutta, where the Christian missionary's first feeling "is the utter helplessness of his outlook in the face of a joyous, idle, universal, self-satisfied, non-Christian life, the streets crowded, the students happy and eager, the idolatrous processions beautiful as a dream, the burning sun, the beautiful flower-trees, the birds singing, the philosophers lightly and airily discussing the religious life of the past and of the future, the missionary thought of either as a needless bore, or a pleasant means of obtaining an hour or two's logical word-play,"[2] and overshadowing all the majestic ægis of a foreign government and a distant sovereign, just as the Roman official exercised dominion over the concourse of mixed multitudes. Or again in Bombay, the Indian Tyre, which, like Calcutta, delights to call itself "the hall of all the nations," and where all varieties of national type and national dress throng the streets, and of the Christians, European or native, the question asks itself, "What are they among so many?"

Capernaum was a suitable base as the home of growing faith (Luke iv. 31). Here lived the court officer and his son. Here, or close by, dwelt the sons of John and the sons of Zebedee.

[1] L. Oliphant, "Haifa," p. 219.
[2] MS. letter from the late Rev. P. S. Smith of the Oxford Mission to Calcutta.

"Here He would on the Sabbath days preach in that synagogue, of which the good centurion was the builder, and Jairus the chief ruler."[1] Here begins a new departure in the life of Jesus. He had been a lonely missionary preacher. He had been scattering the seed. He now begins to gather in. The Organizer of the Church appears for the first time. Simon and Andrew, James and John, form the first community of the new kingdom, the first spiritually specialized to definite office. They are no longer disciples. They are called to the personal fellowship of Messianic work and undivided spiritual industry. On the following Sabbath they witness His words and works of power—the unclean spirit cast out, the mother-in-law of Simon restored by the touch of His hand. The home Simon had given up is already blessed, and the sick in the neighbourhood,

"At even, when the sun was set,"

and the Sabbath over, were graced with the healing touch, one by one.

The Galilean labours which follow, briefly sketched in the Synoptists, produced abundant fruit. Two points specially marked them (Luke v. 17; vi. 7). The Rabbinical party, deputed from, or instigated by, the Jerusalem faction, were in ceaseless and open opposition. The Messianic party was increasing in quantity and quality. Another onward step in "organization" takes place when Jesus, after the long night-prayer, formally selects the Twelve (Luke vi. 12).

[1] Edersheim, i. 457.

CHAPTER XII.

THE DIVINE APOSTLE. THE DIVINE MORALIST.

"And these things He taught, not as contrary to the Law, but as fulfilling the Law, and rooting within us the means whereby the Law maketh righteous" (IRENÆUS IV. XIII. I, translated by Keble).

"What you do not want done to yourself, do not do to others (CONFUCIUS' "Golden Rule").

The selection of the Twelve—Organization of the Divine society—Organization of the life—Code of the New Kingdom in its past, present, and future revelations.

THE site of the selection of the Twelve and the delivery of the Sermon on the Mount was evidently well known in the early Church. It is termed by the Synoptists "the mountain" simply, perhaps as being so well known to Christians as a habitual resort of Christ and His disciples, and possibly, in after-time, as to require no specifying; or there may have been no name to this one of the many heights in the neighbourhood. Tradition regards the Horns of Hattin (Kurun Hattin) as the place, and many moderns are disposed to assent to it.

The appointment of the Twelve Apostles was an example of supernatural rather than natural selection. It was a spiritual differentiation of the fittest of the disciples according to Divine, not human valuation. The chosen of the chosen were summoned to step into the inner circle which should share the Lord's intimacy, and constitute the governing body of the Church. The inclusion of Judas is one of the unsealed mysteries of God's predestination. It was only after a night of prayer that Jesus decided upon His final choice. An unseen Hand pointed them out. They did not choose Him; He chose them. How shall

THE DIVINE APOSTLE.

they preach except they be sent? He was the Apostle of the Father, the authorized and accredited Messenger; they were the Apostle's Apostles (*Malachim*). Their authority was derivative, as their teaching was in His Name. Their present mission and commission was preliminary and local. Their promotion to world-wide jurisdiction was at present unrevealed, and, as the case of the traitor proves, conditioned by their faithfulness in service.

Of these twelve, Judas, the man of Kerioth, alone was of Judean origin; the others were Galileans. The Galilean character formed the best ethical basis for the elevating power of the new kingdom. The Galileans were men of loyal and patriotic spirit, intelligent, active, laborious. They were fashioned of the stolid stuff and high spirit which make good soldiers and merchants, from the days when Zebulon and Napthali jeoparded their lives unto the death in the high places of the field (Judg. v. 18), to the days when the fighting men of Japha beat back the Roman soldiers till twelve thousand of the former fell. They were free children of nature, filled with the sunny breath of their own highlands. Their reality, their manliness, their *perfervidum ingenium*, their zeal for the law apart from tradition, stood in sharp contrast to the artificially religious and self-seeking political Rabbis, who would—

" Make of God their tame confederate,
Purveyor to their appetites."[1]

These Twelve were in an eminent degree meant to be living gospels—personal Christ-forces, Christ-organs. The transmission of the faith was dependent, in the first instance, upon living depositaries, personal eye- and ear-witnesses. The faith and the life are alike one. Christ alone is the source of either. Human *media* are strictly *media* between Him and His. Life and faith were meant to co-exist, hence living agents propagated the Divine life and the Divine faith before any documentary embodiment of either. The Church existed before the Bible. What God hath joined together let not man put asunder.

The number Twelve was significant. It indicated that under the Messianic King they would rule the twelve tribes of Israel. The organization of the official element in the Church to all time

[1] R. Browning, " Pippa Passes.'

lay in this germ. In Christ is the fulness of all functions—ruling, evangelizing, pastoral, prophetic. Church officers claim but delegated authority. The dependence of the Apostles upon Christ was absolute, at first more " outward and unconscious," [1] afterwards more inward, self-intelligible. At first they were servants, they became friends ; they never ceased to be children. The manifestation of His own life and character indirectly, as well as directly, was the leading factor in their moral, spiritual training. Only after He left them visibly did He become an inward formative force. His personal influence was at first outward—an example, a voice, a manner, a temper, a look, a conversation. Later on these passed into the memory and very life as an abiding power. From without He passed within, to interpenetrate, to transform, to spiritualize.

The Sermon on the Mount was the natural and immediate sequel to the nomination of the officers of the kingdom. It was the official manifesto of the moral code of the kingdom. It was addressed, in the first place, to the new officers ; in the second, to all the children and children's children of the kingdom. It was, above all, a definition of character ; a statement of principles, rather than a promulgation of rules. It had relations to the past, to the present, to the future. To the past ; for He, the Lawgiver, came to fulfil all righteousness, to conserve and to reinforce all the moral force, and colour, and authority of the old covenant ; to give finality to what was partial and incomplete ; to develop incipient morals to the full length, and breadth, and depth, and height of a perfect organism To the past ; for all the moral thinkings of all previous non-Jewish moral teachers were here recognized, revised, and re-issued. The Divine Law, as approached in varying degrees in divers ethical schools — Egyptian, Babylonian, Indian, Persian, Greek, Roman—is here, so far as true, and therefore authentically Divine, ratified and confirmed. The moral system of Buddhism, for instance, so far as its theory goes, occupies the highest place among non-Christian religions The five commandments are as follows : "Not to kill (anything that has life) : not to steal : not to lie : not to drink what can intoxicate : not to commit adultery." [2] And the Buddhist commandments,

[1] Neander, p 126.

[2] Professor Kellogg, " The Light of Asia and the Light of the World," p. 270 following

THE DIVINE MORALIST.

just as the Mosaic interpreted by prophet and psalmist in distant approximation to Christ, reached beyond the letter to the disposition of the heart. Thus we read that the Buddha, on one occasion, being asked to declare "the highest blessing," answered in words such as the following:—

"Waiting on father and mother, protecting child and wife, and a quiet calling, this is the highest blessing. 'Giving alms, living religiously, protecting relatives, blameless deeds, this is the highest blessing,'" &c.

But it must be remembered parenthetically, to avoid misunderstanding, that these higher Buddhist flights must be taken in connection with their whole code, which has no conception of a personal God, no conception of a moral obligation, or authoritativeness, which is "law" only by a transference of ideas without a lawgiver. If the Mosaic law could not give life, much less could the highest non-Jewish, such as the Buddhist.[1] And the moral weakness of Buddhism is too notorious and patent to need illustration.

As non-Jewish moral teachings so above all the Jewish law given by Moses, glorified in countless Psalms, vindicated and enforced by prophets and men of God, striven after by the righteous remnant in every generation, was reaffirmed and certified Its inviolability, its absolute validity, its catholicity reasserted and authenticated, not word by word, and detail by detail, but as a whole and by typical examples.

But there was more than reaffirmation of the past righteousness. There was expansion, creative development, progress inward and spiritual. "In five cardinal points of the moral code"[2] the new righteousness is contrasted with the old : in the law of murder, the law of oaths, the law of adultery, the law of retaliation, the law of charity. The public placard of the Decalogue is taken down and rewritten upon the heart. The sources of good and evil, the inward springs of thought and life, are dealt with at their centre and focus. Thought and look and gesture are traversed and scrutinized.

If the Law of Christ had simply been a more stringent provision than the Mosaic, covering a wider field, and penetrating

[1] Professor Kellogg, p. 280 following, and the express declarations of such experienced and credible eye-witnesses of Buddhism, as Bishops Schereschewsky and Copleston, or Dr Edkins

[2] Rev S Cox, D D , "Expository Essays and Discourses," p. 12.

into deeper chambers—where had been the possibility of fulfilling commands which in their earlier form were beyond attainment? With the new law Christ, but not till after His Resurrection, liberated a new power. The Christian's life is a reproduction of Christ's life. His energy is transformed and conveyed into the Christian. Communion with Him is a scientific necessity of spiritual obedience. Faith is the line along which the currents of spiritual energy pass ; and Sacraments are the means of His communications of life.

With regard to the present, its synchronal position, the whole required to be interpreted in the light of the Life of the Lawgiver. He spake by authority and He exemplified by authority. The Blessed above blessed ones revealed and exhibited every beatitude. With Him the law was not external, it was not imposed from without; it was the expression of His own inner nature. The Law Royal was a reflex of the Royal Mind.

In its positive aspects and in its negative the Royal life was the best commentary on the Royal Law. He was Himself the exponent. His example expressed it in the concrete. Whenever the disciples had difficulties about the application of principle to different details, they had the ever-speaking likeness of the Law obeying Himself. The Royal Law was to Him a perfect law of liberty, and became so to all who took the yoke freely upon them of Him, "cui servire libertas."

In this the most effective of all ways, that of personal influence, the apostles were trained to deal with moral problems. The gospel in contact with the degraded morals of corrupt society had, as it often has now, to create moral demands before supplying them. The gospel had to meet most perplexing problems in applying the sweetness and light of moral truth to the various complications of artificial, often highly civilized, but rotten society. One of the sayings of the Lord, unrecorded in the Gospels, capable of wide application, "it is more blessed to give than to receive," is an instance of many others which in His own life-time, and in the life-time of His ear-witnesses, became fruitful principles of action, and useful guides of conduct.

Such difficult questions as those of caste and polygamy which confront the Christian missionary of to-day were present to the after-experience of the apostles and disciples. Those who had occupied the pre-eminent place of being eye-witnesses of the Word of Life had two first principles which they could apply.

THE DIVINE MORALIST.

What did the Lord say? What did the Lord do? Simple, untutored minds, without other culture than that of the Lord's life and words engraven on a memory quick with the strong pulse of love, and fortified by the re-creative influx of the Spirit, were thus enabled to cope with the mental and moral obstacles to belief, and the mental and moral difficulties of planting, preserving, and perpetuating the holy stock of the faith in noisome, unclean social soils, and hotbeds of civilized vice, in nurseries of deeply rooted, widely ramified evil, strong in possession, in interest, in degenerate undisturbed heredity.

And in its immediate applications, the Law had negative relations. It was polemical. It was the unqualified contradiction of the fashionable authorized moral teaching and living. The best Rabbinical ethics may be found in the small Talmudical Tractate Pirke Aboth;[1] and at every point of contact pale in comparison. The moral teaching of the day, allowing for exceptions, resolved itself into personal and national selfishness. Righteousness was an acquisition, not a gift, purchasable by individual merit. Individual merit was consciously created, valued, and asserted. "My humility is my greatness, and my greatness, my humility," said Rabbi Hillel. The famous Rabbi Simeon ben Jochai would say, "I have seen the children of the world to come, and they are few. If there are three. I and my son are of their number; if they are two, I and my son are they."

And not only had the current moral teaching to be negatived, or transformed, where capable of transformation, ethics had to be raised to a new position. An externalism like that of Brahminism had to be dethroned. Rabbinism had debased the whole theocratic system. Morals were enslaved. Action was chained and bound in a systematized machinery of fetters. The polemic of Christ against the Pharisees and Sadducees was the absolutely necessary condition of creating a healthy moral standard. Between Christian law and Rabbinical there was no reconciliation. It was a life-and-death question. One or the other must perish. The Sermon on the Mount was the epoch of the new birth of moral life. It was as life from the dead.

One or two examples of the legalism and formalism from which men were delivered will suffice. No less than twelve treatises

[1] See Dr. Taylor's convenient edition and notes

of the Mishna, filling the whole of the last part, deal with ordinances relating to cleanness and uncleanness, such as the defilement of hollow earthen vessels, of metal vessels of which "the mouth and the hollow are capable of defilement. If they are broken they are clean; if vessels are again made out of them they are in their former uncleanness." The very three mementoes, the *Tsitsith*, the tassels or fringes which every Israelite wore at the four corners of his upper garment; the Mesusa, or box fixed to the doors, containing Deut. vi. 9, and xi. 20; and the Tephillin, or prayer-straps, which every male Israelite put on at morning prayer, except on Sabbaths and holy days, probably of scriptural origin, and of great value rightly used, were debased to a thousand superstitious prescriptions about knots and threads and the like, and were often treated as charms.[1]

In regard to the future the permanent force and value of the Sermon is witnessed by its own perennial freshness and vitality. All moral progress is a pursuit of these ideals. The ideal Christian, the ideal righteousness of the individual, the society, the Church is here outlined. Christ believed in Himself, in His work. He knew His community would last. He knew His work would survive His earthly life. He knew its continuity to the ages of ages. His action and His words were equally prophetic, equally creative, equally indestructible. He could trust in His cause, and in human nature. Knowing humanity as He did, with the perfect insight of intuition, and the experience of active mixture with all classes, and in a country where men of all nations met, knowing its worst and its best, knowing its worst to Himself to the end, He was never a pessimist or a cynic. He was the incarnation of faith and hope in human nature, as well as of faith and hope in God. He was the lover of humanity, whose delight was to be with the sons of men, as well as the destroyer of all the works of the devil, and the supreme hater of evil.

The moral teaching of the Sermon on the Mount is the charter of moral life to all Christians. But its influence has gone far into non-Christian regions. It leaves its impress upon the characters of those who have lost faith in Christian doctrine, and upon non-Christian ethical systems like Comtism. It attracts with a wonder of joy those who have not learned

[1] *Vide* Schurer, ii. 2, § 28.

THE DIVINE MORALIST.

to believe in Christian doctrine, and leads the more honest and enlightened among them on to the full acceptance of the doctrine without which it has but permissive value and force

Many educated Hindus are now adopting some form of Theism. The Brahmo Samaj movement in Calcutta is one of the most striking instances. But it is a Theism which is learned from Christianity, and with or without acknowledgment borrows Christian moral ideas without the sanction upon which they rest. Some have found this out, and have been consistent enough to embrace the creed which underlies the morality. The Rev. Nehemiah Goreh, the eminent missionary, is a notable example, and the promise of more. He affirms, " I know, and am as sure as of my own existence, that I learnt Theism from Christianity, and, I also know, that Christianity alone does teach it, and that from Christianity alone it can be learnt."[1]

In the Sermon on the Mount, the Christ formulated for all time the principles of the Christian character. His faith was a school of character. He Himself was a trainer of special character. Character was to be the human propagating power of His truth. His immediate teaching was a technical education in spirituality. All the graces and gifts of Christian character were perfectly embodied in Him, and transcribed, reproduced in varying approximations by those on whom He stamped the ineffable beauty of His image, and the lustrous light of His native force. His spiritual children were to be His speaking likenesses.

His character, like His truth, was progressively revealed. Cross lights beat upon it ; counter currents, fierce oppositions, fought against it ; but as the darkness increased it shone brighter and brighter, as hatred waxed and wove fresh combinations, newer lights and fuller beauties flashed forth from the furnace. The complete ascendency of His character, the full appreciation of it, the true measure of it were only won by the Resurrection. That was the beginning of the final victory of character which was consummated at Pentecost. From that moment the victory of the Christ, and Christ-derived character over all contradictory ideals, was assured. Human life in all its moral relations has never lost, and can never lose, that ideal.

---

[1] "Occasional Papers of the Oxford Mission to Calcutta," quoted by Rev. E F. Taylor, on Indian Theism, *Mission Life*, Feb., 1883.

It is of eternal validity, of universal worth and potency, and is an everlasting spring and fountain-head of like characters, in all the provinces of human life, in all the possible developments of moral loveliness and strength and truth. While He lived on earth His eye was always upon His pupils. In their missionary works and tentative transient evangelizations, they could always refer to Him. He superintended, He dictated. This revealed His public character under various difficulties and emergencies, and prepared them to deal with the like when He was gone.

The Sermon on the Mount was the official manifesto of incarnate moral truth and life. Viewed in connection with His whole life-work, it was the beginning of the transfiguration of character, of the transformation of morals; the beginning not the end. The end was sacrifice, and that could only be understood after He who pleased not Himself had officially announced:

"IT IS FINISHED."

The Ten Beatitudes are the ten words of the new law corresponding to the ten of the old. They are the prototypal moral ideas of the gospel. They are marks of the ideal Christian; one and all perfectly manifest in the Divine Man. The last two Beatitudes were specially suggestive of suffering, and a prophecy of the progressive victoriousness of suffering. The kingdom was one built upon triumphant pain. "In this world all good, even the fairest and noblest—as love—rests upon a 'dark ground,' which it has to consume with pain and convert into pure spirit."[1] This truth was one which had repeatedly to be pressed upon the disciples. For current Jewish teaching regarded suffering as the reward of sin, and even the pure pre-Christian scriptural sufferers had fallen back baffled before the dark mystery. And in their present stage of Messianic experience the disciples had but tasted the cup, and were sheltered by an overpowering strength and sympathy.

The organization of the Christian body, and the organization of the Christian life, were correlative. The words of the Sermon presupposed in the future an organized community, a recognizable brotherhood. The exact form of the body wherein the

[1] Rothe, quoted by Professor Martineau.

spirit should be ensouled is as yet undefined. It was not the method of Christ to seal systems upon living forces before the spirit within needed some embodiment, visible, social. The Kingdom of God centred in the King while He lived and worked on the earthly scene. He would define in word and create in practice the character and life which should stamp the children of the kingdom. He would breathe into them the breath of the new royal life before any outward organization was dowered with the royal charter.

CHAPTER XIII.

THE DIVINE ART TEACHER.   THE DIVINE NATURE-WORKER.
THE DIVINE MISSIONARY.

> " A sweet attractive kind of grace ;
> A full assurance given by looks ;
> Continual comfort in a face,
> The lineaments of gospel books—
> I trow that countenance cannot lye,
> Whose thoughts are legible in the eye."
> " Friend's Passion for his Astrophel."

Capernaum—Nain—The Baptist in Machærus—The Saviour and the lost woman—Divine self-assertion—Spiritual industry—Parables of Divine art interpret Nature—Miracle of power over Nature—Demonism—Incessant labours – Mission tours—The martyr of Machærus—The Feeding of the Five Thousand—The Bread of Life—The stormy lake—The contradiction of sinners—Passover retreat—Back to work.

JESUS descended from the mountain of Beatitudes, and entered into Capernaum (Luke vii. 1).   The crowds had not dispersed. The spell of His presence and His words lay upon them.   They still followed Him.   They witnessed the prayer of the large-hearted centurion, the wonder of the Lord at his faith connecting itself with the promise of many more of Gentile blood entering into the kingdom of heaven.   This last word, coming upon us as a surprise in the Jewish Gospel (Matt. viii. 11), was one of those germs which would fructify in the after-teaching of the disciples.   The evidential force of it should not be overlooked.   The Divine Galilean boldly announced the world width of the kingdom of heaven, and flatly contradicted the whole stream of current teaching and national jealousy, by not only admitting, but preferring the " children of hell," in Rab-

THE DIVINE ART TEACHER. 107

binical language, to the "royal" posterity of Abraham. The unique faith of the straightforward soldier was the spark which kindled the prophetic fire. By a natural association of ideas, Jesus already saw in him the march of a vast army of likeminded soldiers of Christ.

The reward of faith was followed by a miracle where no faith could have found place, or is unrecorded (Luke vii. 11). Victory over death follows victory over disease. On the next day,[1] or shortly after,[2] still accompanied by crowds, sailing perhaps down the lake, and then, taking one of the still existing roads, Christ came to what was then a city, Nain, some twenty miles from Capernaum. Nain, in "its green nest" on the edge of "Little Hermon," well deserved its descriptive name, "the pleasant."[3] The name Nein still lingers over the squalid huts which mark the site.

The two streams met at the gate, probably on the east, where the "rough rock was full of sepulchral caves, which still exist." The only Son of His Mother feels for the mother of an only son—and she a widow. The body lay face upwards and hands folded on the breast, like an effigy on a cathedral sepulchre. The bier was open. Jesus came and touched it. The initiative was His own. In an instant the spirit of life returned to the dead young man. Fear falls upon the whole multitude, mourners with the tears yet upon their cheeks, and those who had now witnessed a greater triumph than any that went before. What was the spiritual link between the Divine power and the lifeless youth ? Some think[4] he died with an intense prayerful yearning for life. We would rather leave it among the unrevealed mysteries and suggested potencies of blessed hope.

Tidings of Jesus' works came to the heroic spirit whom Herod had cast into his fortress prison. St. John was in the palace fortress of Machærus, now M'Kaur. The castle, standing "starkly bold and clear,"[5] 3,860 feet above the Dead Sea, 2,546 above the Mediterranean, dominated the whole country round like some dark angel. Here Herod occupied at once a splendid palace and a frontier rampart against Arab marauders Within the waste of ruins which now mark the spot the two dungeons of the citadel still remain, "the small holes still visible in the

[1] ἐντῇ ἑξῆς, Gebhardt, Tischendorf.   [2] ἐν τῷ, Hort.
[3] Hugh Macmillan, "Our Lord's Three Raisings from the Dead," p 75.
[4] Godet.   [5] J. G. Whittier.

masonry, where staples of wood and iron had once been fixed "[1] One of these was probably the last home of the free son of the wilderness.

Never did life's work seem a more complete failure. St. John knew how God's people had treated God's messengers of old. But was the kingdom of heaven still but a floating light upon the retreating hills of prophecy? and the immediate future as dark as the mountain walls which girdled his dungeon? The uttermost isolation, bodily and spiritual, the horror of encompassing darkness left its trace upon the strong spirit. The iron entered into his soul. The second Elias, like the first, faltered. To face his own doubts, and to satisfy for ever himself and the faithful disciples, who still sought his rocky cell, he would put the question to Him alone who could answer it. "Art Thou the Coming One (*habba*), the Man of the Future, or do we, I and my school of faith, wait for another?" The answer came, clothed in the language of the Messianic prophet,[2] whose words and spirit were the life-breath of all the creed and teaching of John. The benedictory warning[3] is added rather to hearten the disciples than their master, "Blessed is he, whosoever shall not be offended in Me." The brevity of the dismissal may have been needed to quicken the dull flame of their convictions. When they departed lest their weakness should reflect on the Baptist, Christ lifted up His voice in unqualified praise of him who was a prophet, and more exceeding a prophet. Yet, standing outside His Kingdom, he was less than the lesser within. Holy violence such as his could alone force an entrance into its gates. Yet this generation was like fretful children, who would neither mourn with the ascetic nor rejoice with the joy of the Messiah

In St. Luke's record a dramatic incident follows (vii. 36). Our Lord's dealings with women, and women's dealings with Him, form an instructive study, and show marked contrasts with the Rabbinical theory and practice. The woman who came through the open door into the house of Simon the Pharisee was a fallen one, possibly a notorious professional harlot of the town. It may have been Mary of Magdala, whose name is mentioned so soon afterwards. Three figures are prominent in the company.

[1] Tristram, "Land of Moab," p. 259 , Edersheim.
[2] Isa xxxv 5, *sq*., xxix 18, *sq* , xlii 7 , lxi. 1, *sq*.
[3] Not "public censure," as Keim

The Holy One, all tenderness and truth ; the smooth Pharisee, coldly civil, critically unsympathetic ; the penitent daughter of affliction, gliding in unabashed in the glory of her passion and her tears. Modern verse and art have combined to halo the gently audacious guest raining the dew of her tears and kisses upon His feet, and the perfumed ointment from her flask upon His head.

> "Oh, loose me ! See'st thou not my Bridegroom's face
> That draws me to Him ? For His feet my kiss,
> My hair, my tears, He craves to-day , and oh !
> What words can tell what other day and place
> Shall see me clasp those blood-stained feet of His ?
> He needs me, calls me, loves me , let me go." [1]

Such conduct from her, and towards Him, is unthinkable of any contemporary Rabbi, and was immediately challenged. So, often, the good works of Christ, perhaps always, were accompanied or followed by some revelation of the power of evil, some liberation of defeated spite, to mar His happiness in well-doing, and to counterwork its activity. Criticism turned this time upon a crucial question—" Who is this that even [2] forgiveth sins ? " It was a personal question. The answer turned upon His Nature and Office. Christ indirectly asserts both, and so far from withdrawing or explaining the implied authority, reaffirms it by His dismissal, " Thy faith hath saved thee ; go in peace."

Attention must here be drawn to our Lord's repeated assertions of His own Nature and office. Sometimes directly, sometimes indirectly, sometimes openly, sometimes by implication, sometimes by word, sometimes by deed, He avows Himself more than man, and the equal of God. Unless these assertions were *bonâ fide* Christ was a self-deceived impostor, or a deceiver whose influence was, as His enemies declared, of Satanic origin. We are left in this dilemma. We are shut up between these alternatives. The verdict must rest with the sound heart and pure conscience. To maintain that Christ was a self-deceived enthusiast is an outrage upon common sense. If any man was sane and whole-hearted, clear in mind and purpose, able to convince others of His absolute wisdom,

---

[1] D G Rossetti.
[2] So R V , if as A V., the καί would suggest forgiveth sins, as well as treating sinners thus.

truth, and holiness, it was this Man, it is this Man. Either He was honest, or He was dishonest. In the last resort this is the final issue. Upon the answer to this question, the whole past of Christianity depends, the whole present, and the whole future. The believer echoes St. Paul's "audacious challenge"[1] from the inner heart of His own experience, if Christ be not risen then are we of men most wretched; and so far from admitting it to belong to "a past stage of religious development"[2] regards it as the decisive issue upon which all future history depends, and the pledge of the advancing triumph of Christ's kingdom, as well as the absolute basis of his own inward and outward life.

The rapid ingathering of the multitudes, and the special selection of the Twelve, and the manifold works of healing are indirect evidence of the Lord's intense activity. His work was the travail of a spirit held in leash for thirty silent years of praying, bursting forth with the fire and impetus of economized power. A vast reserve of spiritual energy had been accumulating for the day of work. The springs of love and grace were flowing unchecked. Viewed merely as a piece of human labour, the Lord's industry at this time was that of incarnate Work. While the apostles must have tested the powers which they were "sent" to exercise, He bore the burden and heat of the day, and the solitary diadem of responsibility. Among His helpers we find mention of many women (Luke viii. 2), one of whom, at least Joanna, the wife of Chuza, Herod's steward, was of the upper classes.

The first recorded parable was spoken at this time. Our Lord's sympathy with Nature was not only artistic, it was moral. The poet interprets the beautiful in Nature, the physicist the order of facts; Christ drew out the moral and the spiritual revelation. Job had seen something of this. Isaiah too, and the Psalmists. But Christ was the first to emphasize the unity between Nature and grace. His parables are translations of the order of Nature into the order of grace. He created the parable.[3] Apologues are found such as Judges ix. 8 and foll., 2 Sam xii. 1, but the parable was a spiritual work of art unattempted before. The Buddhist parables of the so-called "Sower" and "Prodigal Son" may be compared not as

[1] J. A Symonds, *Fortnightly Review*, ccxlvi p 895.
[2] Ibid.   [3] Renan, p. 136.

THE DIVINE ART TEACHER.

possessing "exactly the same tone and the same character," as M. Renan affirms, but as allegorical tales and images suggesting doctrinal or moral lessons.[1]

The parable in form is a work of art. Truth is taught mediately; the truth of spirit enshrined in matter. The moral function of art is best taught in one of its highest teacher's words.

> "Why take the artistic way to prove so much?
> Because, it is the glory and good of Art,
> That Art remains the one way possible
> Of speaking truth, to mouths like mine, at least.
> How look a brother in the face and say,
> 'Thy right is wrong, eyes hast thou yet art blind,
> Thine ears are stopped and stuffed, despite their length,
> And, oh, the foolishness thou countest faith!'
> Say this as silverly as tongue can troll—
> The anger of the man may be endured,
> The shrug, the disappointed eyes of him,
> Are not so bad to bear—but there's the plague
> That all this trouble comes of telling truth,
> Which truth, by when it reaches him, looks false,
> Seems to be just the thing it would supplant,
> Nor recognizable by whom it left—
> While falsehood would have done the work of truth."
> But Art, wherein man speaks to men,
> Only to mankind—Art may tell a truth
> Obliquely, do the thing shall breed the thought,
> Nor wrong the thought, missing the mediate word."[2]

The first parable contains under its landscape colouring a complete moral classification. It is a work of the master of spiritual analysis. It is a scientific arrangement, valid for all times and places, of human hearts in experimental contact with the Word of God. That Word is the seed truth of the kingdom, and was spoken in His pre-incarnate days by the Word through human organs, and was now spoken by Himself. All human hearts upon whose soil the word fell, falls, and will fall, from the hand of the Sower, or His ministers and workers, are here classed in four divisions. They are not arranged upon arith-

---

[1] Cf. Rhys Davids, "Buddhism," p. 133 f, his so-called Parable of the Sower is an invidious misnomer, cf. reff. *s. l*, and Pressensé, "The Ancient World and Christianity," p. 241, and Bp. Copleston on Buddhism.

[2] R. Browning, "The Ring and the Book," *ad fin*

metical principles. They are qualitative, not quantitative distinctions.

The first parable was minutely explained by Jesus, in order to supply the key to open others, and with a view to teach His disciples how to clothe His truths in like lively forms, and here in also to discern the inter-relations of Nature and grace in their identity of source, common dependence upon law, and similarity of operation.

A cluster of parables are grouped in the Synoptists with the first, probably spoken at different times. The teaching throughout was one, the word (Mark iv. 33) developed under various aspects, according to the spiritual capabilities of the hearers. The leading idea of the whole was the Kingdom of God, its outward development, its inward development, its absolute worth, its finality, its authoritativeness.

The underlying teaching of Nature was uncovered by Christ in the parables. His spiritual insight into Nature was exhibited that the inward and spiritual might always be detected in and under the outward and visible. "Verily Thou art a God that hidest Thyself," was the summary of prophetic interpretation of Nature under the Law. Verily Thou art a God that revealest Thyself is the Christian version. From the time of Jesus Nature has become a sacrament, whereof artist and poet and man of science have partaken in diverse ways and many parts, a sacrament of life unto life, or of death unto death.

By a harmonious sequence of teaching in word and teaching in work, Jesus exhibited His power over the forces of Nature after He had unfolded the spiritual lights which lay hid within them. He is the Divine Man of Science imposing His laws superphysical, as He is the Divine Artist revealing beauties supersensible. But this miracle was not primarily a lesson, still less a dramatic display of power. It followed in the natural order of events. It was evoked by circumstances; it fell in with the ordinary current of the Galilean trials of life. And it was singularly adapted to impress the hardy fishermen of the lake in the line of their own business and experience. It was one of the casts of the Fisher of men. They had seen a hundred times the majesty, the violence, the sudden impetuosity of the Galilean storms. They had long known the fickle temper of the winds which swept down the gorges of the hills, and left the lake half calm, half riot and confusion. They may have lost dear lives in such storms, on such days or nights when

> "One could not hear
> A word the other said, for wind and sea
> That raged and beat and thundered;"[1]

or waited and watched

> "The awfullest, the longest, lightest night
> That ever parents had to spend—a moon
> That shone like daylight on the breaking wave.
> Ah me! and other men have lost their lads, . . .
> And seen the driftwood lie along the coast."[2]

And now they seem likely to lose their own, for one of those thunder gusts that hurtle across the lake and lash the calm surface into tossing sheets of foam[3] had burst in more than ordinary violence, as is shown by their terror, upon the filling vessel. And the Master slept tranquilly on the steerman's pillow as in His Father's arms. At their cry of alarm He awoke, and the

> "Wild winds hush'd"

in a moment at His breath. It was a double-edged reproof. He smote the winds with a curt rebuke, as if behind the inanimate play of impersonal forces He beheld (as perhaps He did) the active personal control of a guilty spirit. And the disciples were chid for the faith which had not cast out fear.

This victory over Nature was immediately succeeded by a very different one. The psychology of demonism is obscure. Modern lunacy furnishes points of contact, and apparent instances of it now and then.[4] But the two are not to be confounded, as the ordinary lunatic may merely suffer from some

[1] Jean Ingelow, "Brothers, and a Sermon."   [2] Ibid
[3] Compare Captain Conder's graphic account of a storm, "Tent Life," ii. p 340.
[4] The writer believes there is more connection between the two than is usually supposed, and is in possession of evidence indicating that both demoniac possession still exists, especially in uncivilized and unchristianed countries, and that cases of lunacy are sometimes partly, at least, spiritually conditioned.

cerebral disease, while the demonized need have had none, and was conscious of possession by some foul spirit, sometimes losing his consciousness in that of his master fiend, sometimes violently asserting his own separate individuality. Again, the moral connection between demonism and evil was absolute, between lunacy and evil it is partial and relative and occasional.

It must still have been evening when, after the short, stormy passage, the crew landed on the eastern shore. Two demoniacs, one of whom appears to have been the spokesman and leader, immediately (Mark v. 2) came to meet Him. Led by some unaccountable Divine instinct, some far-off vibration of mercy, they saw Him at a distance in the moonlight, and ran and worshipped Him. Unless the sacred narrative be tampered with in the interests of critical presuppositions, the demons recognized Jesus, addressed Him in a loud voice as the Son of the Most High God, and besought permission to enter the swine. And He said unto them, Go. The sharp bluff down which the panic-stricken herd rushed has been easily identified, and the caverns and sepulchral rock-chambers out of which the demonized came abound around. One of the two patients of Jesus clung doglike to his Saviour's presence, clothed, and sane, but he is ordered to leave it and to proclaim God's mercies to his own circle. The owners of the swine and all the city would rather be rid of Him. "Egypt was glad at their departing." The stone of stumbling proved an offence.

The question of Christ's right to destroy, or, more accurately, to suffer the destruction of animal life and property, has been raised. But it is only a part of the larger question of the permission of all evil, moral and physical. In this case moral reasons appear on the surface. It was for the good of the possessed that he should have ocular evidence of the removal of his masters; and the same applies with less force to the disciples. It was for the good of the owners who set so much store upon their swine, and probably in defiance of the law, for the population of Peræa was essentially Jewish,[1] that they should learn by punishment if they would not be taught by mercy.

Jesus returned by sea. Crowds gathered round Him in the morning light. Pushing his way through (Luke viii. 41) with the persistency of an impassioned purpose, Jairus, one of the

[1] Schurer, i. 3, and reff s l to Josephus and the Mishna.

synagogue rulers, lays his father's sorrows at the feet of Jesus. His healing powers were well known; and His words of "comfort ye," and His pitifulness, and sweet compassionateness must have been recognized in the synagogue, and by the bedsides of the sick, most of all by the merciful and the sorrowful. On His way a woman with an issue of blood (Luke viii. 44) touched His tallith, and was healed of the twelve years' incurable malady and consequent Levitical uncleanness. Many of such restored invalids, comforted mourners, and healed sick, if only one in ten like the lepers were grateful, must have formed a nucleus round which the Messianic societies would increase.

The house of Jairus was now reached. Tumult and wail and "the flutes for the dead" sound round the still form. So far from wishing to advertise His recall of the maiden to life, Jesus took apart with the parents only His select three. Peter and John and James were now for the first time taken into the innermost circle of His confidence. It was a spiritual differentiation of the three most like-minded to Himself, and most adapted to respond to the high gift and burden of His special call. "Talyetha Qum"; two words recall the spirit to its forsaken tenement. She awoke from the death which our Lord, in common with Rabbinism, called sleep. Perhaps this, the second, to be followed by a third, return from the kingdom of the departed, prepared the way there for our Lord's mysterious journey from the Cross to Hades, and the proclamation to disembodied spirits. Before His saving death, before the keys of Hades (Rev. i. 18) lay in His victorious hand, the spirits of the departed cannot have been as blessed as after. Since the parting of that soul and body, and the penitent robber's translation into Paradise, a new beatitude has been uttered on them that sleep in Him, and on those who mourn for them. Christ passes from the busy streets of Capernaum. Perhaps He was becoming too famous there, and a continuous presence and work might have precipitated a Messianic movement, and one of the very kind He uniformly rejected. His Messianic policy was founded on a Divine, not a human, basis. Otherwise He might have created a storm of popular enthusiasm in any of the largest towns, and ridden upon the crest of it to the gates of the capital. There are, too, unseen links of spiritual causation in all lives governed by conscious obedience to Divine vocation. Alike in its greater heights and deeps, as in its every-day entrance into commonplace duties, the life of the Divine Being in the flesh is, and must be, a mystery which the highest raptures of faith in its loftiest adoration must approach a great way off. He returns to Nazareth (Mark vi. 1). His own city has a second opportunity offered. The same objection is made. The narrow vulgarity of local self-sufficiency cannot understand His "generation." How could He rise above the level of His "parents" and family? It was a social breach of the laws of Nature. Their unbelief imposed limits upon Christ's power, and He wondered. But the dilemma before them and modern unbelief is the same. His human environment being what it was, how could He rise so infinitely above not His source only, but above His highest contemporaries in the whole world, in thought, and in life, unless He was "before them"? (John i. 15.) What laws of heredity, of environment, of evolution can account for Him? If His origin was not natural, then no account is possible, but that for which His own word is pledged. Either the Nazarenes were right, and are the creditors of the human race, for their superior insight, or He whom they cast out. "We can understand nothing of the works of God, if we do not take it as a principle that He blinds some while He illuminates others."[1] Into the conditions of such blindness we need not now inquire. But so much we may be permitted to observe. That the Nazarenes had, if exceptional difficulty on social ground, exceptional privilege. They had witnessed for years the lovely growth of the tender plant; they, in all the world.

A general missionary tour followed in the immediate neighbourhood. And now as the spiritual harvest lay thick, He called to Him His reapers. Not till the time was come, not till the workers had received some preliminary training, did He send them forth. He sent them two by two (Mark vi. 7 f.; Matt. x. 5 f.; Luke ix. 1 f.) as His missionaries now ought to be, and are more often sent, possibly to regions as yet unvisited by Him. The mission was not final, but temporary; not catholic, but limited to the house of Israel. Their function was to preach the kingdom of God, and to heal, to cast out demons, and to raise the dead. They were royal messengers

[1] Pascal, Thoughts, xviii.

and emissaries accredited with delegated royal authority. They were to go unprepared, unprovided. A Jewish colouring pervades the whole charge of their Master The words in St. Matthew's account go beyond the immediate prospect, and gather up the fragmentary missionary directions of different occasions. This is quite in accordance with the classifying method of the sacred writer. The spirit of all His missionary operations is identical, though the form and manner may differ widely.

The sacred narrative abruptly turns at this point to the heroic spirit who lay forgotten in the rocky dungeon at Machærus (Mark vi. 21 ; Matt. xiv. 6). Spring had come, and with it the approach of Passover. The anniversary of the death of Herod the Great, and of the accession of Antipas to his Tetrarchy has arrived. There is a sound of revelry. Salome, daughter of the adulterous Queen Herodias, descendant of the Asmonæan heroes, granddaughter of a king, dances, like a Nautch girl, before the tetrarch and his lords and courtiers. And the head of the noblest of the pre-Christian white-robed army of martyrs falls as the guerdon of a dancing-girl. But

"Be sure they sleep not whom God needs ! "[1]

The tidings of this event must have moved Jesus deeply. The forerunner had been faithful unto death, and had gone before to the end which awaited his Lord in a greater darkness of foreseen horror. And His immediate plan was adapted to the change. Yielding to the current of events, to escape the danger in which the murder of the Baptist involved Himself and His disciples, and the uprising of popular indignation, Christ retreated across the Sea of Tiberias, outside the jurisdiction of Antipas, to Bethsaida-Julias.

When St. John's voice had been silenced in the prison fortress, and his outward and visible work broken off, the cry of the kingdom was again taken up by Christ, and rung through Galilee. The prophet's work had died only to rise again to a new life of higher and wider fulfilment, and his message to be repeated in louder tones with more peremptory authority. There are no gaps in the continuity of the kingdom, no breaks in the order of Divine development.

[1] R. Browning, "Paracelsus."

> "O power to do ! O baffled will!
> O prayer and action ! ye are one
> Who may not strive, may yet fulfil
> The harder task of standing still,
> And good but wished with God is done."[1]

The news of St. John's death must have spread rapidly among the people, and may have been one element in the motives which brought a vast concourse after Jesus, and suggested the popular rising to make Him king. The miraculous feeding of the five thousand men, without counting women and children, is alone of all the miracles related in full by all four evangelists. Its importance lay in its symbolical meaning. It was an act of Divine compassion, in the first place. They who had hungered after righteousness, and sought first the kingdom of God, did not even lose their daily bread. But the discourse in the synagogue at Capernaum interprets the sacramental prophecy of the miracle. Jesus began both to do and teach. This is His way. First the work, then the doctrinal content. The discourse and the miracle interpret one another. Christ would be the Bread of Life; His apostles and successive ministers would distribute the Bread to His people. His very words and action, the blessing, the breaking, look onward to the Last Supper, as the Last Supper preludes the Marriage Supper of the Lamb. The Passover, too, was nigh, and most of the guests at the table in the wilderness were on their way to partake of the Paschal Lamb in Jerusalem. And was there not also the further thought indicated that all "daily bread" should savour, as in St. Augustine's rendering of the Divine prayer, of the "supersubstantial Bread," and all common food recall Divine, and every Christian table be a table of the Lord?

It was upon the green grass at the north-east corner of the lake, near the eastern Bethsaida, perhaps now Et Tell, or Bethsaida-Julias, upon the present fertile plain of Batîhah, that the multitudes sat down in order. St. Mark, from the graphic stroke of St. Peter, has pictured the scene in a word. Their many-coloured order, their regular arrangement, suggested rows of "garden-beds," bordered by the verdure of the spring grass.

Turning from spiritual to historical sequence, the tumultuous Messianic enthusiasm which broke out after the miracle

[1] J. G. Whittier, "The Waiting."

of feeding forced Jesus to decide between heading the excitable multitude on a royal march to the capital or instantly leaving them. The disciples had been fired by the explosion of popular feeling, and two Gospels significantly report that they were compelled by Jesus to embark while He dismissed the multitude. Here, then, the third temptation had recurred, and His own friends were an instrument in it Had He been a mere social reformer or Nationalist, He would have mounted on the wave of an overpowering popular impulse to the highest place of authority. Not so; He fled to the mountain, to be alone with God, wrapt in the storm, but with a soul bright with the consciousness of duty done and temptation overcome, as lake and shore and windy height with the effulgence of the Paschal moon. Yet in their hour of need unforgetful He walks across the waves to the tossing boat and labouring crew. Perhaps this was rather a work of psychical sympathy than of power.

> " Star to star vibrates light · may soul to soul
> Strike thro' a finer element of her own ?" [1]

Sympathy annihilates distance, and reads the thoughts of the farthest away. They were in actual jeopardy, in fear; perhaps further disheartened at His repulse of an offer which, made by so vast a Galilean multitude, if not national in act, was national in promise. Their faith must be strengthened, their hope confirmed, their love not left comfortless And so, quite naturally, and without effort, He stepped across the moon-lit surge and brought them to the haven where they would be.

The western Bethsaida, or " Fisherton," must have been very near Capernaum, and was probably its fishing suburb.[2] Christ had purposed landing; but the storm-drift had borne them northward, and they made shore at the beautiful "land of Gennesaret," now the marshy plain of El Ghuweir, along the north-western shore. The discourse in the synagogue on the Bread of Life, must have been delivered on the Sabbath, or Saturday; consequently it was early on Friday morning when the Lord landed, and the miraculous meal, like its antitype, took place on Thursday evening. During Friday took place the

[1] Tennyson, "Aylmer's Field."
[2] Comparing Mark vi. 45 and John vi. 17 and Mark i. 29 with John i. 44 · xii. 21.

concourse of out-patients, as if to a living hospital. These must have been happy hours of healing. They were not undisturbed. The evil spirit of opposition rises up in the person of a deputation of Pharisees and Scribes from Jerusalem. Why at this particular crisis is not clear, nor is it material. The question between them was fundamental. Underlying the particular point of complaint, eating with unwashen hands, lay the whole principle at stake, which Western thought would have formulated in exact terms First, what was the relative importance of Scripture and tradition? Second, what was the authority of Christ in comparison with both? Third, what was the spiritual worth and position respectively of the opposite parties? A definite solution of these questions was essential. A point of detail involved the whole principles. Any mode of reconciliation between the contending forces of thought was more of a moral than an intellectual impossibility, because the difference was really spiritual, a difference of character—the final difference of Christ and anti-Christ in all their embodiments of thought and life.

With regard to the first question, Christ appeared to Rabbinism to be taking up a revolutionary position, whereas He really returned to the original and primary prototypal revelation. To this day Christianity is faithful to the first-hand law. The Jews are the representatives of hereditary degenerate Rabbinism. Christ restored the true type. Pharisaism was committed to the degenerate forms. The law of custom (the *Halachah*) was " quite as binding as the written Thorah (law) ; "[1] nay, as the former was the " authentic exposition and completion of the latter," a breach of it was a more serious transgression. While the Law was supreme and final in name, in practice it was superseded and made void. The conscience could not breathe. Religion was adulterated at its source. Christ came to substitute a natural for an artificial conscience, to harmonize nature and grace, or rather to transform nature into grace, mechanical slavery into free-hearted, intelligent obedience ; in short, to substitute the spirit of sonship for the spirit of servitude. The Pharisaic party were too heavily laden with their own fetters to appreciate the sweet air of freedom ; nor could they confess ignorance and sin, and

---

[1] Schurer, 1 334 and reff

humble themselves to the seat of the poor in spirit. Pride was their sin of sins.

With regard to externalism then and thereafter, Christ came to set it upon its right basis. Here again He came not to destroy, but to fulfil; to combine together internal and external truth, as soul and body are united. Spirit and matter coexisting in Him could and should coexist in happy accord, the latter subject to the former, as the body to the soul.

> " Inward evermore
> To outward,—so in life, and so in art,
> Which still is life." [1]

The whole incidental question of ceremonial is here determined. Ceremonies are indifferent in themselves. To eat with unwashen hands defiles not a man. Their moral and spiritual valuation entirely depends upon the spiritual thought they embody, the spiritual life they reveal. Christ Himself used ceremony when He broke bread and blessed it, and likewise the cup. Ceremony was an end in itself in the Judaism of Christ's days, and is still in Brahminism and many forms of non-Christian religions and superstitions, from fetishism upwards. By Christ ceremony was not put out of court, but humbled to a means and instrument.

Two of the dark shadows of the Passion were already falling upon Christ in these victorious hours. One was the contradiction of sinners; the other was the falling away of His own friends. As the Pharisees openly thwarted Him, so the doctrinal discourse upon the Bread of Life was the signal for disaffection and desertion. "Will ye also go away?" was the appeal of human and Divine disappointment to the first, so to speak, of a long series of refusals to His holy table.

The discourse was spoken, partly at least, "in synagogue." The Palestine explorers have discovered eleven synagogues, and Mr. Oliphant another since, at El Dikkeh. The architecture of these is much alike. It is a florid and debased Roman type. The Capernaum synagogue, being built of white limestone blocks, must have formed a conspicuous contrast to the black basalt all round. The pot of manna found engraven on a block may have pointed Christ's very words. Verse 37 and

[1] E. B. Browning, "Aurora Leigh."

following appear to have been spoken in further explanation to the inner circle of the disciples.

The chilling blasts of controversy which had beaten upon them must have deepened our Lord's purpose of seeking a restful shelter for the weary, disappointed spirits. The two miracles, accompanied by the Messianic storms of favour and disfavour, had been an exciting episode, and our Lord and His disciples would be glad of a quiet Passover. He retired to the borders of Tyre and Sidon without leaving the land of Israel proper (Matt. xv. 21 ; Mark vii. 24), and must have kept the feast "in some friendly Jewish home."[1] Here the intercessory faith of the Syro-Phœnician woman was rewarded, after being purified by instruction and whetted by delay, by the dispossession of her daughter. The act was one of the incidental mercies of special Providence, and may have roused the drooping spirits of the disciples. It was another preparatory hint that Samaritan schismatic, Roman or Greek proselyte, and even outer heathen, were to find a place in His household and at His table. It was another indication that the fence of law and privilege and ceremony and tradition was being broken down, that all nations would seek and find the Universal Healer. They were so slow in apprehending the Messianic kingdom that they may have put down to the overflow of gracious sympathy what was a scientific law of the kingdom. That kingdom was to be universal, not natural ; cosmic, not terrene ; eternal, not temporal. Entrance into it, and allegiance to it, demanded spiritual, not natural, affinities. For some such purpose He may have taken the circuitous route of the district of Sidon[2] as His return journey. Another excursion into heathendom follows. Decapolis becomes the scene of missionary activity and of many works of healing. The feeding of the four thousand takes place. Hagaret-en-Nusâra, or "Stones of the Christians," one of the points of the Toran range, is the supposed site.

[1] Edersheim, ii 44.
[2] Mark vii. 31. "Through Sidon," R.V., Tischendorf, Westcott and Hort, &c.

CHAPTER XIV.

THE DIVINE TRANSFIGURATION.

> " Upon a sudden One there entered there
> Whose countenance with marvellous beauty shone,
> More than the sons of men divinely fair,
> And all whose presence did the likeness wear
> Of angel more than men."
> ARCHBISHOP TRENCH, " Gertrude of Saxony."

On the way to Cæsarea Philippi—The Petrine confession—The Rock—
The Divine sign—The excellent glory—The descent—The return—The
predictions.

"THE retreats of Jesus were not merely journeys of flight; they were epochs of reflection,"[1] and, we may add, of revelation, of progressive teaching. The storm of opposition, the ebb of desertion, had not shaken Christ's spirit nor abated His purpose. Cæsarea Philippi, Hermon, were spiritual stages on the road to Jerusalem. Having dismissed the multitudes (Matt. xv. 39), Christ came to the region of Magadan and Dalmanutha (Mark viii. 10), which are unidentified, unless the latter be Tarichæa,[2] *Kerak*, and encountered the Pharisees and Sadducees. They demanded a sign from heaven, perhaps in allusion to the manna feeding. Leaving the issue to be fought out upon another arena, He journeyed on beyond the borders of Israel, past the " lower springs " of Jordan, through a well-wooded, park-like country, rich in varied beauty, forward to Cæsarea Philippi, twenty-five or thirty miles north of the Sea of Galilee.

[1] Keim, iv. 256.
[2] Or Dalmanutha may be the present ruin of Ed Delemiyeh, one mile north of Jarmûk (Dr. Thomson), and Magadan, Megidon (Ewald)

It was another devotional epoch rather than a missionary tour. It was a time of spiritual retreat. The sign refused to unbelief and hardness of heart was to be given to the faithful. The rapture of conscious Divine communion was to forearm Jesus, as if with a second baptismal unction, for the last and worst agonies of labour and suffering, and those who would be with Him in His temptations and drink of His cup.

On the way thither (Mark viii. 27) Christ drew from Peter, the spokesman, the great confession, "Thou art the Christ, the Son of the living God." The rocky base of the great castle frowning ahead may have supplied the material colouring, or pointed the meaning, of the responsive promise of the Messiah, "Upon this rock I will build My Church" (Matt. xvi. 18).

As Moses had hailed God in his triumphant *Nunc Dimittis* again and again as the Rock—

> "The Rock, His work is perfect,—
> Then he forsook God which made him,
> And lightly esteemed the Rock of his salvation ;—
> Of the Rock that begat thee thou art unmindful,
> And hast forgotten God that gave thee birth "—
> (Deut. xxxii. 4, 15, 18)

and so on (verses 30, 31, 37), and Hannah in her *Magnificat*—

> "Neither is there any rock like our God" (1 Sam. ii. 2)—

so did Christ identify Himself with the Rock of Moses and Israel's salvation. Upon His Messianic Divine Nature, *i.e.*, upon Himself, would His Church be built (Heb. xii. 28), "a kingdom that cannot be shaken" as He afterwards told them in the words of the Messianic Psalm. He was the chief cornerstone of the real, true Temple (Psa. cxviii. 22). That His hearers understood Him in this sense then and thereafter is manifest from the use made by St. Peter himself of the word and its underlying thought, conceiving Him "as a living, lifegiving stone, and a stone of stumbling," and a rock of offence; and the Fathers who have regarded the Petrine faith as the rock may be followed if we regard the same subjectively. Faith in Christ is the inward heart foundation upon which the whole life-confession of the Church and the Christian reposes. This is, then, one of the many places where Christ peremptorily

THE DIVINE TRANSFIGURATION.

required immediate and prospective faith in Himself as a spiritual necessity ; and upon this occasion, in surroundings specially heathen, where the temples of Greek, Roman, and Syrian deities uprose like outlying fortresses of error marked out for destruction.

Far from Zion, the city of God, far from the potentates and lords and teachers of Israel, did Messiah receive His due homage. Here another latent prophecy of the incoming of the Gentiles and the Epiphany of the sign from heaven to those whom the stars of righteousness, godly fear, and penitential desire were, and are, leading to the Light.

And now they had come to Cæsarea, or its immediate proximity. At the south-west foot of Hermon were the sources of the Jordan, where the grotto was dedicated to Pan, and the place and surrounding country named after him, Paneas or Panias. Close by, Herod built a splendid temple to Augustus ; Philip rebuilt the place and changed its name to Cæsarea. The place has retained its earlier name, and is now called Banias, and is famed in travellers' descriptions for its beauty and its seclusion.

The rest here, or in the neighbouring villages, attempered their minds for quiet thought undisturbed by controversial heats. Peter's adoring confession of faith and the immediate reward of promise was the preface to the deepening solemnity of the Messiah's forewarnings of His suffering and rejection. These were no instinctive vaticinations, nor the political forecast of a leader who felt his cause was lost. They are the explicit and detailed intimation of His Passion, His Death, and His Resurrection. The prophecy calls out the surprised rebuke of the leading apostle, whom perhaps the promise of the keys had exalted, and who was now humbled. Till the Petrine confession had been made, Jesus had spared them some of the revelation of the Cross. Not till the truth of His Nature was deeply lodged in their faith did He task it with so unwelcome, so novel, and uncontemporaneous a revelation as that of the suffering Messiah. Doubtless they took the truth to heart. But we cannot live in our highest moments, and from this level they fell away in life, as the temporary desertion at the Passion shows, and partly in faith. Nor did they rise to it again till the light and power of the Resurrection transformed their conceptions of His Office, and work, with its own glory, and the majesty stood out before them in the kingly splendour of its proportions, till with the Spirit He passed into them, the hope of glory, the faith of their faith, the life of their life.

Mountain heights have from time been chosen as the scene of supereminent Divine manifestations. The cliffs of Sinai heard and echoed the Ten Words which were the crown of the older Covenant. Upon Hattin the new Law was delivered by the Prophet of the New Covenant. Upon one of the elevations of the snowy height of triple Hermon Christ was transfigured. From a mount He ascended. The solitude of the lofty mountain, the stillness of the night, or possibly the early dawn, befitted this more than

"Bridal of the earth and sky,"

when the Shechinah came down and the Voice was heard out of the cloud. It was the supreme moment of spiritual elevation in the life of Jesus. It was a prelude of the Ascension. Jesus was never nearer Heaven, nor farther above earth, alike in body and in spirit than upon this night. Hermon shares in Scripture with the mount of the first Divine Epiphany the title which one of the eye-witnesses of the excellent glory applied to it—"the holy mountain" (Ezek xxviii. 14 ; 2 St. Peter i. 18).

Jesus took with Him the three chosen disciples. They who witnessed and shared the prayer of the Garden of Agony, witnessed and shared the prayer of the Mountain of Glory. The immediate purpose of this evening journey was, St. Luke alone characteristically informs us, prayer. The snowy dome of Hermon is the most conspicuous object of the landscape from almost any point of the country. And now it rises before them—

"A kingly spirit throned among the hills,"[1]

as they leave Cæsarea Philippi and climb its steep heights and ridges. How long the silent prayer of Jesus had lasted we know not. The heights and depths of that incense offering upon that midnight mountain altar pass human thought. Even devotion gives place to weariness. It is a very true touch of nature and physical infirmity that the disciples exhibit. The time, the fatigue of the climb, the drowsy effects of the snow,

[1] Coleridge, to Mount Blanc, changing "Thou" to "A."

THE DIVINE TRANSFIGURATION.

and the keen mountain air, tell upon their senses, and they are heavy with sleep. When they have become wide awake they perceive that a change had come over the Lord. He was transfigured before them. His face shone as the sun, His garments were white as the light, such as no fuller on earth could whiten them. And within the circle of glory were two human forms, recognized by their words or signs as the great Lawgiver and the first great Prophet. Law and Prophecy in their persons rendered homage to the fulfiller of both, whose words should not pass away. Moses and Elias had broken, as it were, away from Sheol upon the wings of this "light unspeakable and full of glory," to speak with Jesus of His Exodus which He should accomplish at Jerusalem. The communion of saints was for the time visible. The word exodus carried with it all the types and predictions of Israel's history of conflict and deliverance and victory, and pointed the way to their definite fulfilment at Jerusalem in the second Moses, and to the promised city of glory beyond, which was the inheritance of the spiritual Israel, whose glory they already beheld in foretaste.

While they were still looking in wonder the three disciples were parted asunder from Jesus. "The extreme rapidity of the formation of cloud on the summit" of Hermon has been noticed. In a few minutes a thick cap forms over the top of the mountain, and as quickly disperses and entirely disappears. Such may have formed the material basis of the cloud of light which overshadowed them. As St. Peter, the spokesman, in confusion and fear suggested that they should make three tabernacles, or arbours, from the boughs of the trees, for it was good to be there, in this heavenly society and effulgence, they entered into the cloud. The simplicity and materiality, so to speak, of the plain Peter are marks of the truth. The writer of a myth or fairy-tale legend would never have invented so prosaic a statement. They were afraid. The climax of glory was reached, the same Voice which had attested the Divinity of the Messiah at His Baptism, commanded them to hear Him, as the authentic Prophet of God, because He was the Beloved Son of God.

To Jesus the recognition of His Father's voice must have been a repetition of the transcendant joy of the baptismal greeting. Must we not say that for the moment all else was forgotten, or in that absorbed, that—

"He heard not, saw not, felt not aught beside,
Through the wide worlds of pleasure and of pain,
Save the full flowing and the ample tide
Of that celestial strain "? [1]

Must it not have been for His sake as well as for the disciples? The irresistible outflow of Divine approval and attestation, the surpassing benediction of the Father upon the Son of His love? There is no mention, as in the Baptism, of the Third Person of the Holy Trinity. But the presence of Moses and Elias suggests far-off, unknowable relations to, and vibrations of joy to, the pre-Messianic children of light.

The Divine Voice, the burden of joy and glory, were too tremendous for human nature. The three witnesses fell on their faces with terror. It was necessary for Jesus to come near and touch them, as the Angel of the Covenant touched Daniel, and set him upright, before they could look up (cf. Jer. i. 9 ; Ezek. i. 3, ii 2). And when they had lifted up their eyes the glory had passed away like a pageant, and they saw no man but Jesus only.

The veracity of the account stands or falls with that of the rest of the Gospels. Its spiritual fitness at the time, and importance in the drama of the Christ life, are better understood the more they are studied in the after-light of the Passion, Resurrection, and Ascension. The Transfiguration looks before and after. Before to the glory of the Only-Begotten of the Father, before to the triumphant confession of Simon Bar Jonah crowned with unsought proof (Matt xvi. 17) ; after to the resumption of the same glory with the Father, after to the communion in glory of all the sons of God.

In indirect support of the gospel veracity and in general remark two observations may be made. First, that of all un-Jewish incidents in the life of Jesus this is the most un-Jewish ; of all words or deeds unexpected of, out of correspondence with, and indeed impossible to a Messiah of contemporary Jewish conception, this was up to this time the most remarkable. The kingliest Messiah of the highest Jewish conception would never have made this expedition to Cæsarea, and the promises uttered upon the occasion. The revelation of glory upon the mountain none but a Divine Messiah could have made. Yet, secondly,

[1] Abp Trench, " The Monk and the Bird."

THE DIVINE TRANSFIGURATION.

that revelation bears on the face of it, in the light of its before and after, its own explanation. The Transfiguration must be viewed in strict connection with the preceding confession. They are chronologically two scenes in one act, but spiritually undivided. It was the Divine answer to the divinely-inspired avowal of the disciples, and the authentication of Jesus' claim to be Messiah by the Divine sign, withheld from unbelief. Eye *hath* seen, and ear *hath* heard, not all, but some of the things which God hath prepared for them that love Him. The kingdom of God was seen in power by three of those who had heard the King speak of His departing to Jerusalem, His Cross, and His Passion. The very words were, so to speak, overheard by, or the teaching knowable to, the pre-Messianic saints, and formed the subject of their talk with the transfigured Messiah. The continuity of God's plan of redemption is illustrated as it moves on from stage to stage in the gradual, timed, localized evolution of His Divine eternal purpose.

The glory had passed away. Jesus and the three descended from the mount of God to the valley of tears, from spiritual rapture and exaltation to the broken cries and discords of tuneless, half-articulate humanity.

The first incident jarred. Even the nine apostles were of a faithless generation (Luke ix. 41), and could not cast the demon out of the lunatic child. The crowd which had gathered round the famous Prophet must have been deeply impressed at the Lord's work of power and sympathy. In the grateful father, the healed son, and the sympathetic crowd, undisturbed by Rabbinical cross-fires, we discern the germ of an outlying mission church, to the very early existence of which the after-legend of Jesus' statue points.

Without any record of the intervening journey we find Him again in Galilee. Very solemnly He again warns the disciples (Luke ix. 44, 45, and Synoptists) of the approaching Passion and Resurrection, to which now He was consciously approaching, and for which He was deliberately preparing them. How much they needed preparations of heart and head after-events disclose.

At Capernaum was made of St. Peter the demand for the payment of the national Temple-contribution, with which the public sacrifices were bought (Exod. xxx. 13 f. ; 2 Chron. xxiv. 6). This consisted of two Attic drachmas, *i.e.*, one common shekel, or Sanctuary half-skekel. The stater in the fish yielded up by a Providential coincidence, paid in full for St. Peter and for Christ. Jesus pointed out, too, that He paid it, not as an obligation, but as a concession to misunderstanding. The Prince was free of the king's taxes. The payment should not therefore come out of the common fund, but from an extraordinary source.

Lessons on the spirit of the new kingdom follow according to natural suggestions of circumstances. The lesson of humility and simplicity of heart like that of the child set in their midst. The lesson of largeness of heart, which sinks itself in the advance of the kingdom so far as to overlook an imperfect sanction and authority when devils are cast out and good works are done in Christ's Name outside the Apostolate. The lesson of mortification, or sacrifice of any line of thought, word, or deed which imperilled the spiritual life and threatened the ruin of the whole nature in Gehenna fire. The lesson of brotherly forgiveness, which forgets as well as forgives; the true altruism, or spirit of brotherliness, which does not efface "reasonable self-love,"[1] but extends it to the other self. Each of these lessons was complete in itself, and part of a whole.

[1] Bishop Butler, "Sermons."

CHAPTER XV.

THE ASCENSION JOURNEY. THE DIVINE MISSIONARY IN PERÆA.

"I was glad when they said unto me,
Let us go unto the house of the Lord "
A Song of Ascents , of David (Psa. cxxii. 1).

" And every thought and word,
And all things seen,
And every passion which his heart has stirred,
And every joy and sorrow which has been,
And every step of life his feet have trod,
Lead by broad stairs of glory up to God."
LEWIS MORRIS, "The Food of Song."

The days of going up—Peremptory claims—The Feast of Tabernacles—
The adulteress—The Light of the World—The Shepherd of Israel—
Pastor pastorum—Peræan Mission—The seventy missionaries—The
Good Samaritan—The devout home scene—The prayer of prayers—
Peræan work resumed—The Feast of Dedication—Return to Peræa—
Incarnate energy—Missionary parables—Parables of the Unseen
World.

A PREGNANT phrase of St. Luke's shows that a new chapter
(Luke ix. 51), and that the last, of Jesus' life now opens. The
rest of His life constituted the days of His receiving up.
From the height of that crowning event, the writer looks back
upon the different incidents as so many stages linked in spiritual
order and sequence. The unity of the purpose is the key to
the whole. The Christ who said and did and suffered what the
following record reports is now in glory. To that Ascension
glory He was moving. The Ascended Lord is the thought
which fills the mind of St. Luke even while he relates His

earthly ministry ; so he spoke of His exodus, not of His death. So St. John's picture of the earthly life is dominated by his conception of the Eternal Word manifesting Himself humanly in the world and then returning to His glory.

If, as seems likely from the Mishna, the Temple tax was due about the Passover, the date of the journeys to and from Hermon is approximately fixed, and followed immediately upon the events before narrated. An interval of silence occurs in the fourfold history. From the Passover of John vi. to the Feast of Tabernacles of John vii. 2, *i.e.*, from Nisan 15 to Tishri 15, was a period of half a year. The months that followed the return to Galilee after the Transfiguration are passed over in a single connecting verse (John vii 1). To go up to the Feast of Tabernacles with the pilgrim company which His "brethren" joined Jesus refused (John vii. 9). They did not, as yet, believe in Him. Their Messianic conceptions were of the purely Jewish order. They could not be in sympathy with Him; their paths must lie apart. After they had gone Jesus began His "Ascension" journey privately (Luke ix. 51) with His disciples, and by a different route. For instead of going through Peræa to avoid schismatic Samaria, His first intention was to go direct by way of Samaria. The first incident on the journey showed that the seed sown in Samaria had not ripened sufficiently, or spread widely enough, to dispel Samaritan hatred ; nor had the sons of thunder who wanted to bring fire down from heaven[1] learnt yet to apply the lesson of forgiveness. Further on a scribe, unique in his calling, said he would follow the Master. He Himself bade another. A third offered Himself. All three meet with searching half-repellent answers. From the last two Christ claims a peremptory obedience overleaping the dearest natural ties, such as only the Divine Being and the Divine cause could justify. It was an application of the precept, "Seek ye first the kingdom of God." His own homelessness, outward, as the first was reminded, inward, as His own spirit knew, was His own more than fulfilment in example.

Whether the mission of the Seventy took place before or after the Feast of Tabernacles is much disputed. We put it ater. The Feast of Tabernacles, the Harvest Festival of the Jewish Church, was the most popular and important festival

[1] Even as Elijah did—om R V , Tischendorf, Hort, Gebhardt.

THE ASCENSION JOURNEY.

after the Captivity. It was observed in the month Tishri. It began on the fifteenth day, five days after the Day of Atonement, and lasted eight days. At Jerusalem it was a gala time. It was to the autumn pilgrims, who arrived on the fourteenth, like entrance into a sylvan city. Roofs and courtyards, streets and squares, roads and gardens, were green with boughs of citron and myrtle, palm and willow. The booths recalled the pilgrimage through the wilderness. The ingathering of fruits prophesied of the spiritual harvest already beginning.

As Jesus did not arrive in Jerusalem till the middle of the Feast of Tabernacles, He cannot have been there for the Day of Atonement. St. John (vii. 11) especially intent upon the conflict of faith of which He was the centre describes the questioning and murmuring among the different knots of Jews, Jerusalemite or Galilean. Feeling was divided, but those who were well disposed towards Him knew too well the mind of the hierarchy to express openly their sentiments. While men speculated and questioned, Jesus came up Himself in the middle of the feast, and resumed His teaching in the Temple. The oft-repeated question "How," takes another form. How knoweth this man letters, having never learned in any recognized school of thought? The answer is a plain, unevasive appeal to first principles. His teaching was derivative, not humanly, but divinely, and assigned the highest place in appraising spiritual evidence to the will honestly bent upon doing God's will. His doctrine was knowable to doer, not dreamer. Up to this point the argument is universal in scope, and appeals broadly to mankind. It is spiritual, superhistorical. It then takes a Jewish turn—an *argumentum ad hominem*—an appeal to Moses. Which showed the true Mosaic spirit, those who broke the Law they professed, those who sought to kill, or He who wrought a greater work of healing and mercy than the circumcision which was permissible on the Sabbath day? The dilemma was a personal one. It was the alternative of the Messianic, or the anti-Messianic party, the invariable, the final alternative set before the Jews.

The bold stand made by Christ was the next object of remark (vii. 25). There was no shade of concession on His part, no pretension to a compromise with the dominant party. The scabbard had been thrown away. An ineffectual order for His arrest followed.

The last, or great day, of the feast came, the seventh, "the great Hosannah" (John vii. 37). When the voice of Jesus rang loudly through the Temple, " If any man thirst let him come and drink." This must have been after the symbolic pouring, at the Altar of Burnt Offering, of the water solemnly brought from Siloam, with its thanksgiving choral song, the great Hallel (Psa. cxiii.–cxviii.). It was the Divine answer to the supplication of the ingathered thousands of far-scattered Israel, " with palms in their hands." Another ferment breaks out. The crowds are convulsed with a rush of conflicting movements of thought and feeling. Is, or is not, this the Christ? The faltering Nicodemus was a type of those who would give Him fair play, but were slow in forming their convictions, and timid in acting upon them. Many believed in Him (John vii. 31 and viii. 31), and were at various stations on the road towards the light, others waxed in unbelief and hostility. The line of division became more marked. Several futile attempts were made to seize Him. The Temple officers themselves confessed to the hierarchial party, " Never man spake like this Man."

The episode of the woman taken in adultery is no part of St. John's original gospel (John vii. 53). All internal and external evidence is against it. The moral evidence is admittedly for it. It is just one of those anecdotes which would be remembered and handed down. That some incident took place of the kind may well be supposed. But the time of it is quite uncertain, and the details appear to be un-Jewish and inaccurate. It may have crept into the fourth Gospel from a lost work of Papias of Hierapolis, who collected various discourses of our Lord, with comments, gathering them from the reports of primitive disciples.

Probably on the next day, or Octave, Jesus spake in the Treasury, within the Court of the Women. Another of the festal rites supplied Him with a text. The nightly illumination of that court symbolized Him who was the Light of the world. The light was a Messianic title, and would have been Messianically understood, as in the vesper hymn of the aged Simeon. Both this and the following discourse, reported in a summary by St. John, travel along, yet infinitely above and beyond, Jewish modes of thought and argument, but utter eternal truth. His own claim was self-evidential of Divine. That truth could only be appropriated spiritually Truth carried with it freedom.

THE ASCENSION JOURNEY. 135

The children of Abraham were those who shared his faith. Abraham himself had spiritual sympathy with Him. Christ here strikes out the great doctrine developed by St. Paul. They must be taught of God. Christ's words became more and more decisive, and the dilemma before His adversaries increasingly peremptory. He ended with the assertion of His eternal existence (John viii. 58). Before Abraham was, I am. It was brought out by the stress of controversy, like all great truths. It set the issue straight before all. They answered with stones. But He was not to die like St. Stephen, and hid Himself and withdrew

If, as seems likely,[1] St. John's narrative is here strictly continous, the healing of the blind man took place on the next day (ix. 1). The connection of doing and teaching,[2] as ever, and the correlation of thought between moral and physical blindness and enlightening, necessitate the inference as to chronological connection. And the Sabbath sheltered Him from renewed violence. The miracle took place probably at the entrance[3] to the Temple. Again St John, as so often,[4] fixes our attention on the mental and spiritual forces at work. Again he dwells minutely on the history of an individual. It is the inward scenery of the moral life as every soul passed across the penetrating Light. and revealed itself to which he is sensitive. His intense moral realism is the secret of the vividness of the dialogue. The whole scene is not a triumph of artistic imagination, but the vivid expression of what he saw and remembered, outward and inward. The eye- and ear-witness records, whose eye and ear have been opened. Were not this the explanation, St. John must be placed at the head of all dramatic artists. Christ was the Master light of all his seeing; in that Light he saw the light, the Light Himself and that on which He shone, and, by shining upon, made transparent. But upon the enemies of the Light the darkness was now sinking.

St. John's tenth chapter contains our Lord's address to the shepherds of Israel,[5] and the flock which had become a prey to them. There is nothing arbitrary in the choice of the figure of the shepherd. He identifies Himself with God the Shepherd

---
[1] Reading δὲ in John x 22 with R V , Gebhardt, Tischendorf, &c , ii τότε be read with Westcott and Hort, then Dr Westcott's inference may be correct, that John ix 1-x 21 all belong to the Feast of Dedication.
[2] Cf Acts i 1.   [3] Cf. Ibid iii 2.   [4] Cf. vii 43 , viii. 30 , x. 19, &c.
[5] Cf. all Ezek. xxxiv.

of Israel in the past ;[1] and promises the universal extension of His one flock. So with the flock He identifies Himself elsewhere as the Lamb of God. He knows the Shepherd will die for the sheep ; but His death is a voluntary self-surrender, and He will take His life back again. Such teaching must have prepared the apostles for their own work of shepherding. Again, the continuity of God's purpose reveals itself. He had been, and is, the One True Shepherd all along, the *Pastor pastorum*. His under-shepherds, His flock, belong to Him only, and by their character and work set forth the pastoral aspect of God's character, revealed fully in Christ. Under the figures of Shepherd and Lamb, combining both lines of thought, we have the full expression of the doctrine of Christ's mediation. And the figure of the Shepherd would remind the more cultivated of Enoch's pre-Messianic vision of God as the " Lord of the sheep," calling seventy shepherds and committing to them the punishment of the sheep. The recognition of other sheep not of the Jewish fold was a very un-Jewish statement. Such an implied prophecy revealed His pastoral love and yearning sympathy over the unshepherded flocks of universal humanity, for whom He laid down His shepherd life. And the prophecy speaks of His personal bringing them, and the becoming, how slowly, how gradually, He knows, one flock under One Shepherd. Such words must have been one of the inspirations of the first apostolic missionaries, as they have been of the latest. " He loved all men alike, and he never despised any one," were the words of the Melanesian boy over the body of Bishop Patteson, lying with its five wounds before him. So after the death of the Rev. Philip S. Smith, of the Oxford Mission to Calcutta, at a meeting held a few days after that event had brought mourning to many non-Christians, Mr. Protap Chunder Mozoomdar, a leader in the Brahmo Samaj since the death of Keshub Chunder Sen, spoke of him as follows : " Truly did the Rev. Philip Smith imitate the glorious Ideal by whose name he was known, by living in this country a life deep and profound. What shall we say of his life ? It was so gentle, so good that his features have painted themselves upon our mental vision for all time. Manhood and womanhood, tenderness and strength, blended in his sweet character. I, thinking of him,

---

[1] Psa. lxxx. 1, xxiii. 1 , Ezek. xxxvii. 24 , Zech. x. 3.

am reminded of some mediæval saint, overflowing with kindness to bird, and beast, and man."[1]

Such overflowing love to peoples of strange heart and tongue and colour has been the uniform characteristic of those who have carried on the Messianic tradition of love beyond the bounds of national creeds and the home centres of the faith.

Love was the inspiring motive of the Incarnation, of the Atonement. Love is the central fire of the sacrificial energies of the Christ-bearers. The passion to spread the kingdom of love is the master passion in the hierarchy of noble ambitions. The love of the Chief Shepherd propagates and repeats itself in thousands of hearts, and wings flights upon flights of prayer.

> "The world is used to have its business done
> On other grounds, find great effects produced
> For power's sake, fame's sake, motives in men's mouth.
> Truth is the strong thing. Let man's life be true!
> And love's the truth of mine"[2]

The view taken of St. Luke ix. 51 negatives the opinion of some that Christ now returned to Galilee. Of Galilee He had taken farewell. Nor is it likely that He can have remained tranquilly working in Judæa after so determined a declaration of hostility. And the woe upon Chorazin and Bethsaida loses its point away from their neighbourhood. We agree then with those who place his Peræan ministry here lasting with the break of the Feast of the Dedication about six months. Some place the mission of the Seventy[3] on the journey to the Feast of Tabernacles. But there seems more time for it now, and as a missionary campaign of ingathering it fitly follows on that festival. We are wholly without geographical details in St. Luke's account. His bias is towards missionary history and spiritual expansion. The personal colouring shows itself here. For the writer was an evangelist and a fellow-worker with St. Paul. Just those details of Christ's discourse or work which he had laid under contribution in his own labours would naturally collect in his memory, or in his notes and manuscripts. This will account for the universality, the humanity of his

---

[1] Oxford Mission to Calcutta Report, June, 1888, compare Sir W. Hunter in *The Nineteenth Century*, July, 1888, in reference to "the young Oxford ascetic."

[2] R. Browning, "In a Balcony."   [3] With Tischendorf, &c.

Gospel, for its Pauline character, its especial attention to the home and foreign missions of Christ. His is the Gospel of the Good Samaritan, of the Prodigal Son.

The mission of the Seventy was a new departure, both in the constructive organization and in the outward expansion of the kingdom. They were sent in pairs. This society and fellowship provided for spiritual sympathy and co-operation, for practical efficiency, and also formed a knot of so-to-speak churches, where two were gathered together into a nidus or centre, and the whole co-ordinated under the Supreme Missionary. The occasion was temporary. The underlying principles were permanent, and are specially suggestive of the importance of sending out missionaries, two by two, or in brotherhoods and societies. The concise practical directions given to the evangelists show that the Christ, as Administrator, did not despise attending to minor details of order and method. Economy of time, of equipment, and healing of the sick were especially insisted on.

The number seventy was not a statistical accident. It was a sacred number, and bore the dignity of honourable and historic precedents. Moses had organized seventy elders. The Sanhedrin, when instituted or reorganized, numbered seventy. The number seven again and again recurs in the cycle of Jewish religious observances.

The Mission was successful. The Seventy returned with joy, and reported that even the demons were subject to them in His Name. Jesus had identified Himself with His workers in the impressive words, "He that heareth you heareth Me, and he that rejecteth you rejecteth Me," implying thereby their plenary authority and representative commission. Now after the declaration of Satan's fall from heaven, as if He beheld behind the visible scene the prehistoric downfall of the Evil Spirit repeating itself in spiritual dethronements, He renews, and confirms, and extends their delegated authority over all the power of the enemy. And more than the disciples their Master in that same hour rejoiced (according to the right, newly recovered, and most remarkable reading, Luke x. 21, R. V.) "in the Holy Spirit." Were not such hours when He saw of the travail of His soul and was satisfied but few?

At this time the question of the lawyer elicited the parable of the Good Samaritan. Some episode in the lawyer's own life,

THE DIVINE MISSIONARY IN PERÆA.

or some well-known incident of the day, may have formed the basis of the story. It was entirely un-Jewish; just as now it would be un-Mahommedan, for a Mahommedan Sunni would leave a Mahommedan Persian Shi'ah to perish unheeded on the roadside.[1] It taught the spirit of brotherhood of which He gave so many examples. Perhaps some of the Seventy were Samaritans. The parable is, as it were, the foundation-stone of all Christian hospitals, and the equalization in treatment of all sects and faiths within the walls where Christian doctors and nurses often exemplify the power of His faith and fraternity.

The visit to the home of Mary and Martha at Bethany may have been just before, or just after the feast. Its interest lies in its revelation of the Lord in the retirement of home life, and in His intercourse with women. The anecdote of Mary and Martha is inserted by St. Luke for some purpose other than biographical. Mary and Martha are representatives of two orders of human character.[2] One was absorbed, preoccupied, distracted; the other was concentrated and single-hearted. Her own world was the all of Martha; Christ was the first thought with Mary. They did not necessarily represent the laborious and the contemplative types of life. The former was divided; the latter, one. To Martha life was "a succession of particular businesses"; to Mary life "was rather the flow of one spirit."[3] Martha was Petrine, Mary was Johannine. St. Luke gives us a moral as well as a domestic interior. The one was a well-meaning, bustling busybody; the other was a reverent disciple, a wistful listener.[4] Did not the first miss the Divinity of the guest, and the other go far towards recognition and worship? As a rare glimpse of family life in the Gospels, and Christ's presence in the home we gladly dwell upon it. We shall hardly do wrong to notice a certain touch of humour in the Lord's reproof of the "distracted" mistress of the household St Paul had such a picture in his mind when he spoke of attending upon the Lord "without distraction" (1 Cor. vii. 38).

---

[1] Sir F Goldsmid gives an example in his own experience at a Turkish caravansera near Baghdad, "On Islam," *Mission Field*, May, 1888.
[2] Cf. J. Martineau, "Hours of Thought," p 59.   [3] Ibid
[4] Cf. "Pirke Aboth " 4 , Taylor, "Let thy house be a meeting-house for the wise , and powder thyself in the dust of their feet , and drink their words with thirstiness."

By the law of association of ideas it is likely that the prayer of the disciples (Luke xi. 1) to be taught to pray, took place in some spot where John, like any other Rabbi, had taught his disciples a form of prayer, or where our Lord Himself had been seen, or heard, offering the calves of the lips. It is well known that the Lord's prayer was based upon pre-existent Jewish prayers. But there was transformation as well as conservation. In the first place, no orthodox Israelite could have sincerely prayed "Forgive us our trespasses as we forgive them that trespass against us," any more than an orthodox modern Mahommedan. In the second place, Christ laid down no rules as to posture and ceremony. The prayer was internal—without implying or excusing irreverence. The Rabbinical prayers were too often external. "This appears from the Talmudic tractate specially devoted to that subject (Berakhoth), where the exact position, the degree of inclination, and other trivialities, never referred to by Christ, are dwelt upon at length as of primary importance."[1] The universality of its content, "Our Father," was also as un-Rabbinical as un-Mahommedan, and another indication of the fraternity and interdependence of the members of the kingdom one with another. The clause, "Thy kingdom come," may have been a devotional creation of the Baptist, and adopted by Jesus. "Thy will be done on earth as it is in heaven," could only have been born of a mind conversant with heaven and earth. "Give us this day our daily bread," was a practical confession of faith in the minute providential superintendence of the bodily needs of those who sought first the kingdom of God and His righteousness. "Deliver us from the Evil One,"[2] had special point in times and seasons of conscious warfare with the ubiquitous works of the devil, and in relation to thanksgivings such as "I beheld Satan as lightning fall from heaven," and prayers such as that of the Great Intercession. The personality of the Evil One comes into very distinct view in the New Testament. He had been a figure in the background under the Old Covenant revelations. But when the intense light of the gospel was shed with increasing power on things unseen and seen, the figure, the character, the work of Satan emerged more and more clearly.

[1] Edersheim, i. 536.
[2] For this rendering see the Bishop of Durham's (to the writer's mind) conclusive essay

THE DIVINE MISSIONARY IN PERÆA.

The work of Christ as a personal antagonism, past, present, future, and as a chronic victory over a personal enemy, can only be fully understood by reading it in the light of His own prayer, His own words, and in those of the men whom He taught. He knew He was contending not with the *vis inertiæ* of evil, with mechanical masses of death and corruption, but with a superhuman personal will and intellect at the head and front of others like him, many as those who fell from heaven like stars.

The Peræan ministry was not rich in noticeable incident. Christ's teaching was public and open. The masses flocked to Him. The words of the prophet Jeremiah (xv. 10), " Woe is me, my mother, that thou hast born me a man of strife and a man of contention to the whole earth," describe the tone and spirit which pervade His teaching in the face of Pharisaic opposition. The necessities of spiritual polemics drove Him into open denunciation of those whose spiritual disestablishment was necessary in the interests of their own souls, and of those who looked up to them. Even at the friendly meal, out of season as well as in season, the Pharisaic host must be taught to unlearn his externalism, if he would be a child of the prophets and not of their murderers.

A prophetic outlook underlies His teaching to the disciples. With regard to the nation his call to repentance becomes more and more accentuated ; with regard to the disciples, more and more illuminative. The burden of coming events seems to weigh every word. The night was coming when no man could work.

Our Lord's warnings became increasingly severe. His invective breathes the thunder of the prophets, and predicts the wrath of the Lamb. Mighty works and deeds, of which the former are selected rather than the latter by St. Luke, lose evidential force for, and judiciously harden, hearts encrusted with guilt and blackened with hatred. The climax of warning sin the against Holy Ghost (Luke xii. 10), in the face of myriads of was reached in the declaration of the unpardonableness of the the multitude, so closely packed that they trod on one another (Luke xii. 1), and emphasized by the preceding tenderness of the context which spake of the unforgotten sparrows, and the hairs of the head all numbered.

This Peræan ministry was interrupted by the Feast of

Dedication (John x. 22). Christ was not afraid to face His enemies again in the heart of a hostile territory. The feast was not one of Divine, but of national institution. After the desecration of the Temple by Antiochus Epiphanes, Judas Maccabæus had dedicated the altar "with songs, and citherns, and harps, and cymbals" (1 Macc iv 54). The spirit of patriotism, the wish to render honour to national feeling and civil authority, animated the Ideal Son of Abraham. Both as Messiah Prince demanding the allegiance of Israel, as Son of God always and everywhere declaring His Father's glory, and as Child of Israel, He would discharge the duty of an Israelite indeed, and show His fellowship with His people. Under the last aspect we have the consecration of patriotism. Upon the altar of the Divine heart that flame burned brightly. Christ accepted His place in the organism of the State, and discharged His civil obligations with the fullest recognition of the Divinity of their claims. When Judas "decked the forefront of the Temple with crowns of gold and with shields" (1 Macc. iv. 57), he was champion alike of Church and State, and in both characters a vicegerent of God.

Not till the Temple of Christ's Body had been restored and reconsecrated by the Resurrection, after the desecrating violence and profane destruction at the hands of the wicked, did the figurative prophecy of the Maccabean restoration come to a fulfilment. The festival probably took place at the Christian Christmastide, but the twenty-fifth of Chislev that year, according to some, fell earlier in December. The wintry season is especially noted by St John, and accounts for Christ's walking under the shelter of Solomon's Porch.

The teaching contained no new elements, but re-emphasized and reiterated old truths. The consistency of Christ's claim through evil report, and through good report, with opposition or without it, the steadiness of His front, and the calm decided insistence of assured conviction, must have deepened the favourable impression of honest inquirers wavering towards the light. Here was One who never quailed, who never abated, who never lost dignity nor temper, whose looks and mien towards high or low breathed tenderness, sincerity, holy force, whom no one could detect in any weakness, compromise, or concession, whose words of grace and truth seconded works of power and love. Character is a potent force, often

THE DIVINE MISSIONARY IN PERÆA.

when and where least acknowledged, or openly decried. The character of Christ must have made itself felt with increasing clearness, and farther range of influence, as He became more and more a public Man and the great question of the day, in Temple Court, in crowded street, in upper chamber gatherings, and in the private musings and heart-searchings which come to all but the careless and profane.

The great point in His statement He presses again and again —His works. It is still the evidence of the Christian life which tells most among non-Christians, or half-believers.

Again He employs the familiar figure of His sheep, but makes a magnificent addition, which implies that the turning point had come to some of them, and the great decision made—"I give unto them eternal life," not I will give. The gift is theirs for a present possession, the free, unbought guerdon of the saving Giver.

His unequivocal statement of unity of nature with the Father was understood, and rightly understood, in the only sense it could bear. It was a more categorical statement of what had been implied and indeed asserted before. Again the threatening stones were taken up Again they sought to arrest Him, and He escaped from their hands.

The change to Peræa was as sudden as it was welcome. In the capital the more He loves the less He is loved. In Peræa He again reaps where the Baptist had sown. In Jerusalem the tide of hatred is rising to the flood. In Peræa "many believed on Him" (John x. 42). Wherever He is His presence cannot be "put by." His character, and the work which is the necessary outflow of it into His social environment, is strong to repel or to attract. Neutrality was impossible. The question of the day, in public debate, in private self-examination, was approaching solution. Every other question, national and political, social and sectional, religious and spiritual, general and individual, turned upon this. Eyes and ears were opening to this fact everywhere in Jewry. We constantly meet evidence of our Lord's physical activity. Here in Peræa (Luke xiii. 22), as formerly in Galilee, a round of cities and villages is visited. Everywhere the new teaching is heard, and the same results took place on small fields which the scanty records and the incidental hints of the Gospel memoirs depict in the larger centres of population.

We feel again in the presence of incarnate earnestness and energy. The drain upon the Lord's physical and spiritual resources at this time must have been unceasing. Religious work is especially exacting. The flow of feeling, the pressure of responsibility, the excitement of aggressive labour, which His workers knew, and know, and which we see so luminously reflected in the pages of the Pauline Epistles in every phase of high emotion, and breathed in the thousand diverse harmonies of the Psalter, must have been as real, and as exhausting, in the perfect Missionary and Christian Worker, at least as in any of His followers, or in many put together.

But to balance the pressure of over-work there was the perfect trust in God, the casting of all care upon Him, the rest under the shadow of His hand. When He bade His "little flock" "fear not," or " be of good cheer," or " be not overanxious," He spoke straight from the heart of His own experience. He revealed therein indirectly the inner springs of His own spiritual strength and peace, and the outward demeanour of the Blessed of all His own beatitudes must of itself have been an outward and visible sign of inward and spiritual grace and light.

The parables of the Peræan ministry are transcripts from the Divine experience. They all illustrate the seeking and saving love (Luke xv.), the redemptive forces of God, seen actually and visibly in Christ's own life, secondarily and derivatively in the lives of those He taught and inspired. They harmonize in place and time with the specially missionary character of this Peræan episode. These discourses may be viewed under three aspects —as they bore upon the apostles, upon the general body of the disciples and hearers, and upon the Church of God. Under all aspects they pourtray the eternal character of God, as the deepening light of ages has shed the lustre of progressive revelation upon it from glory to glory.

In reference to the apostles the parables had an educational value. Christ was gradually transforming the false Messianic ideal of their minds into the true. He was educating their consciences at the same time to a higher level and an acuter vision. Their whole mental horizon had to be universalized. The parables paved the way for the teaching of St. Stephen as that contained in germ the full flower of the Pauline Gospel. The Messianic message to all nations, and the sacredness of the individual in God's right, the absolute annihilation of prerogative and privilege in the election of grace, the freedom of salvation, and over all the yearning heart of God willing all men to be saved and to come to the full knowledge of the truth—these are the truths which flowed naturally from these doings and sayings, and sunk imperceptibly with fructifying power into the hearts of the disciples. And they were lit up at every point by a host of unrecorded words, looks, acts, which even the Catholic Gospel of St. Luke has left for future resurrection and the historians of other worlds.

So to the general body of followers, hearers, inquirers, unorganized as yet, and unshepherded, this Peræan ministry must have opened a new world. All men need Christ, but not all seek Him. Of those who seek Him many seek blindly or unconsciously. The history of modern missions supplies examples of what went on on a grander scale where Christ and His apostles laboured. Much, most, of the work had to be left for future labourers. But an impression must have been left, a mark greater and deeper than the Baptist's made in the same region, which broke ground for the coming harvests.

With regard to the Church of the ages, it is needless to dwell upon the force and meaning. Every missionary effort has drawn upon the stories of the lost sheep, the lost coin, the lost son, as a fund of inspiration and energy.

> "Out in the desert He heard its cry—
> Sick and helpless, and ready to die."

A pair of parables follow in St. Luke's sixteenth chapter, which would not be placed there except for chronological or spiritual fitness. As the preceding triad threw open the gates of the Messianic kingdom, so these close them. Even the spiritually dead might revive, the lost might be found, but there were limits imposed by character, in this department of the kingdom, and in that province which lay beyond the grave. The moral of the parable of the unjust steward was that all property—intellectual, spiritual, material—is a trust to be used in the interest of the kingdom to come. The "other-worldliness" with which George Eliot taxes Christianity might be a true charge if there were no moral connection between the kingdom that now is visible and that now is invisible. On the contrary,

Christ emphasizes the absoluteness of that connection. Use this world aright, because it is the school for another. Here lay His heaviest charge against Pharisaism. All the things in the world, even religion, the most sacred of all, ministered to their selfishness and personal exaltation. They claimed the praise of men here, and the praise of God hereafter. They would step grandly from their popular thrones below to loftier pedestals above. They sat in the seats of learning and knowledge, religious honour, wealth, and social esteem; and every one of these trusts was perverted and abused to their own glory and self-righteousness.

The second parable changes the scene with terrible irony to the next world. The conditions of Dives and Lazarus are exchanged, but the characters of each are unchanged. Dives still justifies himself, and under the cover of a plea for his own brothers, impugns the righteousness of God in not giving himself and them a fair chance. Dives still regards Lazarus as an inferior being, who should be summoned at his beck. Dives still views his environment from the centre of himself and his family. It is a shallow exegesis which here discovers moral improvement in the rich man.

"Cœlum non animum mutant qui trans mare currunt."[1]

Character becomes eternal, independent of space and time.

The personal point of the parable cannot be missed. The Pharisees and Sadducees were warned and exposed. They were the rich men, who fared sumptuously in the palaces of religion, knowledge, and material luxury, and left the "accursed" rabble, Am-ha-aretz, to starve. The drama ends in the prophecy that the resurrection would fail to elicit the moral obedience of those who were deaf to Moses and the prophets. The last words establish and re-affirm the moral continuity and unity of the law and character of God, under its three successive stages of the Law, the Gospel, and the kingdom of the Unseen. God is always true to Himself. According as men were true to Him or untrue, they fell on either side. The Messianic advent was a preliminary judgment and division, reversing the false ideals of the day, and affirming the true. The death of Christ was the cli-

Hor.

max which both sides were approaching. Viewed as to their need of salvation and moral culpability, mankind as a mass were arrayed in hostility to Him, and in varying degrees were guilty of that death. Viewed as confessing or disowning their guilt, as accepting or rejecting a Saviour, mankind fell into two classes before the dividing presence of Christ. In the long run man must admit his own sinfulness, or impute it to God. So the Pharisees established their own righteousness, and imputed to Christ unrighteousness.

CHAPTER XVI.

GATHERING SHADOWS.

"'Mere reason' cannot be tolerated in religion, even as it cannot in the sanctities of home. For religion is truly the home-feeling of the universe. The Church is the home. Here comes feeble, weary, jaded humanity, to seek its rest" (JAS. HINTON, "Philosophy and Religion," p. 187).

The resurrection of Lazarus—Back to Peræa—Divorce and marriage—The rights of woman—The rights of children—Behold, we go up to Jerusalem!—Jericho—Zacchæus and the service of man—The blind healed—The pilgrims in debate—The Sabbath rest and unction.

THE Peræan ministry was now broken by an appeal which could not be set aside. Tidings of Lazarus' dangerous illness reached Christ from some trusted messenger of his sisters. "He whom thou lovest is sick." The message was short and anxious, as a sick bulletin and a virtual prayer. The Lord's answer is a key to the whole of His conduct. Had this sickness—and death—not been for the glory of God we can hardly have believed that Christ would have placed the dearest claims of private friendship above the "bitter cry" of Peræan Messianic need. But there is no real clash of duties. Duty is one. The record of St. John has all the fulness and picturesque minuteness of the memory of the eye-witness. The objections of the disciples to His returning to Judæa and certain death by stoning were the common-sense objections of the natural man. Our Lord's appeal to the preordained limits of His working-day removes the ground of duty to the region of that faith which reads off the invisible. The human, the Divine, move with perfect harmony in the mysterious music of the unity of the Divine Person who is of both. Human affection and sympathy prelude the outburst of Divine power. The silent tear, the loud cry. The word of Christ was a discharge of spiritual force, a supernatural vibration to the unknown regions of the spiritual cosmos. It was the inner current of volition, rather than the loud wave of sound, which was heard by the disembodied spirit. The latter was spoken for the witnesses, or possibly as the discharge of deep feeling, like that of the one grateful leper. Might not unbelief urge, has it not urged that here was imposture? or credit to the evangelist the creation of "a masterpiece of allegorical fiction"? The answer depends upon the presuppositions. This miracle directly declares Christ's independence of the laws of nature and of human nature more emphatically than any preceding one. It was the prelude to the Royal Resurrection. It was a great sign of the greatest sign of all at hand.

Its credibility externally rests upon that of the Fourth Evangelist. Its internal credibility is swallowed up in the larger proposition of Christ's own resurrection. The effect of the resurrection of Lazarus was decisive upon many of the eye-witnesses (John xi. 45). Many of the Jews, *i.e.*, as usually in St. John, the anti-Christian Jewish party, believed on Him. But "some," contrasted with "many" must mean a minority, carried their report to the Pharisees. This miracle more than any other up to the greater one it prefaced, is not only a help to certify Christ's revelation, and itself a means by which in part it is made, " but also a pledge of our final restoration and victory over sin and disease and death."[1]

Such a majestic sign of power was decisive. Lazarus was a living witness who could not be gainsaid before friend or foe. In the heart of Jewry, in the streets of Jerusalem, in the courts of the Temple, could henceforth be seen and heard a man who had returned to this corruptible life in the flesh at the bidding of Him who declared Himself the Messiah. Either His Messianic challenge must be accepted, or He must be finally silenced. At this juncture a council was held to consider. There was no hesitation among the Sanhedrists, no change of mind. Their hearts were too hardened to listen to evidence. The one question was not, is He after all the Messiah? but, what can we do? The one danger, their personal ruin before the rising tide of

[1] Stanton, p. 17.

popular belief, and in the near distance the annihilation of Temple, and city, and nation, of Church and State, by the Roman power. It is one of the Divine ironies of history that the fate they would avert by the sacrifice of principle to policy was that which befell them. The Romans took away their name and nation, and destroyed the Temple which they falsely accused the Lord of wishing to destroy. The wailing-place of the Jews in modern Jerusalem, viewed in its past spiritual and historic relations, and from Christian Jewish sympathies, is indeed the saddest nook in this vale of tears.

Tidings of the decision of the council reached Jesus. He retired to the obscure Ephraim, probably Ophrah, of Benjamin, afterwards Epherema, a village thirteen miles north of Jerusalem, now Taiyibeh. Here He stayed with His disciples. Such a rest may have been needful to them and to Him.

From Ophrah He could get by Roman roads to one of the Jordan bridges, and must have gone, for once more He is in half-heathen Peræa, at a safer distance, and goes as far as Galilee (Matt xix. 1), perhaps to some rendezvous where He might join Galilean pilgrims to the Passover. From the frontier of Galilee (Luke xvii. 11) He passed between Galilee and Samaria,[1] perhaps because rejected at En-gannim (Jenîn), the northern frontier town of Samaria, into Peræa. His previous missionary work had left a deep and wide impression. Great multitudes again came round Him, and He healed and taught them (Mark x 1). Again we may compare His Peræan to the foreign mission, His Judæan and Galilean to the home work of the Church.

The union here, as usual, perhaps always, of the ministry of healing with the ministry of teaching suggests the importance of combining medical[2] with directly spiritual work in the missionary operations of the Church. Modern missions lack the extraordinary gifts of healing. If apostolic faith and unity of heart be restored to Christendom, why should not this missing weapon return to the armoury of Christian aggression? Without it, at least the best resources of medical science should contribute to the holy warfare of heathen evangelization. Some of the most

---

[1] διὰ μέσον as Hort, Tischendorf, Gebhardt, "between" margin R V.

[2] Cf. especially the decisive utterances, exemplified by their own experiences, of the Bishop of Rangoon, J M Strachan, M D., and the late Bishop of Sarawak, and that of medical missionaries of the Church Missionary Society and Scottish Medical Missions.

GATHERING SHADOWS.

satisfactory results of evangelization have followed in the wake of missionary philanthropy, ministering, in the true spirit of love, to the wants of diseased limbs and famishing bodies. The annals of such missions as those of Nazareth, Tinnevelly, and of the ingatherings after the waifs and strays of the Indian famine had tasted the kindness of those who gave bread to the hungry, furnish cogent evidence. The lives of such men, as Dr. Henderson and Dr. Lockhart in China, Dr. Elmslie in Kashmir, show how deep an impression may be made, and how the gospel way may be prepared by medical skill moved, hallowed, blessed by prayer, and followed up by teaching.

The first noteworthy incident was the healing of the ten lepers.[1] The watchful opposition of the Pharisees lay in wait for Him at every place. The nearer He drew to Jerusalem the hotter was the fire of criticism. Opposition to the truth does truth great service. Attack calls forth defence. Criticism enforces explanation, arrests attention. "These men are full of new wine," said the negative critics at Pentecost. An answer to the charge vindicated the truth and published it abroad. Frequently the Pharisaic attacks supplied Jesus with a text and an opportunity for declaring the kingdom of God. Such questions as that may have sometimes been the expression of honest difficulty and single-hearted inquiry (Luke xvii. 20). But that stage was long past with the Pharisees—

> "Sin of self-love possesseth all mine eye,
> And all my soul, and all my every part:
> And for this sin there is no remedy,
> It is so grounded inward in my heart."[2]

Any questions put by them were the explosion of bitter animus, and of the desire to involve Jesus either with the Roman government, or with the masses, or with both.

The question of divorce was cunningly raised about the same time by a Pharisaic deputation. Whatever answer our Lord returned He would come into conflict with Rabbinical practice and popular belief. It was the deepest of all questions pertaining to family life As Prince of Israel, as the Divine head of society,

---

[1] On leprosy, past and present, see an article by Agnes Lambert in *The Nineteenth Century*, August, 1884.
[2] Shakespeare, Sonnet 62.

152   JESUS CHRIST.

as the reformer both of the individual and of human society, He resolved a question which touched many human interests. To this current of controversial inquiry we owe Christ's reaffirmation of the primitive Divine law of the unity effected by holy matrimony, and of its indissolubility. The Mosaic permission of legal[1] divorce was, He said, a provisional concession to their hardness of heart. No teaching could have been more against the grain of contemporary practice. The school of Shammai counselled divorce only on the ground of unchastity, "a matter of shame" (Deut. xxiv. 1). The school of Hillel interpreted the latter clause in any and every sense. "A man," said Hillel, "may put away his wife if she prepares a dish badly ; if she makes a blunder ; if she lets the meat burn." Rabbi Akibah allows it if he sees a fairer woman. But in any case divorce "was obtained with an ease and frequency quite revolting."[2]

That some of the nobler minds took a higher view in principle and in practice is proved by clear evidence, as by the saying of Rabbi Eliezer, "Whosoever divorces his first wife, even the (very) altar sheds tears over him, for it is said" (Mal. ii. 13, 14), &c., &c.[3] But whatever may have been exceptional practice on the whole "the Jewish Law unquestionably allowed divorce on almost any ground."[4] In no respect was Jesus more above and beyond and contrary to His time than in the matter of marriage. In no respect less conceivably the creature and the exponent of His age and environment. To this positive and negative elevation of marriage to a level worthy of symbolizing in His apostle's language, "Christi et ecclesiæ sacramentum,"[5] the Lord added a sanction to celibacy, and a virtual blessing upon it undertaken for the kingdom of God's sake by those to whom it is given. Buddhism, on the other hand, regards celibacy as all but essential to the attainment of Nirvana, and invariably discourages the married life.[6]

Christ's teaching on marriage was very different to that of the Rabbis. It stands still farther apart from that of the sanc-

---

[1] The Talmudic letter of divorcement may be seen in Stapfer, p. 154, E. T.
[2] Stapfer, p. 153.
[3] Hershon, p 239 p., and Stapfer, p. 153 q., "Gittin," 10 b, "Sanhed." 22 a.
[4] Edersheim, ii 333, Stapfer, s. l. [5] Mediæval marriage service.
[6] Cf. Kellogg, p. 313 following.

tioned polygamies of Mahommedanism. It breathes a wholly different air. The whole conception of marriage was more than restored to its original ideal. It was transformed and heightened and consecrated.

The general position of woman towards man, both in the particular matrimonial relation, and in all the social and domestic relations, was raised in conception infinitely, and gradually has risen in practice as Christian ideas have taken effect. Christ's own demeanour towards woman, His birth of the holy virgin, His honour and compassion to the outcast and the influential alike, were repaid by the abundant devotion of daughters of Israel. His conduct and bearing were the first movement towards their emancipation. His attitude towards divorce, a question in which woman has always been the greater sufferer, was in itself an incalculable advance of their rights.

He was never sick. He never needed those gentle ministries of mercy where women all the world over are angels of compassion and skill. But His wounded Body was reverently handled at the rocky sepulchre by those whom His love and respect had won.

But His Incarnation was the honour of honours paid to womanhood Women henceforward were all implicated in the sacred dignity of her

> "Who born of Eve, high mercy won,
> To bear and nurse the Eternal Son,
> O awful station to no Seraph given,
> On this side touching Sin, on th' other Heaven." [1]

And the long submission in gentleness and patience to the mother's love and empire in the cottage home has brightened Christian homes and Christian motherhood with a glory of consecration and pre-figurements of heaven. For Christian women are not likely to forget, nor Christian men who honour a mother's name with filial devotion, and secret incense of homage when only the name and memory are left, nor Christian children most of all to whom the mother is an earthly divinity—to forget how

> "Thenceforth, whom thousand worlds adore,
> He calls thee mother evermore,
> Angel nor saint His face may see,
> Apart from what He took of thee." [1]

---

[1] J. Keble.

And as He honoured the higher and holier provinces of woman's empire, the marriage union, the home, so He shed the rays of His compassion upon the dishonoured and the self-degraded. Such He won back to self-respect, to usefulness, to devoted service ; of such materials as the harlot He could manufacture saints.

Side by side with the Christian homage of women, from the days of chivalry to those of their intellectual emancipation, may be placed by way of contrast the Jewish Morning Prayer, where the men in three consecutive benedictions, bless God " who hath not made me a Gentile—a slave—a woman."[1] Or we may compare such a high non-Christian religion as that of China, where the feet of girls are bound and cramped, and where " no generous sentiment tending to the amelioration of the social position of woman ever came from either " Confucius or Mencius.[2] Possibly the respect shown to women may have been at times pushed too far in the next Christian generation. For in the Corinthian Church there are indications of feminine usurpations of ecclesiastical authority in St. Paul's Epistles. And in the remarkable Epistle of St. Clement of Rome to the same Church about forty years later, the same irregularity calls for severe censure.

And in this love and respect shown to those who have lost all, even for themselves, Christians have from the first seen an example. Christ could not only wash away guilt, He could renovate and re-create. And so the weak are made strong, the unclean clean, the sensual spiritual. In this way the moral laws of nature are constantly broken. The chains of evil habit and circumstance are snapped, sometimes by a sudden resurrection, more commonly as in the history of society as a whole so in that of its units, by gradual disintegration of evil and integration of good. The waifs of passion, the wrecks of stormy lust, the prodigal daughters, are sought and saved by Christ's workers, not in the contemptuous spirit of the proselytizer, or in the interests of sanitary science and public health, but by those who are armed with the purity of the One Pure and His compassionate love, or by those who have been rescued from the like dregs by His sweet mastery.

---

[1] Cf. Taylor, " Pirke Aboth," 5, " prolong not converse with a woman."
[2] Prof. Legge, " Religions of China," p. 111

One of the greatest contrasts between Christianity as it now is, with all its imperfections and unrealized ideals, and non-Christianity may be seen to the advantage of the former, in the moral and social position, or no position, of women, where there has been no Christian influence to disenslave them. And where, as in India, there is beginning to show itself a tendency to raise them in the social, intellectual, and spiritual scale, it is, directly or indirectly, traceable, beyond any shadow of doubt, to the working of Christian teaching and practice in social and individual life. In the instruction and elevation of Indian women in their zenanas lies one of the most open doors to the entrance of the one faith which leaves no fragment of life, social or individual, ungoverned, unpurified, unenfranchized, uncrowned.

The holy charm, the loveable attractiveness of Christ's character is exemplified by the next incident. Perhaps a spectator of the un-Rabinnical tenderness to the children, or of some similar unconventional emotionalism, a young ruler threw himself impetuously at the Lord's feet (Mark x. 13 ; x. 17, and Synoptists). His haste, his question, his spirit, revealed the presence of a deep moral need shaking his soul. The answer of our Lord contained no new revelation, but a re-affirmation of the old. Let the young man examine himself and so let him prepare for eternal life. His conscience certified that he had been obedient after a Jewish manner. Christ then lifts the veil of the higher life. He was eternal life ; union with Him implied there and then the loss of all things. Such a demand could only be justified if the good Master were really God. The rich man must return to his original question and decide who He was—who made a claim so sweeping.

The tremendous decision shown and demanded by Christ foreshadowed the approach of the final crisis. The time was very short, the fire would be very hot, only the whole-hearted would bear the strain. The same spirit breathes in the following warning about and to the wealthy. Times of dilemma come when the Christ follower will be called to sacrifice everything to Him. They may come to all. All then must share the sacrificial spirit and be ready, if called upon, for the forlorn hope. Such surrender brings its own reward. What has been given up is received again many times over [1]—with persecutions—in this

---

[1] The present writer heard a Colonial bishop (Rawle of Trinidad) dwell upon his own experience of the fulfilment of this promise—but without the darker side, persecutions

present life. These words form another important contribution to the missionary charter of the Church; for to the foreign warfare of Christ's soldiers they most literally apply.

The many indirect warnings are now clenched by His reiterated prediction of the Passion. "Behold we go up to Jerusalem" (Luke xviii. 31, and Synoptists)—this, the long silent master-thought, now finds utterance. The details of the scene rise up minutely before Him even as they had flashed

"In outline, dim, and vast,"

in fragmentary intuitions and scattered half-lights upon the prophets. What they saw in parts He saw wholly, but the disciples vaguely or not at all. So completely had the suffering aspect of Messiah's work crumbled away from Jewish memory that this detailed statement, and that too doubtless in a manner indescribably solemn, failed to be intelligible to them; and the next question asked was the petition for pre-eminence, in the Messianic kingdom, by Zebedee's wife and her two sons (Mark x. 35).

Jesus now crossed the Jordan. It was His Rubicon. A march across an arid waste brought the festal band to Jericho. (Luke xviii. 35 and Synoptists). A gleam of sunshine lighted up the way to storm and darkness. For the beautiful city of Palms and the plain of Jericho recalled warm and verdurous Galilean home, and the salvation of Zacchæus, the healing of the blind, the joyous crowds of pilgrims, suggest an interval of inward and outward gladness. There are no signs here of the rejection of the Messiah. Officials from the grand palace and gardens of Archelaus, soldiers from the forts of Herod which guarded the death-bed of their builder, merchants who have stopped to purchase balsam on their route to or from Arabia and Damascus, priests from the priestly city or their rural homes, and a many-coloured stream of Galilean and Peræan pilgrims, form a crowd of questioning onlookers as the Nazarene Prophet passes through the midst. The question of all questions was the absorbing one of the hour. All the minutiæ of triviality which fill the minds of many even at great times, and moving moments, must have vanished at the living presence of the great Mystery passing on to the threatened death or to the crest of a Messianic revolution.

GATHERING SHADOWS.

"All cognition is recognition."[1] For the most part unknown, because unrecognized in His fulfilments of Messianic law and prophecy, the Master of hearts stepped out into the fierce light that beats upon a public man by a direct challenge to social prejudice and local pique. The head of the customs is directly invited to become his host for the night, the most unpopular man in a focus of national life and prejudice. The spiritual intensity of the incident is shown in the instantaneousness of the publican's conversion. The corrupt child of an age of corruption and fraud, steeped in an atmosphere of oppression on the one side, social suspicion, national aversion, and individual opposition on the other, is confronted for the first time of his life with absolute personal honesty, transparent truth, and single-mindedness. The hardened man of the world openly confessed his guilt to the world. Heart and life were changed at a stroke before the burning gaze of Incarnate Honour. Many previous doubtings of heart may have led up to this happy catastrophe.

Jericho, as a place, is now a desolate wilderness. "The Bedouin lead the flocks across the plain as did the patriarchs of old." "But there is no other sign of human life."[2] The soil, as in so many parts of Palestine, is said to be as fertile as ever. A good government in that afflicted country would be as life from the dead in a land where Nature opens a bountiful bosom to farmer and agriculturist and engineer. The redemption of the soil of the Holy Land, its restoration to fruitfulness, to sanitary well-being, to freedom from ruinous oppression, venial administration, and financial tyranny, is a worthier cause of a Crusade than even the recovery of the questioned site of the Holy Sepulchre. Christian politicians have here a golden opportunity for putting unexceptionable pressure upon the Porte; Christian commerce and science an inviting field for regenerating efforts and richly rewarding work. May the Lord who there brought us salvation of body and soul help us to extend to it material salvation!

The discrepancies in the accounts of the healing of the two blind men at Jericho must be left as they are. At all events they prove the independence of the narratives, and the absence of collusion. The general credibility of the evangelists will not be destroyed by minute differences of detail, here or elsewhere.

[1] H. Spencer.   [2] S. Manning, "Those Holy Fields," p. 77.

The absence of any such differences would be far more suspicious than the presence. Some have supposed that the Old Testament and the Herodian Jericho are here confused in the accounts, but a brief examination of the passages negatives that hypothesis. Bengel's solution is more probable, that Christ heard one man cry for mercy as He entered and healed him, and Bartimæus as He left the city. But common as blindness was, and is, in the East generally, and in Palestine, it is not improbable that He healed one on the way to Jericho, and that he told his recovery and the method of it, to two fellow sufferers. So the same scene may have taken place again as He left.

A crowd of pilgrims had come up early to purify themselves before the feast. As they stood in groups in the Temple (John xi. 56) the uppermost question in their minds was where is Jesus? St. John sketches this scene as illustrating his general plan of pourtraying the spiritual attitude of the people towards the Messiah, and as prelusive of the final decision. That decision was the last result of a long series of intermediate rejections. It was deliberate on the part of the leaders at least. The causes which led up to it are indicated at every turn of the history. It was not a momentary outburst of temper, nor the rabid fury of blind fanaticism mistaken in means while worthy in ends. It was the climax of all the struggles in which the most favoured branch of fallen humanity had contended against God.

While Jewish pilgrims were speculating about His coming to the passover Jesus spent the last Friday before the Passion in the now dearer home of Bethany. On the following day He shared the Sabbath feast with Mary and Martha and Lazarus, and apparently other guests, in the house of Simon the Leper (Matt. xxvi. 6; Mark xiv. 3; John xii. 1). Mary's anointing may have been prompted by some reference to His self-consecration by death, or the simple outpouring of a sisterly love made more fragrant by gratitude for a brother restored from the grave. But Christ saw a higher end fulfilled, as all action passes beyond itself to unseen Divine issues. He was already being embalmed for His burial, and some of it may actually have been used. The words were mysterious and suggestive. Yet only a week lay between the symbolic and actual unction. The outspoken objection of Judas is reported by St. John, not as a mere detail, but to reveal the hidden man of the heart. The moral attitude of Judas was no more sudden than that of the chief priests and Pharisees, or Mary and Martha's. The importance of this incident in its after-lights explains the Johannine repetition of the two previous Synoptist accounts in fuller personal portraiture.

CHAPTER XVII.

THE MESSIANIC ENTRY. THE CONTRADICTION OF SINNERS.

> "Now I behold how worldly gain is loss,—
> That weeks and days and hours that by us fleet,
> Must wear the Royal impress of the Cross"
>
> ISAAC WILLIAMS.

The Triumphal Entry—The Devil's stand—The Second Temple cleansing—The barren figtree—The "Day of Questions"—The Divine Controversialist—The Divine Apocalypse—Jewish Eschatology.

THE offering of Mary's homage is followed by the acclaiming welcome of the people. For one day He came unto His own and His own received Him—even on that day a minority despised and rejected Him.

The importance, present and prospective, of the Triumphal Entry of the Messiah appears from the fourfold minuteness of the report.

With the patient foresight of details, and the orderly method which marked the march of Jesus' plans, He sent forward two pioneers to loose and bring the ass's foal.[1] This detail of Zachariah's prophecy had not escaped His memory, nor failed of its aim. The Prince of Peace could not ride on the horse, the beast of war, into the City of Peace.

The final decision was now coming. The King makes His

---

[1] The actual and metaphorical use by Christ of the animal world suggests *per se* its participation in man's recovery, and in the resurrection to a new earth of "glorious liberty," as was suggested before at the manger.

THE MESSIANIC ENTRY.

last offer to the Royal City. For once He will enter in royalty and imposing pageant. They had rejected Him upon His own evidence of dignity and worth. Will they accept Him at the head of an army of peace, supported by serried troops of Galilean pilgrims, their acknowledged Lord and Prince Messiah? Even the people are declaring for Him. Will they change their minds? The verdict must be given this day. The last plea is uttered. The last witness has been called. The question is now set before the nation, and the Holy City especially, for the last time. Jesus asks it in word. Jesus asks it in action. In word and in action the all but universal reply is made. There is not the slightest evidence that Jesus expected to take the allegiance of the people by storm "by suddenly unfurling the Messianic banner and overwhelming the murmurs of opposition by the rejoicing shouts of the people."

From first to last He knew perfectly well how it would end. The temporary enthusiasm of the pilgrims did not confuse Him. Nor did He turn bitterly away with cynical contempt for mob acclamations. The vision of a fallen Jerusalem, a desolate city, a ruined house of God, shows that His eyes were looking beyond the gates of the present, and that His heart was brooding over His people's sorrows, not His own. We need not therefore suppose that the cheers of the festal crowd were ungenuine or uncomforting. We may rather see "in part," and prophesy "in part," a vision of a Royal entry into the antitypal City of God, of waving palms, and multitudinous concordant voices, greeting and accompanying the King of Glory.

It is impossible to read the long and darkening tragedy of Jewish rejections of God, first in His messengers, and last in His Son, without detecting a superhuman influence at work. Behind his unconscious instruments the master of evil was busy. Annas and Caiaphas, Pontius Pilate, Judas, were tools of the anti-Messiah. He was at bay. The gates of hell were threatened; the whole hierarchy of hell mustered for defence. Jesus Christ came to destroy the works of the devil. The devil may be credited with a better contemporary knowledge of that fact than ignorant erring humanity. Whatever power he could exercise over a fallen and partly enslaved race in the plenitude of his spiritual intelligence, in the fulness of his command of all the resources and powers of evil, he must have put out in his self-defence. He carried the war into the enemy's country. The loss of Judas, the breaking of the apostolic company, the denial of the leading apostle, and the desertion of all of them, are tributes to the vast organized activity of Satan's final stand. After three years of the transcendent personal influence which had been acting upon them night and day, he succeeded in wresting one captive from the strong grasp of Christ, and in shaking the allegiance of His chosen. He had already succeeded in turning the Messianic nation from the Divine Messianic Ideal. He had blinded the most enlightened, he had turned religion itself into an anti-Messianic engine. He had corrupted and perverted the truth; he had maintained an unbroken hostility to it through the dominant party. He had united every worldly interest in a common league. He had by masterly manœuvres, bound together in a common cause and a common course, persons and interests so antagonistic as the Roman governor, the Idumean king, the Jewish high priesthood, and the masses. All hated one another but shook hands. And now the final issue of ages of progressing evil, advancing corruption, and accumulating falsehood, had reached its climax, and the full volume of the gathered momentum of actual and transmitted evil under its acknowledged and, so to speak, lawful head, guided by a superhuman will, ordered by a stupendous intellect enriched with incalculable experience of all the sciences and successes of wrong, was launched at the head, and at the heart, and at the life of one devoted Man. The Week of the Passion was the time of times. The field of battle was the City of God. Humanity was the prize of the Victor. Till the hour and in the hour of his absolute rout the victory appeared to rest with the Prince of Darkness.

The Triumphal Entry need not be described in detail. The picture is well known, and Dean Stanley's memorable contrast of the scene that then was and the scene that now is is too perfect for broken quotation.

We pass on with the silent King and shouting crowd to the Temple. He looked round about on all. He might have seen a Temple still cleansed and for ever purified, the home of a repentant people, ready to welcome the Messiah on their knees. But Temple and people were uncleansed. The irreverence of the Temple represented a people who had a name but not a life.

The night was spent at Bethany. Sleepless watch and

THE MESSIANIC ENTRY.

prayer may have caused the hunger of the early morrow. Very early Jesus left the village, well known as the modern El Aziriyeh, in its sheltered peace. A single figtree stood out on the skyline as they walked on to the city, like the "one tree" on a Kentish hill.

It bore neither new nor old fruit, but leaves only. The curse of Christ blasted the false tree; it was barren, so untrue to its mission, it had not yielded its life in the labour of bearing the fruit; it was false in its display of leaves, instead of, or without, fruit. In both respects it typified the people, for whose fruits the Lord hungered unsatisfied. It was an object-lesson, an acted parable, a re-telling of the story of the Fall, and a rehearsal of the Last Judgment, "Depart from Me, ye cursed."

The second Messianic cleansing of the Temple follows. The first had been that of the Messiah Prophet, the Messiah Patriot. The second was that of the Messiah Judge, the Messiah King. It was a repeated miracle of moral impetus, an outburst of "sublime and generous anger."[1] Those who look only at the gentle and meek lights in the human character of Christ, forget the fire and victorious force which lay hid in the reserves of His strength. His was neither the meekness of resigned, Hindu-like inactivity, nor the nerveless gentleness of the spiritless, but the tenderness of the strongest of the strong under the restraint of self-governing love and unfathomed compassion. And His words were as trenchant, as incisive, as powerful, as His deeds. The robbers were cast out from the House of Prayer. The carriers of vessels were stopped on their profane walk. The place was cleared, and as quickly refilled with the blind and lame, who came to be healed.

"How soon a smile of God can change the world!"[2]

And to the noise of wrangling traffic succeeded the ringing acclamations of childish hosannas. Up the porticoes and through court to court sounded the welcome of the only lips in Jerusalem, outside the Christian company, which did not cry Crucify. Perhaps they were Galilean children; "perhaps those children of the Levites who acted as choristers in the Temple."[3]

---

[1] J. A. Symonds on Dante's "Divine Comedy."
[2] R. Browning, "In a Balcony."   [3] Edersheim, ii. 381.

The remainder of the day was occupied in teaching. The approaching feast and its Messianic applications must have pointed its drift. A very deep impression was made upon the Paschal multitudes. The after-labours of the apostles must have profited by these lessons to large audiences. Their rapid successes on and after Pentecost were prepared for, and they themselves were being made ready for ministries of healing and preaching in large centres of population, and before mixed crowds, as they had already been in training for missionary tours and rural evangelizing. Again Christ left the city and sought a night's shelter at Bethany. Perhaps the rest was necessary to Himself and His apostles; for the night was coming when no man could work, and for the work of the remaining hours of life's day all His strength was needed.

The third day opened with the early morning walk over the verdurous Mount of Olives. The figtree, now withered, was again passed, and made the text of a lesson in the power of prayer; its destructive power over evil and difficulty conditioned by the faith and forgiving love of the supplicant. "We remember, that the promise had a special application to the apostles and early disciples; we also remember, how difficult to them was the thought of full forgiveness of offenders and persecutors: and again, how great the temptation to avenge wrongs and to wield miraculous power in the vindication of their authority."[1] And as aggressiveness was to be the constant policy of Christian warfare, the temper must be of impersonal, selfless aggression.

When Jesus had entered the Temple Courts and was walking about and teaching, the Chief Priests and scribes and elders came up to Him. This was the first result of the party deliberations which had been taking place since the raising of Lazarus, which had been embittered by the Triumphal Entry, and exasperated by the second implied denunciation of the priestly profits made by the Temple traffic, which latter must have been seriously diminished and perhaps entirely stopped for this Passover. They put a question to Jesus. It was the first of a series which has given to the day the name of the "Day of Questions." It was no new one, nor asked for the first time. What was His authority? The Lord's answer was the same as before. He identified His authority with John's,

[1] Edersheim, ii. p 377

so far as the greater more than covers the less. They stood upon the same platform, authenticated by the same direct inspiration, and accredited by the same Power. If John was of God, Jesus was of God. If John was of God, what he said of Jesus was of God. An acceptance of John's baptism and teaching as heavenly, involved the acceptance of the claims of Jesus, who was the end of all John's preaching. Whose duty was it but theirs to examine the evidence and to pronounce official judgment? Their answer " we know not" condemned themselves. They abdicated their position and evaded their duty, and denied their moral and social responsibility. It was an Agnostic attitude to adopt towards God, who had, or had not, sent John ; who had, or had not, sent Jesus.

They feared the people and durst not before them publicly pronounce the claim of the great prophet invalid. They acted upon policy. Expediency was their touchstone. Truth was a matter of indifference. The venue must be changed; the ground of controversy shifted ; another issue raised. To appeal to Rome upon any religious question was a national apostasy. It was to betray the Church to the State, and that State, heathen, hostile, idolatrous, and impersonated in hated, guilty, and corrupt officials. To an honest and patriotic Jew it was a downright appeal to the devil. Yet would Annas and Caiaphas, and their tools, shrink from calling in upon an ecclesiastical question the very power which had invested them with rank and office ?

But Jesus did not act upon the defensive only. The three parables from Matt. xxi. 28–xxii. 14, were a counter attack. The burden of the prophets was taken up, the familiar imagery of the vineyard was adopted as the veil of a personal denunciation ; and in no softened tones or hesitating accents the judicial wrath of the king was sternly announced.

Neither entreaty nor menace, neither gentleness nor anger, equally proceeding from a love which would leave no stone unturned, no moral lever unapplied to petrified hearts and darkened understandings, had any effect upon the set hatred of the Pharisees.

They were past repentance. But the people were not impenetrable. For the sake of the sheep their shepherds must be publicly exposed and shamed. The direct, or indirect, polemics of Jesus were dictated by necessity, not opportunism.

They were the utterance of uniform charity, not the explosion of party passion or outraged feelings. They were the utterance of plain truth by One who knew the whole truth and for truth's sake must speak it—in behalf of God, for the sake of the false hypocrites themselves, and for the sake of those whom they had deceived, and would deceive. The Jewish nation of to-day suggests the most cogent evidence of the necessity of the withering exposure of the hierarchy. They have inherited the Rabbinical learning, and perpetuated the Rabbinical traditionalism; they have as a nation adopted the debased Rabbinical Messiah for the true and Scriptural Christ. But signs are not wanting that the hearts of Israel are beginning to be drawn to the true Messiah.

On the same day two cheering incidents occurred. In the storm of judicial wrath which swept over the soul of the Messiah in the face of the enemies of God's righteousness there were bright interludes. There was the poor widow in the Court of the Women, who cast in her "two Perutahs"—all she had, the germ of the goodly company of mothers and daughters of Christ who spend and are spent for their Master. There was the momentous and fruitful inquiry of certain Greeks. They must have been seekers after truth, who had found in Jewish Scripture, doubtless in the Septuagint version, or in later pseudepigraphic writing, or among Jewish home influences, some satisfaction of their spiritual wants. Greek thought could lead them to moral and asthetic self-culture, Greek art could lead them to the beautiful, but no abstract or impersonal ideals can satisfy a hungry soul. The Law brought before them an Ideal Personality, but must have, even in the watered Septuagint, created the sense of infinite distance between Him and men accustomed to anthropomorphic conceptions of God. The Law could not solve the question, it could only point to its solution. Some such lines of inquiry, whether morally or intellectually, must have been followed by the Greeks who pressed Philip for a personal interview with Jesus. Philip may have been passing through the Court of the Gentiles. A stone balustrade (Soreg) parted the Greeks from Jesus in the Court of the Women, which was open to both sexes, and where public meetings took place. The Greek inscription it bore has been lately discovered by M. Clermont Ganneau, and ran as follows—

THE CONTRADICTION OF SINNERS. 167

> " NO FOREIGNER TO PROCEED
> WITHIN THE PARTITION WALL
> AND ENCLOSURE AROUND THE
> SANCTUARY, WHOEVER IS
> CAUGHT IN THE SAME
> WILL ON THAT ACCOUNT BE LIABLE
> TO INCUR DEATH."

The news of the quest of the Greek proselytes made a very deep impression upon Jesus. Since the Magians sought His infant bed it was the first Christward movement of the Gentile world. It was spontaneous and self-originated. Jesus must have stepped down into the Court of the Gentiles and in their presence delivered His soul of the Creed of the Cross. The grain of wheat was a single example of the universal law of self-sacrifice, which beginning in Nature, ascended to human nature. The Son of Man Himself obeyed that law; His service required it; God would honour it. The death He would die, and the life it would bring and the power of His own attraction thereby and thereafter over all, came vividly before Him. And a voice from heaven authenticated His prophetic word and prayer. Here was another missionary lesson to those who would soon welcome the men of Corinth and Ephesus, Rome and Alexandria, Antioch and Babylon, into the liberty, fraternity, and equality of the faith. Those Greeks and that crowd which heard of Christ's lifting up must have been prepared to put His word and act together, when they saw it in three days with their own eyes. But the Christian syllogism requires the touch of the Holy Spirit to connect the premises. In His light would they see the Light.

This Tuesday was possibly the most laborious day, excepting the last, in the earthly life of Jesus. He met in turn every assailant. He silenced Pharisees, Scribes, Herodians, Sadducees. He lifted up His voice to the crowds. It was the final day of debate. He was compelled to be a man of strife and contention. Such a day of mental and physical exertion must have exhausted the human spirit of Jesus. It was a spiritual martyrdom for the truth's sake. Mind and body were much more than overworked. Yet as He went homeward on His way out of the Temple He had more to say, and it must be said. What it must have cost Him can only be faintly realized by prophets whose hearts break at the message they cannot muffle. Necessity was laid upon Him. Christ felt what He said, but said little of what He felt. The deeps of His sympathetic sorrow and yearning desire agonized His soul before the final darkness encompassed Him round.

As they were leaving the Holy City it was evening. They walked up the Mount of Olives, perhaps to rest, perhaps to look at the crimson flushing the white and gold of the Temple mount, and the long shadows of the massy walls. The red rays lingered over the royal city as its Sun of righteousness was departing,

> "an awful sign and tender,
> Like the Blood of the Redeemer shown on earth and sky." [1]

They had often seen the Temple in its glory before. But just now, perhaps under some such striking atmospheric effect, and with the connecting thread of some lingering ill-understood words of the day in their mind as they went out of the Temple, they came to the Lord and directed His particular attention.

Christ's own Messianic predictions and their sense of His prophetic powers supplied a basis for a lesson upon this majestic text. The flames of Jerusalem would re-write it in letters of fire. The early Christian Church would never be able to forget that the direst calamity that ever fell upon the house of Israel was clearly predicted by Him who wept over its coming shadows. The crash and downfall of the Jewish Church reverberated through the Jewish and Christian world. And the prophetic discourses of the Lord, which must at the time have thrilled the disciples with wondering awe and horror, must have come to the ears and minds of many, and accentuated in their creed the belief in that Second Coming foreshadowed in the same visions of judgment. This may help to account for the wide and strong feeling which filled early Christians of the nearness of the Lord's return.

Christ had declared Himself a Prophet all His life. The great prophecy on the Mount of Olives marks the climax of His prophesyings. It was the great Messianic Apocalypse. The occasion, the associations, would impress the memory of His words, while the surprising novelty and un-Jewish originality of them would shock. Voice and manner were as sublime as the burden of His prophecy, with some touches, it may be, of the

[1] Jean Ingelow, "Requiescat in pace."

rapture of prophetic ecstasy, without any loss of self-command or merely emotional excitement ; and underlying all, streaming over all, the fulness of perfect sympathy, Divine and human, with all that was on His side in the time to come, lighted by perfect insight, welling from a heart at one with God. If the style is the man, the Man Jesus was not less great than His words, as from the mountain over against the Temple He looked down the horizons of the æons—the holy city, in division and fratricidal strife, a ruin and desolation where the Temple was, a scattered people, the world a greater city of confusion and division, but in its midst a fair Temple, made without hands, gradually rising, bearing the Name of names ; and, in the farther distance, the lightning rush of angels, the shaking of the powers of heaven, the Son of Man descending with power and great glory, the Judgment, the Trial, the passing away of all but words eternal with the breath of His eternity.

Upon the devout imagination of one apostle the visions of judgment made the deepest mark. In the Apocalypse of the Messiah we have the germ of the Apocalypse of John. But the Lord from heaven supplemented and authenticated what the Lord on earth had outlined.

Nor were the disciples altogether unprepared on purely Jewish grounds for eschatological Messianic conceptions. The disciples must have known the Book of Daniel, which exercised so great an influence upon Jewish thought that it became the parent of a long line of Apocalypses with symbolical historic pictures and vaticinations. The visions of Ezekiel were, by St. John at least, minutely known and realized. The ideas expressed in the Apocalyptic and Pseudepigraphic literature must have assisted in the formation of their Messianic conceptions in this as in other aspects. The way then was prepared for the conception of the Son of Man in His glory as Judge.

Pictorial visions had been made public of wars and confusions and iniquity abounding among men, hostilities between God's people and the nations, and the overthrow of the latter ; in later documents by the Messiah Himself, or by the Most High to usher in His coming. "The slaughter of enemies before the Messianic era would be at once consummated by a universal judgment, or something very like it, on men and fallen angels ;"[1]

[1] Stanton, p. 299, foll. for detailed quotation and comparison, and Edersheim ii. 433, foll.

or else, and more commonly, the Messiah's reign was of fixed duration, "and the universal judgment was placed at the conclusion of it, after which would follow finally 'the world to come.'"[1] The woes of the Messiah (*Chebley shel Mashiach*) were a common theme. The future blessedness of the righteous, "the accursed valley" for "all those who speak with their mouths unseemly words against God, and speak impudently concerning His majesty" (Enoch xxvii. 2, 3). In connection with the Day of Judgment, "The gulf of torments shall appear, and opposite to it the place of rest; the furnace of Gehenna shall be revealed, and opposite to it the paradise of pleasures" (4 Esdras vi. 1–4).

Yet comparison of Jewish and Christian eschatology shows that where the former left the language of psalmists and prophets, it often fell from the sublime into the grotesque, from the spiritual to the material and earthly. The Christian conception corrected, refined, simplified, purified, dignified, ennobled, spiritualized in the process of transformation and promotion. The Christian conception was a much higher and deeper and larger structure than the Jewish. The distance between the two is measurable by reading the Book of Enoch side by side with the visions on Patmos.

The double aspect of the Lord's Apocalyptic discourse is plain upon the face of it. It was both historical and spiritual. Historical, in so far as it bore upon the immediate dangers and difficulties of the early Church, and especially upon the catastrophe which would swallow up Jerusalem and the whole fabric of Church and State which centred in the Temple; it was spiritual and unchronological, so far as it pourtrayed in vivid colours, but in outline only, the militant condition of the Church of Christ, its sufferings, its enemies, its unceasing progress from nation to nation, till the consummation of the age, and the Parousia of the Messiah in His glory. The object of the address was not to satisfy the speculative superstitiousness which is always peering into the darkness of the unrevealed, but to create a character unshaken by chance and change, a temper of spirit and life not changing with changing environments, but permament and unalterable.[2] It was also calculated to destroy falsified,

---

[1] Edersheim.

[2] Gordon's watchword, "Be not greatly moved," expresses the passive side of this truth, the Christian's defensive position

THE CONTRADICTION OF SINNERS.

materialized, and realistic conceptions of "the days of the Messiah." The "coming age" (*Athid labho*) merging into "the world to come" (*Olam habba*) was very different from any of Rabbinical fancy.

The Messianic yoke had as yet been comparatively light and easy. The disciples had been in "the boyhood of religion."[1] The fiery trial awaited them. They were now entering into the troubled waters of storm and shadow, through which the gospel fishing-vessel would fight its peaceless way of peace to the haven. The life of the Master, looked back over from the brightened heights of adoring memory, flooded the whole of His words with light. As He had been, so they would be in the world. Their past, and yet more their future experience with Him, first visibly, then invisibly, would be a repetition of His. The false Christs, the false prophets, the persecutors, the physical, the mental, the social, the spiritual adversities and adversaries, were not the accidental difficulties of the childhood of the Church and the faith. They were the inseparable environment of the warfare of the Christ and of the Christ's, whereby a process of selection[2] and elimination would sift the strong and true.

The great shock of conflict between the Christian and the Judaizer has been better understood of late, however magnified into irreconcilable antagonisms. Within the precincts of the faith there would be the dissensions which even the living presence of the absolute Master did not entirely check. Without there would be the active hostility of disintegrated cults and philosophies, and the *vis inertiæ* of deadened indifference. Yet in the calm presage of certain progressive victory, the Messiah armed His Messianic community for a world-wide warfare. The parables enforce the same practical and doctrinal truths as the apocalyptic discourse. The reiteration, the fulness, the peremptoriness of style and description, indicate the strength of the impression the Lord wished to make and His own assured confidence.

[1] Bp. Milman, "Love of the Atonement."
[2] "The elect" (Matt. xxiv. 29).

CHAPTER XVIII.

THE DIVINE SACRIFICE.

" What marvel, when the Lord our God most High,
Clothed in our flesh, was lifted up to die,
If then His Godhead to His Manhood gave,
Merit and force a thousand worlds to save ? "

W. BRIGHT, D.D.

Judas traitor—Wednesday in retreat—The Last Supper—Gethsemane—
The arrest—The Divine Prisoner before Annas, before Caiaphas, before
Pilate, before Herod—Judas' end—Before Pilate again—Ecce Homo !—
Round the Cross—The Seven Words—The Atonement.

ONCE more Jesus withdrew Himself. A Jewish Messiah would have raised the popular tumult dreaded by the Rabbis. The Son of Man refuses the opportunity and passes into a sacred silence of preparation. The day of apocalypse, of warning, of prophecy, is followed by a day perhaps of prayer and sacred conversation with the disciples. We can hardly be wrong in finding here the explanation of Judas' final change. Under the plain outspokenness of the Lord's Tuesday words, the last shred of a hope of a Jewish and a worldly Messiah had been destroyed. Judas wanted a version of the Satanic Messiah of the Third Temptation. Failing that He would join the anti-Messianic party. So far from being false to himself he would be false to his Master, and true to himself. There is not the slightest evidence to support recent attempts to whitewash the traitor. Whether he ever made such excuses to himself as that the Master would be able to deliver Himself by His own wonder-working power, or had any secondary intention of forcing His

THE DIVINE SACRIFICE.

hand, and compelling Him to declare Himself as the Messiah, it is bootless to inquire. The psychological gospel shows the real spring of his action (Luke xxii. 3 ; and later John xiii. 27) : Satan entered into him. He decided for evil. Love, honour, conscience, benefits, and blessings, common prayers, a common hope, were not worth thirty pieces of silver. His Messianic ideal had all along been self. His Messiah must enrich and advance His friends. He had been mercifully denounced as a devil. The plain personal truth had not won him "the grace of repentance."[1] He had stolen from the common fund which had been entrusted to him as the man of business capacity. What should have been and was meant for his wealth became an occasion of falling.

His illusion was over. His ambitious hopes were broken. In bitter disappointment, and the low cunning of hate, he would make a bargain and save something for himself out of the coming wreck. Secretly he steals away from the little company, perhaps pleading Paschal preparations, and makes his offer to the priestly council. "From the very Temple Treasury,"[2] with the sacrifical money, at the hands of the responsible officers of the Church, the apostate apostle is paid for the blood of the Redeemer. The legal price of a slave is "weighed out" (Zech. xi. 12) piece by piece, thirty shekels.[3] It is not to be wondered at that Wednesday as well as Friday were kept as fasts by the early Church.

Wednesday was the 13th Nisan. On the evening, the 14th, began and with it the Passover, "in the popular and canonical sense."[4] This was the Day of Unleavened Bread (Luke xxii. 7). Peter and John were sent to slay the lamb and to make ready the Paschal Supper. Armed with provident instructions Judas may have bought the lamb on the previous day, and "on his way from the sheep-market to the Temple, to have his lamb inspected, may have learned that the chief priests and and Sanhedrists were just then in session in the palace of the high priest close by."[5] Some of its blood was cast at the base of the altar, and amongst thousands of other worshippers and Paschal pilgrims, going to and fro the Court of the Priests, the two bore the lamb to the large upper chamber of the unnamed friend.

The Paschal Supper was the highest point reached in the

[1] Clement of Rome.   [2] Edersheim, ii. 477.
[3] Worth about 2s. 6d. each.   [4] Edersheim, ii. 479.   [5] Ibid, ii. 486

self-revelation of Christ to heart believers, as the Cross was the highest point in His revelation to all the world. All sweet and holy communions with Him, in prayer and in sacrifice, in chanted psalm and quiet song of praise, in teaching and in learning, in still meditation, in suasive discourse, public or private, in mighty works and ministries of miracle, met here in a central core. The discourse at Capernaum had prepared their minds for the truth of spiritually receiving the Bread of Life, the miracles upon the loaves had interpreted His power and bounty of supply even of daily bread. The frequency of His bodily contact with the sick in His healing treatments had revealed glimpses of the mysterious and benedictory Divinity outflowing from His Body. The Lord's prayer for daily bread and the beatitude upon the hungry and thirsty after righteousness suggested more than the supply of physical want. The Paschal meal itself, the sacrificial time and place and act, the common feast, the broken bread, the outpoured wine—all under the historic, under the devotional associations which they conveyed to Israelites steeped in the lore of their fathers, worshipping with their worship, taught in part their Christward application, went to their deepest heart of memory, of devotion.

There was the still fresh impression of the burning words and works of Tuesday, and the restful prayers or communings of the day before. There was the dark sweet shadow of the Cross bathing the whole scene in its coming glory, and breaking in a flood of inexpressible tenderness upon the sacrificial Lamb Himself. Laden with the weight of such high and holy, such sad and joyous memories, it was but natural that every day in the week, which became the Lord's own, became a day for representing the memorial of His death, and the witness to His resurrection, and the medium of His imparted life. The Holy Communion and the Commemorative Sacrifice, the Lord's Supper and the Eucharist or Thanksgiving, are names which express aspects of priceless truth and beauty impossible for Christian devotion, unheated by controversial discords, to spare. Many are the dear memorials of Christ. This the chiefest.

Viewed under these converging lights of the past, in its present cheer and solace to Himself and His faithful, in its future blessedness to the children of His kingdom, and its typical relation to yet far-off Supper of the Lamb, we understand in part how the Passover was by the rd desired with desire. And this

THE DIVINE SACRIFICE.

sacrament, like its twin sister of the gospel, was into His death but into His life, into His suffering and into His glory, into His humiliation and into His exaltation.

At the Supper Christ took the head of the low table, St. John was on His right.[1] "But the chief place next to the Master would be that to His left, or above Him. In the strife of the disciples which should be accounted the greatest this had been claimed, and we believe it to have been actually occupied, by Judas." After the foot-washing[2] and its speaking humility and its gentle pathetic warning to the traitor, and the scriptural appeal to his conscience in the language of the psalmist, the next incident of moment where every detail is most precious was the plain public declaration of the betrayal. It is spoken of as still in the future, for though more than begun, there was still the hope of leaving the last blow unstruck. The words and the sop struck home to a heart which had now ceased to be human. Satan and his own hell were there, and even the final thunder of woe upon that man by whom the Son of Man is betrayed fell harmless upon it. There is no text in the Bible so awful as that which follows in the record of him who lay upon the Lord's bosom, and was parted by Him only from the one apostle who was never seen again—"He then having received the sop went out straightway: and it was night."

And now the atmosphere was changed. There was room for that Christian Passover which should take the place of the Jewish, but much more than surpass it. "If we are asked what part of the Paschal Service corresponds to the 'Breaking of Bread,' we answer, that this being really the last Pascha, and the cessation of it, our Lord anticipated the later rite, introduced when, with the destruction of the Temple, the Paschal as all other sacrifices ceased," anticipated, *i.e.*, the custom after the meal of breaking and partaking "as *aphiqomon*, or after-dish, of that half of the unleavened cake which had been broken and put aside at the beginning of the Supper." So too with the third cup at the close of the Supper, or Cup of Blessing, was connected the institution of the cup.

A fourth cup followed, and the remainder of the Hallel (Psa. cxv.–cxviii.) formed the Eucharistic Hymn of Thanksgiving.

---

[1] For diagram and details see Edersheim, ii 494.
[2] Still practised among the Greeks and Latins in Jerusalem.

This was followed by the spoken thoughts which St. John alone brought out from the treasure of his memories of that

"Food, so awful and so sweet"[1]

and of His words of after-communion. We have, as it were, a continuation of the prophetic utterances of the Tuesday. But the tone is different. He has now not the world in view, but His own redeemed children and faithful friends. He speaks heart to heart, soul to soul. He dwells not so much on conflict and opposition, and on the forces of evil in their progressive manifestation, as on the inward glory and light and peace of His own in the midst of the world, in spite of the Evil One. Above all, He prepares them for the coming Paraklete,[2] Advocate, Comforter, Spirit of Truth. No words of Christ are sweeter with the breath of love, none clearer or more definite in doctrine. Christianity was never so tender, as when it was most doctrinal, on the lips of its Head; but, alas, speaking the truth and speaking it in love have at times parted company.

After listening to the Lord's words of communion with His friends, we are suffered, as they were, or one of them, to draw nearer still and hear His words of communion with the Father. It is the high-priestly prayer of self-consecration, and of the consecration of those whom the Father had given Him. The intercession in their behalf follows—that they may be one. Whether in the Temple, as some suppose, or in the open air, or more probably in the stillness of the same chamber which would so often afterwards be perfumed with the incense of Christian devotion, the Divine Prayer was breathed, is unknowable. Alike in communion with the Father and in communion with the disciples, there breathes the same tender tone of strong hope. Jesus calmly, in the felt shadow of the Passion, looks forward and upward in the certitude of triumph.

Cheered and strengthened by the sweet song of praise, if the One Hundred and Eighteenth Psalm, laden with Messianic music,[3] the little company passed out of the still crowded city, across the torrent Kidron, which separated the Mount of Olives from the Temple mount, to the garden of the oil press, even now, possibly, rocognizable at the traditional site. The un-

---

[1] Hymns Ancient and Modern, 322, by Dr. Bright.
[2] On Paraklete, *vide* Watkins on St. John, appendix.
[3] See especially vers. 22 to end.

speakable horror of darkness into which Christ's soul entered is past human thought. Soul and Body could not have endured the strain but for the brief respites of return to the sleeping disciples, and the more strengthening visit of one pitiful angel. Here we are in the deep of "the unknown sufferings" and the dissection of such incalculable anguish may be spared, noting only for devotional attention the agonizing wrestle of the human soul in the full force of redemptive desire, the absolute meek submission of the human will to the Father's will, the spiritual and inward torture pervading even the whole prostrate body of the Divine Son of Man.

And now the solemn silence of the garden is broken. Nearer and nearer draws the hurrying of a crowd, the tramp of armed feet, a confused tumult of lights and arms flashing through the trees. The calm words of the Master, *Arise, let us go hence*, fall clearly, like thunder drops before a storm, on the ears of the aroused sleeper. " It is well known that there is seldom any strictly defined account of moments such as these and those which followed it. The terrible deed is accomplished by one stroke after another ; and before full consciousness of the situation could be attained, Jesus had fallen into the hands of His enemies."[1] "All the disciples forsook Him and fled ;" but one young man, who some believe to be Mark, and others Lazarus, casting his sindon about him, began to follow Him, only to flee, too, leaving his garment behind.

The Divine Prisoner is led to Annas. Annas, like all the members of the Temple aristocracy, was a Sadducee. Doubtless the vast wealth his family derived from their famous booths, and the cunning intrigues they carried on with the Roman power, won the High Priesthood for Annas, for his five sons, for his son-in-law, Caiaphas, and for his grandson. The Pontificate and the Temple traffic had almost become a monopoly, " and the family of Hanan and their serpent hissings" were accursed of the people. What passed between Jesus and the anti-Messianic leader was brief, but decisive. The High Priest questioned Jesus about His disciples and His doctrine (John xviii. 19-23). The former part of the question may have been directed to ascertain what social or political support He might be thought to count upon. The preliminary examination was informal and private and was, after an interval, followed

[1] Weiss, iii. 326.

by the formal examination before Caiaphas. All discrepancies [1] disappear if, as is not unreasonable to suppose, Annas had lodgings in the official residence of the High Priest, Caiaphas, and that consequently both were present at both examinations.

Two of the disciples had soon recovered from their panic. John obtained entrance into the inner court. Peter stood without, till he too was let in by the maid who kept the door. John was unnoticed, and had perhaps gone to the upper gallery, in one of whose apartments the prisoner was being tried. Peter mingled with the crowd of menials round the coal fire, which the chilly spring night made welcome. It was a time of intense depression. From the heavenly altitudes of the holy Paschal communion the apostles had sunk to the lowest deeps of sorrowing disappointment. Unnerved, unstrung, out of heart, borne down on a wave of violent reaction, without any sensible spiritual support, the apostle who had not watched in the garden and prayed in the hour of temptation flinched and fell.

At the first flush of dawn the leading priests, elders, and Sanhedrists came hurrying to the High Priest's palace. "Thus much, at least, is certain, that it was no formal, regular meeting of the Sanhedrin. All Jewish order and law would have been grossly infringed in almost every particular if this had been so." [2] Both time and place and procedure are proof of this. But it was the expression of the mind and will of the Sanhedrists, the official leaders of the people, and their representatives. The death of Christ was predetermined. The capital sentence could only be executed by the Roman power. It was their work to establish a capital charge. The false witnesses contradicted one another. At last two, possibly among those who had suffered loss from the purifications of the Temple, arose and perverted the Lord's statement about destroying the Temple, yet without agreeing. And the Lord preserved a merciful silence, like the long-suffering voicelessness of God when His rights are trampled on, His honour outraged, His love scorned, by the devil born. The holy dignity of the Prisoner, and the confused contradictions of the witnesses,

---

[1] The other alternatives (Edersheim and others), to press the aorist, $ἀπέστειλεν$ (John xviii. 24), into a pluperfect, referring to verse 14, and to ignore the $οὖν$ (Hort, Tischendorf, Gebhardt, R. V.), or omit it with Tregelles, is too violent.

[2] Edersheim, ii 557 foll., for proofs.

THE DIVINE SACRIFICE. 179

drive Caiaphas to his last stake. He must put the question of all questions, under the most awful sanction possible, in the name of the living God : Art Thou the Messiah, the Son of the living God? The two questions were rightly put in one Many would have accepted Jesus as a Messiah upon their own terms. But the whole of Jesus' Messianic claim was, and is, indivisible from His assertion of His Divinity. The answer to the question was as unmistakable as it was solemn. Question and answer still ring through the world, and leave the everlasting dilemma, Is, or is not, Jesus the Divine Christ? Is He what He said He was? Or was He a liar and blasphemer? If the answer of Caiaphas be right, His death and execution were right. For us, apart from and in addition to other currents of evidence, the moral and spiritual evidence is His own character, which intentionally overshadows all the rest, and it is inconceivable that He should have made a false claim.[1]

The scene changes from palace to palace, from judge to judge. Whether Pilate occupied the palace of Herod at the north-western angle of the upper city, or the barracks of the castle at Antonia, is a question still in debate ; but the balance of opinion favours the former locality. It must have been about five or six in the morning that the Sanhedrists arrived at the gates of the Prætorium, and refused to enter in because they would be defiled by entering a heathen dwelling, and so be prevented from offering and eating the *Chagigah*.[2] Here took place what St. John describes (xviii. 33–38, and St. Luke xxiii. 2)—the first formal civil charge against the Messiah, and their openly-expressed resolution to have Him put to death. Pilate was not unprepared for the encounter. He could not have been in total ignorance of so notorious a movement, and his own soldiers had been called out ; and he had the insight of Jewish experience of the unscrupulous Annas party. The message from his wife came at a later stage, but may have been the emphatic accent of a repeated warning. Certainly Pilate hesitated even in the face of so serious a charge as that of Jesus' aspiring to royalty. Nor could the influence of the Prisoner's demeanour, so unlike a criminal's, so gently fearless, so noble in transparent innocence and wan

[1] Bp. Temple, The Relations between Religion and Science, p. 216
[2] This view of φάγωσιν τὸ πάσχα (John xviii. 28) of course follows upon that of regarding the Lord's Supper as the real Paschal supper.

dignity, have been wholly lost upon one who was Roman enough to know a man, and whom magisterial and Roman bias would have prepossessed in favour, not in disfavour, of an object of Rabbinical odium. Had he come to the issue with the cleaner hands and truer heart of a Cato or a Cicero, Pilate would have been steadier to face so unexpected and overwhelming a responsibility. But the Son of Man came unawares. Temptations are apt to mask themselves under the guise of a surprise, which the ordinary discharge of daily duty would have forestalled or disarmed. And what shreds of rectitude or tenderness of honour or of heart were left to one whose official career had been one long murder, whose cruelty had been "unceasing and most vexatious"?[1] Roman statecraft of the best was unable to fathom such a character and such a policy. A kingdom of truth, not of this world, was an intangible, unpractical idea to a man of the world, much more to such a man of such a world. It was a far-off Divine idea which a practical, business-like officer could not attach any workable meaning to. It never occurred even to cynical Pilate that there was delusion or imposture. Here was One whose every word and look breathed manly dignity, appealing tenderness, and reserved force. Here was no slavish cringing, no hot fanaticism, no stubborn defiance. Jesus already bore the marks of cowardly insult; but no suspicion of a quailing spirit or a resentful temper lurked under the open grandeur of the Perfect Sufferer. While Pilate wavered,

"Letting 'I dare not' wait upon 'I would,'"

the storm of accusation waxed louder and fiercer, and the man whose root-motive was selfishness dashed with expediency, with all the power of Rome at his back—

"Parcere subjectis, et debellare superbos,"

quailed before those who never turned his helpless Prisoner a hair's breadth, and caught at the word Galilee tossed up on the surging multitudinous roar. Let the Galilean go to the Galilean Tetrarch, and a troublesome case be got rid of, and a politic compliment paid to the hostile provincial potentate!

Another figure has seen afar off or has learnt in his hiding-

[1] Philo.

THE DIVINE SACRIFICE. 181

place, what is coming to Him who had received the traitor's kiss. The pains of hell have gat hold of him. He would rid himself of the accursed wages.

> " His lust and greed
> Whom thou abettest thou dost make thine own,
> And nothing gett'st but wages of thy work
> To pay thy sin. What ! is't not shame on shame
> Thou puttest thine immortal soul to sale
> For profit of another? . . .
> Oh soil of bad men's service . . .
> Oh curse of bad men's hire." [1]

He would own to the high priests, unmoved as the rocky walls of the Temple, that he had betrayed innocent blood. But the repentance of Judas was a sorrow of this world, which worketh death. Away from the Temple, away from the holy city, away

> " Anywhere, anywhere out of the world ! " [2]

In the old palace of the Asmonæans Jesus confronted Herod and his men of war. Never did He break into his flippant volubility with a word. " Herod was provoked by the obstinate silence of the gentle Galilean. But not one stripe was laid upon His shoulders by the order of Antipas. . . . He had had enough of murdering prophets." [3] Arrayed in the mockery of gorgeous apparel, possibly purple, or a candidate's white toga, the Prisoner was remitted to Pilate ; and the Roman again discovers the piteous figure of Incarnate Suffering which no caricature could unking of royalty.

Pilate has not yet succeeded in shaking off the impression made by his Prisoner's words and demeanour. The " august authority of righteousness " cannot have been unfelt by one trained in Roman law. He was not wholly unpenetrated by "a secret worship of honour, truth, and might." [4] His conscience had been hardly used, but not destroyed. His repeated efforts are the measure of its mute force, and his unwonted scrupulosity a tribute to the moral ascendency of the humiliated and insulted Prisoner. It would be difficult in any

---

[1] Sir H. Taylor, "Philip van Artevelde"   [2] T. Hood.
[3] Bp. Alexander, "The Great Question," p. 174.
[4] Martineau, "A Study of Religion," i. 21.

calculus of guilt to place a Pilate as low as a Judas or a Caiaphas. Our Lord Himself judicially differentiates them. Pilate was an indifferentist, Judas an apostate traitor, Caiaphas high priest to the devil.

Pilate again endeavours to release Him after a special summons of the Sanhedrists and the populace. He tries another shift. But from one centre he can never move. His basal principle is self-servient expediency, and no power in heaven or earth can unseat it. He will not now unconditionally release a Prisoner whose innocence he admits as expressly as he knows the envy which moved His adversaries. He offers them an alternative. He will try and shift the responsibility to their shoulders. Bar-Abbas or Jesus? The kingdom of truth was a visionary empire. To the kingdom of justice Pilate pronounces himself as strange. Nor were his effortless efforts without moral support. His wife's dream startled a conscience open to fear. A minority of the crowd desired the release of Jesus, but obduracy and hatred were the stronger power; the voices of the high-priestly party prevailed.

"Once more. If Pilate cannot move the Jews to a sense of justice (and how should he, when setting them an example of injustice?), or even to self-respect (and how should he, when neglecting to respect his own authority?), he may yet move them, as he thinks, to pity. . . . He will fulfil half their wish; he will execute part of their vengeance. He will torment Jesus, but stop short of destroying Him. 'The tender mercies of the wicked are cruel.' He bids Jesus to be scourged, and it is done. Torn, bleeding, crowned with thorns, in purple rags, amid scorn and shouting, Pilate brings Him forth. 'Behold the Man!' The sight awakens no compassion; only a tenfold storm of wrath."[1]

But the varying details of the Divine tragedy call for larger and stronger colours than the few bare outlines possible here; and we hurry on with hushed steps and penitential spirit to the last scene, leaving the majesty of the Gospel accounts undisturbed in their controlled reticence, pathetic in speech and silence, with the impress of Him at whose feet they are written.

The record of the last scene of the Passion owes several distinctive particulars to one who was, of part at least, an eye-

[1] Bp. Milman, "Love of the Atonement," where a most spiritual account of the Passion is to be found. Cf. Westcott, John, *s l.*

THE DIVINE SACRIFICE. 183

witness and, so far as a man could be, a fellow-sufferer. St. John's account is first-hand. Along the Way of Sorrows to the place of execution outside the gate, like His own apostles [1] at Rome, nigh to the city, Jesus goes. Golgotha may have been rightly identified with the rounded knoll near Jeremiah's Grotto, just outside the present " Damascus gate." But the excavation of the newly-discovered wall must be completed before opinion can utter its last word. The knoll is higher than the sacred rock of the Temple. " A sort of amphitheatre is formed by the gentle slopes on the west ; and the whole population of the city might easily witness from the vicinity anything taking place on the top of the cliff. The knoll is just beside the main north road."[2] " The hill is now quite bare, with scanty grass covering its rocky soil."[3] It has been discovered to be the traditional place of stoning. And the probability of the identification gains ground. It is generally agreed that it was the usual place of execution. And so Jesus identified Himself with criminals in the mystery of His representative sacrifice in the very place as well as mode of punishment.

Around the Cross the world was grouped by representation. For at the Passover members of all nations, faiths, cultures, gathered. The Paschal Supper was over, and the Jews had leisure for a spectacle of momentous interest to all who had heard of the Messianic claims of Jesus. How many of the converts of Pentecost and after were actual spectators ; how many of the pitiful daughters of Jerusalem gathered round the stricken group of holy women ; how many children who cried Hosanna, but never Crucify ; how many devout disciples of the Baptist, or taught of them ; how many Gentiles convicted of righteousness like the centurion of the Cross ; how many priests unforgetful of type and shadow, of sacrifice and prophesy, and specially impressed with the rending of the Temple Veil ; how many awestruck by the physical wonders to a sense of the supersensible and the eternal Power ; how many, in short, the Son of Man lifted up began to draw to Himself, and prepare for the victorious ingress of the Spirit, and His own invisible return—is written only in the archives of the angels and the spiritual histories of the conquering travail of Christ.

[1] St. Peter and St. Paul.
[2] "Survey" , and Henderson, " Palestine," p. 164.
[3] " Cruise of the *Bacchante*," ii. 586

Two groups stand out from the Cross with intense vividness of contrast; the heart of the Messianic and the heart of the anti-Messianic parties; the children of light fellow-suffering, the children of darkness rejoicing. The mother with the sword passing through her heart in incomparable anguish, the beloved apostle, the holy women. And within their sight and hearing and His the still-scoffing, evilly-rejoicing Caiaphas and Annas party, the elect of the Wicked One. It was, and is, the eternal touchstone; the rock of faith or of offence, where the waves of good and evil meet in eternal conflict.

The Seven sacred Words from the Cross are each and altogether an organic whole. The intercession of the High Priest, the royal pardon and the absolution of the High Priest, the filial love of the Son of Mary, the brotherly love of the Friend of friends, the bodily and spiritual thirst of the Son of Man, the forsakenness of the atoning Sin-bearer, the finished work of the Divine Apostle and Victim and Mediator, the final farewell when the human soul passed on its journey to the Father's hands, and the weary Head bowed itself on His Father's bosom. Alike of each word, and of every word and work of Christ it may be equally said, "It is finished." For nothing broken, fragmentary, incomplete, in the wrong time, place, or manner, was thought, said, or done by the Perfect Man. Nothing of Messianic fore-ideals had been unfulfilled by the Messiah. Everything was timed to a second, and finished to a hair. And round the broken fragments of broken hours, broken lives, broken thoughts, broken prayers, in Nature and in human nature, is wrapped the blood-stained mantle of the perfect righteousness of the High Priest of both.

When we ask the wherefore of so stupendous a Sacrifice, gleams of light break from the fountains of revealed truth, but partial only. We know that the Cross revealed God's love, God's righteousness, God's holiness, God's truth. It was man's necessity, man's need, that drew the Son, a willing Sacrifice for life and death, from the bosom of the Father. God was in Christ reconciling the world to Himself. "The human blood of the Eternal God was the ransom paid to God for our eternal redemption from the curse of the Law and from the wrath of God, and from the claims of Satan, and from the power of sin."[1] "How His life and death and resurrection accomplished

[1] Canon Evans on 1 Cor. vi. 20.

our salvation, what share they each or all together had in making Him our propitiation they (the creeds) tell us not. They teach an Atonement; but theory of Atonement, God be praised, they give us none."[1]

Looking upon the Atonement in its practical result as a spiritual dynamic, it "stamps upon the mind with a power, with which no other fact could, the righteousness of God. To trifle with a Being who has demanded this Sacrifice is madness, and hence arises awe: but from the acceptance of the Atonement arises the love of God."[2] The love and fear of God actuated men before the Atonement in Israel. The fear of God was the supreme practical religious virtue of the old Covenant. The righteous man feared God. The love of God breathes in the Psalter, and in the highest visions of the Prophets breaks through the stormy voices like the clear shining after rain with the promise of brighter morrows. And the fear of God or Gods is the dominant religious motive of non-Christian religions. The Atonement has deepened the fear of God, and set it upon a more intelligible basis; the love of God the thought of the Crucified has not only made an infinitely real conception, but inconceivably the strongest active principle and inspiring motive of all Christian life Godward and manward. "For if when we were enemies we were reconciled to God by the death of His Son, much more being reconciled we shall be saved by His life" (Rom. v. 10.). "From that event dates his [3] adoption, his glorious liberty, the law of the Spirit of life, the witness of that Spirit in his own heart, the expectation of that glory which shall be revealed in him, and the gift of eternal life."[4] From that

"Fountain filled with blood"

have flowed the countless streams of Christian self-devotion; from that Sacrifice all other sacrifices have derived their moral strength and substance; from that blood-shedding "all sacraments, all prayers, all authoritative words of pardon, all sanctifying works of mercy, draw whatever they have of power or virtue."[4] To suppose that all that has been consciously or

---

[1] Bp. Magee, "The Atonement," p. 111.
[2] Dr. Mozley, Bampton Lecture, vii. p. 139.   [3] *I e.*, man's.
[4] Dr. Liddon, "University Sermons," i. p. 246, "The Divine Victim."

unconsciously, directly or indirectly, based upon and sanctioned by the Atonement is based upon and sanctioned by a delusion which would be criminal, or a "legend of pity" which would be fictitious, is an outrage to the soberest human reason, the deepest human piety, the tenderest human love, and the strongest human lives.

> "Upon the ground
> That in the story had been found
> Too much love! How could God love so?"[1]

[1] R. Browning, "Easter Day."

CHAPTER XIX.

THE DIVINE SABBATH.

"Where the wicked cease from troubling and the weary are at rest."
                              TENNYSON, from Job iii. 17.

The marred Body—The Soul free among the dead—Easter Eve.

EVENING was approaching, and with it the Sabbath and the second Paschal Day. St. John had escorted the mother, and perhaps the other women with her, to his own home, and returned in time to see the dead Body of the Lord still hanging and the soldier drive his spear deep into His side. Suffering is the best teacher. Latent or recognized truths flash into light and burning reality. Then and there he saw the Messianic fulfilments of type and prophecy in the pierced form with bone unbroken. Then and there Joseph of Arimathea was lifted from a secret to an open disciple; Nicodemus from a night seeker to a day-believer. Reverently the two Sanhedrists bear the marred Body to Joseph's new rock-hewn tomb hard by, and lay it in one of the niches (Kukhin). Many of these have been excavated and described, and it is yet possible [1] that the very one which sheltered the Body may be found. Present opinion is divided between the Holy Sepulchre and a spot near the Damascus Gate. The opening of the whole course of the newly-discovered wall will throw light on the problem, and if the wall run outside the present "Holy Sepulchre" negative the tradition which gives it its name, if within, confirm it. There was the Body of the Divine Sufferer left in lonely repose, guarded by a great sealed stone, and apparently all through the Sabbath day of rest by a detachment of Roman soldiers.

[1] "Twenty-One Years," p 62 foll.

And whither, happy Soul, free among the dead didst Thou go? What parts of Sheol didst Thou traverse in triumph? Were the Antediluvians the only hearers of Thy proclamation? Or rather not all the dead?[1] Did not Moses and Elias who had been with Thee at the Mountain of Transfiguration to speak of Thine Exodus now greet Thee; and Abraham, and in Abraham, Abraham's children, exult to see Thy day? Thou alone knowest, who didst descend into Hades and hast the keys of death and of Hades!

Silence and darkness fell around the Holy Sepulchre. Silence and darkness lay over the hearts and homes of the mourners in Zion. But the love, the force, the work, the truth lost to the earth was gained by the other world. And those who were asleep in death and had laid them down to the long rest in their hope full of immortality had not gone to utter destruction, but were in the hand of God. They were in peace, and to them the Peacemaker came. So the energies of human love and blessed endeavour are not spent shot, but transmutable to "unimpeded activities,"[2] beatifying and beatified, in the brighter and more populous half of the one kingdom. Such is the teaching of the physical analogies. Energy passes off to other transmigrations. Nothing is lost. The departed soul enriches another kingdom, and increases its working power—the kingdom of light or the princedom of darkness.

Nor has the night of Easter Eve been unremembered by Christian devotion. It has been a night vocal with praise. It has been the night celebrated by such accents of adoration as these:—

"It is very meet and right, with all powers of heart and mind, and with the service of the lips, to praise the invisible God, the Father Almighty, and His only begotten Son our Lord Jesus Christ, who paid the debt of Adam for us to the Eternal Father, and effaced the bond of the ancient guilt by the blood poured forth in loving-kindness. For this is the Paschal festival in which that true Lamb is slain, and the door-posts hallowed by His blood: in which first Thou didst bring our fathers, the children of Israel, out of Egypt, and madest them to pass over the Red Sea dry-shod. This, then, is the night which now throughout the world restores to grace and unites

[1] 1 Peter iv 6 (F. C Cook, s. l.). [2] Aristotle, N Eth , vii , xii. 3, &c.

THE DIVINE SABBATH. 189

to holiness believers in Christ, separated from worldly vices and from the gloom of sin. This is the night in which Christ broke the bonds of death, and ascended a Conqueror from the grave. For to be born had been no blessing to us, unless we could have been redeemed. O the wondrous condescension of Thy loving-kindness towards us ! O the inestimable tenderness of Thy love ! To redeem the servant, Thou gavest up the Son. This holy night, then, puts to flight offences, washes away sins, and restores innocence to the fallen, and joyousness to the sad. O truly blessed night, which spoiled the Egyptians and enriched the Hebrews—the night in which heaven and earth are reconciled! We pray Thee therefore, O Lord, that Thou wouldest preserve Thy servants in the peaceful enjoyment of this Easter happiness, through Jesus Christ our Lord."[1]

That night has been a "watch night" to many hearts who look for the uprising of the Resurrection morning, and listen for the trumpet blast of the Resurrection Angel.

[1] Ancient Gregorian prayer preserved in Bright's "Ancient Collects," p. 52.

CHAPTER XX.

THE RESURRECTION AND THE FORTY DAYS.

" Thou know'st He died not for Himself, nor for Himself arose :
Millions of souls were in His heart, and thee for one He chose.
Upon the palms of His pierc'd hand engraven was thy name,
He for thy cleansing had prepar d His water and His flame."
J. KEBLE, " Lyra Innocentium," " Easter Day."

Τὴν ζωηφόρον ἀνάστασιν.
CHRYSOSTOM in Princip., Act vi.

The Resurrection—*Magdalena dolorosa*—The Resurrection unexpected, a Divine must be—Emmaus—Appearance to the eleven apostles and other brethren—Differentiation of offices—Doubter Thomas—Messianic critical difficulties—Celsus's objection—Vision hypothesis — Galilee again—The fishers on the sea again—All authority—Undetailed appearances—The great Forty Days—Divine organization—Development of order—Development of faith—Continuity, both of soul and body—The four distinct Evangelic reports.

THE darkness, but not the silence, was burst when the angel of the Resurrection came to the Holy Sepulchre. God's mightiest physical agencies are silent.

"There is neither speech nor language" (Psa xix 3)

and His spiritual activities are for the most part inaudible here as the songs of angels.

One human being was the meeting-point between heaven and earth, the instrument of the Incarnation. No human eye witnessed the Resurrection. Out of the guilty sleeping city stole a little band of women like shadows. By the time Mary Magdalene, "last at the cross, first at the grave," had reached the rock-hewn sepulchre, the light had flashed over the eastern sea, and the Lord had risen. She hurries back from the untenanted tomb, and her companions reach the spot and see an angel. "In their affliction they will seek Me early" (Hosea v. 15). St. Luke may be describing another and later party which sees two angels. The two apostles arrive and see the threefold sign, the stone removed, the sepulchre empty, the grave clothes in order. The writer records his eye-witness and his belief. His was the first act of faith. It was a germ which bore the fruit of knowledge. To know[1] was the end of the Johannine creed.

After the running apostles Mary Magdalene returns untold or unconvinced. The angels comfort her not. Only when He calls her by name does the penitent recognize her Saviour. The first to see the risen Lord is the most blessed of them that mourn. Soon after, as it seems, He goes forward to meet the returning company of women and reveals Himself, and charges the brethren to go to Galilee and await Him.

Several points call for attention. Not one soul expected the Resurrection. The fact is not creditable to the disciples, and certainly prejudices in favour of the honesty of the report. Their Messianic belief was derived from two sources, their Jewish preconceptions and Christ's teaching. Their Jewish preconceptions were partly Scriptural, partly traditional. In the Old Testament they had not noticed the types and figures or direct prophecies, which Christian light afterwards illuminated. Extra Scriptural Jewish thought less increased than diminished any belief in a Messianic resurrection. The notion of a pre-existent Messiah was vague and colourless at the best, and such as it was, supplied no basis whatever for belief in a return to life.

It is difficult to see how any honest mind can shake off the impression of transparent veracity and artless truth to nature in the fourfold narrative. The faith of the disciples was at its lowest pressure. The grief, the surprise, the indignation, the physical pain, which overwhelmed them on Friday stifled hope. The Lord's promises were forgotten, crowded out by the stress and storm of present affliction. Great grief has no past or future. It is all present, overwhelming, catastrophic. The sufferings and death of Christ were the greatest trial the dis-

[1] Cf. 1 Ep *passim*

ciples ever underwent. Not only did they suffer with Him, drink His cup of shame and ignominy, sorrow in His sorrow, not only were they baffled, beaten, defeated as a party, dispirited, disintegrated as a body, not only were they wounded in their tenderest affections, but their Messianic beliefs and hopes were assailed at all points. The more heartily they believed in His Messiahship the more difficult and disappointing did the end seem. The further they had reached in acceptance of the mystery of His Divinity, the greater did the mystery of His suffering humanity seem. That their Messianic prejudices had not died the long death of mistake is abundantly apparent. The shock to their faith might have been overwhelming had the Lord not risen again. The Resurrection was the final and conclusive, but not the only, proof of His Divinity. By it He vindicated His claims, fulfilled His promises, verified His words. Without it His life might have been regarded as a magnificent dream, and an unparalleled venture of heroism. With it His life descends into the regions of sound reason and verifiable fact. The Resurrection "should not perhaps have been necessary. The loftiness and purity and humility of His character should have been enough to prove that He only spoke what was true."[1] But there are many aspects to the Divine "must be." Among the many human necessities of the Divine "must" here was one.[2] The moral and spiritual resurrection followed naturally and inevitably. After the shock the recovery was instantaneous and absolute. Henceforward Christian conviction stood upon unassailable ground, and transmits itself by its own inherent force. The evidential power of the Resurrection stands its ground. Upon it is built the whole historic fabric of Christianity. Invalidate that evidence and Christianity is dead.

All the appearances are not recorded in detail. There was one revelation incidentally mentioned by St. Luke, and at an earlier date by St. Paul (1 Cor. xv. 5), which a legendary writer could not have failed to embellish. He appeared to Cephas. This was before the evening appearance to the Twelve. Who

[1] Stanton, p. 253

[2] Cf St. Bernard on the Atonement, in his wonderful letter, "De erroribus Abælardi," Tom ii , Opusc xi , Ep cxc , ch viii., § 19 "Respondemus ; Necessitas nostra fuit, et necessitas dura sedentibus in tenebris et umbra mortis Opus æque nostrum, et Dei nostri, et sanctorum Angelorum," &c

THE RESURRECTION AND THE FORTY DAYS.

would not be glad to know what words, or speaking silence, passed at that interview?

The Lord's self-manifestation to the two disciples on the way to Emmaus is related with some minuteness by St. Luke. He would "travel with the travellers," to adopt the words of ancient liturgical prayer. Of the two disciples one was Cleopas, the other may have been the narrator himself. Either they had not heard at first hand, or had not fully credited, the tidings that the Lord had really and indeed risen. Their state of downcast ignorance and disappointed half hope evidently represented the mental and spiritual condition of many of the faithful in Jerusalem, as the first undulations of the report reached them, and required the confirmation of the Lord's Person to carry conviction.

St. Matthew, the writer of the Jewish Gospel, naturally gives the Jewish version of the Resurrection. It was the authorized anti-Messianic version; he may have often heard and answered it by the appeal to personal testimony. The high priests and elders bribed the soldiers to say that the disciples came and stole the Body away while the guards slept. It is surprising that any revivals of this story could have found credit since; it would seem a far more reasonable hypothesis altogether to deny the fact by discrediting the witnesses. But the difficulties of unbelief are greater than those of belief, and labour under the superincumbent addition of the contradictory theories, clashing hypotheses, and changing no-creeds, which confront the unchanging and unchangeable faith of Christendom in a risen and living Christ.

On the afternoon of the Resurrection another appearance of the Lord took place. Much interesting discussion of the site of Emmaus has taken place in the columns of the Quarterly Journal of the Palestine Exploration Society, and various identifications have been suggested. St. Luke's careful note of its distance, sixty furlongs, negatives the identification with the Emmaus, afterwards Nicopolis, now Amwas, which is one hundred and sixty furlongs distant. The alternative lies between three: (1) Khurbet el Khamasa, "the ruins of Khamasa," "from the Arabic Hammath." It lies close beside "one of the ancient roads leading from the capital to the plain near Beit Jibrin,"[1] and is distant eight miles from the capital.

[1] "Survey," iii. 36 and foll.

Ancient rock-cut sepulchres and a causeway mark the site as being of considerable antiquity, and the vicinity is still remarkable for its fine supply of spring water.[1] But springs do not necessarily suggest the "hot spring" (Khammath) or "medicinal spring," implied by its name; and the identification is open to this objection. (2) El Kubeibeh, the Crusaders' Emmaus, is situate sixty stades north-west of Jerusalem. This site is supported by the proximity of Kolonieh, *i.e.*, Colonia. As Josephus mentions the plantation of a military colony of eight hnndred Roman soldiers at Emmaus, the retention of the name, in addition to that of El Hummâm hard by, constitutes a strong claim. The still-existing ruin Beit-Mizza, near Kolonieh, may represent the "Ammaous" of Josephus ("Amosa" of the Septuagint; Ham-Môtsah, Hebrew), "and be the southernmost trace[2] of the old name"[3] of the district, as Josephus calls it. (3) Urtas,[4] in the valley of Etham, near Bethlehem, a possible corruption of Hortus. At present the second alternative seems the one which combines most of the lines of identification.

The conversation of Christ with the two bears all the internal marks of genuineness. It is natural, it is simple. It is just a Bible lesson which the unknown Stranger gives. They ought not to have required the detailed explanations of prophecy. They ought to have remembered, or others ought to have remembered and reminded them, of the Lord's own repeated prediction of His Passion and His Resurrection. As the Passion had taken place, they should have been the readier to believe in the Resurrection. But Scripture does not idealize its characters like ancient myths or modern novels. They had to unlearn so much before they knew their own Scriptures. "Even in the case of the few who believed in Him, faith was not the effect of the proof from prophecy. Believers did not first study the prophecies, and then come to Jesus as disciples; they first came to Jesus, and then learnt how to interpret the prophecies. The proper interpretation of prophecy was not the cause, but the effect, of their faith."[5] What was true of prophecy in its strict sense was true of the underlying prophetic and priestly element of all the old Covenant revela-

---

[1] "Twenty-one Years," p 120. [2] Being only four miles off.
[3] Rev R. F. Hutchinson and Rev. A. Henderson.
[4] Mrs. Finn and Rev P Mearns.
[5] Dr. A. B. Bruce, "The Chief End of Revelation," p. 257.

tion in its Messianic relation. The kingly element had been better understood, but distorted and secularized. The explanations given by St. Peter notably, and the other disciples, of which the Acts gives us but bare outlines, and suggestive specimens, were doubtless grounded upon the Bible lessons they had personally received from Christ, before and, more especially, after the Resurrection, when His whole earthly time was taken up, not in mighty works, not in preaching to the masses, but in instruction of His believers in the things pertaining to the kingdom of God. Before the Resurrection the disciples had but imperfect appreciation of the Old Testament. In the intellectual and spiritual resurrection which followed upon that of the Messiah the whole of God's dealings became illuminated; and the older inspiration was Targumed in the fulness of its Messianic wealth.

Such re-revelations of old truths renewed, but not understood till a living voice, or a new inspiration, had interpreted, enforced, and cleared up, is not without many parallels in the history of the Church and of the individual. The struggles of the first four Christian centuries involved a constant return to old truths, re-reading of familiar but unperceived or unformulated doctrines. And in the spiritual histories of the aged there is a tendency to revert to the familiar hymns or texts learned in childhood, little understood at the time, but lying hid and bursting into life and flower, just when many anchors are slipping away. St. John himself, in his old age, as we read his latest utterances, his Epistles, seems to be clinging round a few old truths, and old formulæ. They have become fuller and fuller of meaning and light, like songs of childhood charged with the sweetest memories, or treasured letters embalming the most deeply-rooted fibres of the personal life.

It is remarkable that the eyes of the disciples were first spiritually opened when the Lord sat with them at supper and took the bread, and blessed, and brake it, and gave it to them.

> "He blessed the bread, but vanished at the word,
> And left them both exclaiming, ''Twas the Lord.'"[1]

The act of Christ was quasi-sacramental. He did what He

[1] Cowper, "Conversation."

had done at the Last Supper, but whether He gave the cup or not, we are not told. Perhaps the supper then stands midway between a communion and an agape. Though the two disciples were not present at the Last Supper, they may have been familiar with its details, and may have been among the five thousand or the four thousand. Or they may have been like those in whom ignorance is no bar to the benefits of the Holy Communion, where spiritual preparedness exists. Certainly at this moment of, on the lowest ground, social communion their eyes were opened to the Light. And they are soon on their way back to Jerusalem with the glad tidings.

The same night, perhaps about 8 P.M., when the two had returned with their joyful evidence to the eleven apostles and others gathered with them, He Himself stood in their midst. He had appeared to individual believers; He now appeared to the Church. Resurrection had not been a mere revival. His body had "put on" new conditions and higher powers. It was now a spiritual body, entirely indifferent to material limitations. And so the way was paved for the conception of a heavenly bodily organism fitted to be the perfected instrument and organ of a glorified spirit; and for the presence of His own body "after an heavenly and spiritual manner."[1]

The passing of the real substantial body through the closed door was both an evidence and a prophecy. After giving the senses of sight, and hearing, and feeling independent evidence of His continued humanity and unbroken identity, He now formally renewed and ratified the commission they had before received. But it was a grant of enlarged powers upon the basis of His increased authority. It was the grant of a King distributing His functions of government according to His royal will and power with primary reference to the spiritual domain. He gave them mission identical with His own. To send in itself carries with it no powers. But authority in addition was delegated. And under the outward sign of breathing the inward grace of the Holy Spirit was imparted for the discharge of apostolic and ecclesiastical functions, with especial reference to the remitting and retaining of sins. Christ was, and is, the Minister and High Priest of the Church. All offices are actually, as well as ideally, contained in His Person. Out of His fulness He differentiates selected offices,

[1] Art. xxviii. of the Thirty-nine Articles.

THE RESURRECTION AND THE FORTY DAYS. 197

functions, powers, gifts. The Church as a whole and the apostles most nearly were to represent Him in the world, His life, work, authority; not to speak now of His mind and character.

There was one absentee upon this occasion. The doubting Thomas peremptorily demanded rigorous first-hand, sensible experience of the reality of the Resurrection. All appear to have doubted in differing degrees. Doubt was characteristic of the most unhopeful but straightforward apostle. What were the especial difficulties of his faith we are not told. Probably they were in the main physical, for physical proof satisfied his doubt. And the Messianic hope may have taken more definitely local and national outlines with him. Thomas was the impersonation of the doubt of the dull, matter-of-fact character which sinks under the pressure of overpowering environments, but does not cease to love. Thomas wanted imagination; he could see only straight before him; he wanted faith in others because he wanted faith in God. And so, though he honestly loved,

> " Doubt, a blank twilight of the heart, which mars
> All sweetest colours in its dimness same ,
> A soul-mist, through whose rifts familiar stars
> Beholding we misname," [1]

clouded his mind, as it shook, if we mistook not, even the strong grip and single eye of the prophet in Machærus.

Our Lord's reproaches (Mark xvi. 14 ; Luke xxiv. 25) upon this and other occasions would not have contained that element of bitterness which usually characterizes deserved, or undeserved, human reproachfulness. They were the chidings of them that "smite me friendly." And we know not how much His manner and tone sweetened and solemnized the lash which revealed the moral source, the hard-heartedness and slow-heartedness, of their intellectual sins. But what of those whose faith and love retreat in company at quick march? What of those who seal their eyes and heart to evidence within and without, who create difficulties, instead of waiting their approach, with an increasing appetite for negatives, and an unchecked passion to hear all that can be said against the

[1] Jean Ingelow, " Honours."

old story, who "blaspheme dignities," or halve and distort in order to scorn,

> "E'en those, Thine own in earlier youth,
> Now coldly asking, 'What is truth?'
> Who spurn the way their fathers trod,
> Forego their faith, and lose their God"?[1]

Are such Thomases?

A week passed. The news must have spread and brought Thomas to the weekly gathering, which anticipated evidently another appearance when the day of Resurrection came again. Here is the instinctive and unconscious consecration of the Lord's Day of subsequent observance. Again the Lord appears Thomas receives the verification he had desired, and the "ninth beatitude" is pronounced upon those who had not seen the "atoning wounds," but would believe. The falling Church had now become the standing Church. The spiritual and intellectual victory of the Resurrection was now complete. The rising or falling of the Churches to the end depends upon their response to the power of the Resurrection, and their increasing or decreasing in the life of the Risen.

Contrary to their own preconceived opinions of the Jewish Messiah, contrary to their own prejudices, unbroken by the repeated waves of surprise in Christ's conduct, character, and teaching, the disciples believed in the return of Jesus to life, and that life in their belief belonged to a wholly higher order of being. And what was the next step taken in the progress of their conviction? They believed in the return to a pre-existent earthly life, followed by a return to a pre-existent heavenly life. They believed that Jesus was alive in heaven at the right hand of God, in the plentitude of power and glory, and yet in immediate relation and minute contact with His earthly friends, officers, representatives. The excited hallucinations of enthusiasts might have restored to an imaginary life a beloved form. But how could the fondest flights of fancy appeal to His presence above by His works beneath? How could they deepen and widen and strengthen their convictions with the lapse of time? And in the face of hostile criticism and sleepless persecution maintain unshaken their own conviction of His present, energizing power, and afford sufficient proof of the same

[1] Dr. Bright.

THE RESURRECTION AND THE FORTY DAYS. 199

to others to gradually convince many of their own people, including a leading opponent, and many in different places, and of divers tongues, cultures, environments, beliefs, that their faith was not an open question, not a religious novelty, or a tenable hypothesis, or a fanciful superstition, but an absolutely peremptory fact? It is unhistoric, unscientific to isolate the evidence of the Resurrection to its bare context. The whole line of result must be measured from the conviction of the first convinced woman of tears to the still throbbing life and hope of Christendom. It must be remembered that the scientific difficulties of belief were as serious, if not as clearly defined, for them as for us. In addition to that they had greater difficulties of their own. The rejection of the Messiah by all the influence and authority of Jerusalem; His unresisting submission to the Gentile powers; the defection of His nearest disciples; the contradiction to all their hopes and Messianic preconceptions—and all coming when the crown of popular favour had been set upon His brow by the Messianic exultation on the Day of Palms. The reaction to faith required a tremendous impetus. The recoil was by degrees.

Jewish preconception had so far from created a bias in favour of a risen Messiah, that it increased the difficulty of belief. The notion of a pre-existent Messiah [1] was vague and colourless at the best, and even where it existed failed to suggest a resurrection. The only basis of faith was derivable from the predictions of Jesus Himself. The Old Testament itself contained the truth. But it was hidden and unsuspected. Christ's definite promise was forgotten. His words would rise again. They had died and been buried. The change in the disciples' life, outward and inward, in their aggressive militancy, in their power of conviction and producing conviction, is absolutely unintelligible, unless an adequate cause be found. That cause— the resurrection of the Master—carried with it the resurrection of their hearts and lives, of their convictions and powers.

From Celsus onwards the objection has been raised that Christ did not appear to any but believers. But the time for evidential miracles was past. Nor were miracles ever wrought by Christ without obedience to law. That law was God's will and character on the one side, with which He was in constant touch; human spiritual affinity on the other. The universal

[1] Cf Stanton, p. 130 f.

vindication of His claims before believers and unbelievers is held in reserve by the Father.

There was assuredly a judicial element in His withdrawal.[1] It was a *pœna damni*. Was there not here a touch of mercy —lest they should sin too awfully against the light? " If a man love Me I will manifest Myself to him." But where was the promise of manifestation to those who loved Him not? Love opens God's heart as well as man's. And where the initial at once and final gift of love was wanting, what good could mere intellectual coercion have done?

" Had Jesus showed Himself not to disciples only, witnesses chosen before of God, but to all the people—to the Pharisees and Sadducees, to the judges who condemned Him, and to the soldiers who nailed Him to the cross," it would have been, as has been well said,[2] " to renew His Passion." "That Passion consisted in other things besides sufferings deliberately inflicted on Him by the world. Mere intercourse with the world caused no small part of it To have His aims misunderstood, His motives misinterpreted, His revelations scorned; to have the very works in which the glory of His Father most conspicuously appeared traced to a league on His part with Beelzebub : to find that much of the Divine seed sown by Him fell upon the hard wayside, and was taken away before it could penetrate the heart; to come into hourly contact with ignorance instead of knowledge, selfishness instead of love, oppression instead of justice, formalism instead of piety, truth perverted by its appointed guardians, His Father's house turned into a den of thieves, the wretched denied consolation, man living without God and dying without hope—all this was suffering and sorrow ; it was His burden and His cup of woe. No approach even to a fresh experience of a like kind was possible after the burden had been borne and the cup drained to the dregs. From the very nature of the case, the risen Lord could come in contact only with disciples—with those in whom, instead of finding cause for a renewal of His pain, He might ' see of the travail of His soul and be satisfied.' If His resurrection was the beginning of His glory, it would have been a reversal of the whole plan of our redemption, a confounding of the different steps of the economy

---

[1] Cf Tert Apol 21, "ne impii errore liberarentur"
[2] Prof Milligan, 'The Resurrection of our Lord," p. 33.

of grace, had He 'after His passion' presented Himself alive to any but disciples.

Negative criticism still has to content itself with the vision hypothesis. It shatters itself historically upon the evidence of the undisputed epistles of St. Paul. Morally and psychologically it totally fails to account for the rapid, decided, and permanent moral and spiritual resurrection of the believers, and the present power and working of the Church of Jesus. If the Resurrection were a visionary hallucination, the whole of Christian devotion and life rests upon the baseless fabric of a vision; and a vast stream of moral and spiritual energy flows from an inanimate object of worship. A delirium which has flooded the world with seas of prayer, crowded it with churches, girdled it with armies of workers in every field of human activity, leaves the world more insane every day ! So vast an effect requires an adequate cause, and that cause is pronounced to be a dream " of the feverish moods of evening ! "[1]

It does not seem difficult to follow the Lord's reasons for sending the disciples into Galilee, which to negative criticism has been suggestive of suspicion. Galilee was the centre of the faith. The apostles were Galileans. Old associations would be renewed. Old ties riveted. In sight of the old places, on the ground redolent of word and deed and a thousand minutiæ of tones and looks, the old truths would come home with gathered interest. The continuity of the pre-Resurrection and post-Resurrection teaching would be shown to be as consistent as the continuity of the pre- and post-Resurrection life. Scenes of home affections, consecrated and doubly endeared, or freely surrendered, scenes of spiritual birth and conversion, times and places which were landmarks to be unforgotten in heaven, would reinvest the old teaching, and connect it with the new, in a network of hallowed environment.

In Galilee the sentiment of attachment, the affection of personal loyalty, gained the accumulated and organized authority of past association. "It is undeniable that, taken in its widest acceptation, the feeling of the community is the sole source of political power."[2] Feeling, as a source of moral, spiritual, and social power in the Christian body, would be invigorated and

[1] Keim, vi 345, though he disclaims in words adopting the vision theory

[2] Herbert Spencer, "Political Institutions," p. 327.

refreshed. The resurrection both of emotion and of intellect would be completed where eyes and ears told a thousand unforgotten tales of the Master's past works and words. Galilee was the real home, the dear home, both of the Master and of His disciples ; and the resurrection of all Christian home life which began in the Incarnation was now perfected. And with the love of home in their hearts His teachers would go forth to bring all families into one, and show them the way to the Home of homes.

The home feeling would cling around the remembered form of the beloved Master, and all of His, when He had left them for the silence.

The first Galilean scene is a prose idyll. They are in the thick of the old work, just as if nothing had occurred to break it off, and the three last years had been a dream. With the three fishers of the lake in the old place are Galilean Nathanael and Thomas and two disciples—a company forming the mystic number seven. They had fished all the night and had caught nothing. Parting the fresh morning air like a cheery good morning came the hail from the Stranger on the shore, " Cast the net on the right side of the ship and ye shall find." The successful haul was a speaking sign. Love is quick of memory and recognition. It is the beloved apostle who at once understands, and characteristically says to Peter, " It is the Lord !" It is Peter who characteristically springs into the sea, respectfully putting on his fisher's coat, to swim or wade the hundred yards to His Master's feet.

The dragging in of the loaded net follows ; and the exact counting of the fish. Considering the importance of numerical combinations in Scripture the symbolical interpretation of the number, supported as it is by names so weighty as Augustine, and so devout as Isaac Williams, claims a respectful hearing. The meal upon the shore is irresistibly suggestive of prophetic import. The Rabbinical and extra-canonical pictures of Messianic banquets under spiritualized applications find some scriptural countenance, and the figures, or whatever the truths that underlie them be, of eating and drinking in the kingdom, recur in the Apocalypse of St. John.

After the meal follows the memorable dialogue with the son of John. He had been reinstated with the others in office. He is now formally reinstated in confidence before himself and his fellows.

"He can forgive, we never can forget." His own future uplifting on the martyr's cross is shadowed forth. Such a touching exhibition of unbroken loyalty to His friends, such a more than *redintegratio amoris*, restored the apostle to his own self-respect, and left no doubt resting upon his future priority in the society. His friend too, and his Lord's, unforgotten of either, must tarry on till the judgment thunders broke over Jerusalem, a real judicial coming of the Christ, and a type and shadow of the Last.

"The spell of the mountains seems to have been on St. Matthew, and he loved to contemplate the Son of God in those solemn sanctuaries."[1] The spell was upon the disciple because it was upon his Galilean Master. Upon some Galilean height, it may well have been the mountain of the Sermon, for it was specially appointed by Jesus, and would have been well-known ground, Christ came to them. It was the time for a Royal proclamation. All authority in heaven and earth was His by gift. He now issues His royal commission to baptize in the threefold Name and disciple the world, and pledged His word that the Royal presence would accompany the faithful to the consummation of the world. The circle of victory widened through unknown reaches to invisible shores of hope. The Messianic hope was lifted and extended beyond national borders and temporal royalties to the regions of the Infinite and the Eternal. Earth and heaven were different provinces of one Empire. The Head over all, blessed for ever, stood before them.

It would be travelling out of our way to point out how this truth was only gradually realized through the shock of party conflicts, voices of debate and discord in the apostolic company, the disseminating effect of persecution, the rise of a personality of unique power and unclouded vision upon the scene of Christian warfare, and the direct visions and revelations of the Lord from heaven : so slow is human nature to rise to the supernatural, so ready to lapse from its highest moments of conviction, and to fall into moral disintegration and spiritual disorder.

No details remain of other manifestations. He appeared to "above five hundred brethren at once" (1 Cor. xv. 6), of whom more than two hundred and fifty were alive twenty-eight years after. Such a large company of witnesses of the Resurrection must have disseminated the seeds of faith far and wide, especi-

[1] Bp. Alexander, "Leading Ideas," p. 16.

ally when the persecution of which St. Stephen was the first victim scattered the faithful. We also learn from St. Paul (1 Cor xv. 7) of an appearance to James. "At the time when St Paul wrote, there was but one person eminent enough in the Church to be called James simply without any distinguishing epithet—the Lord's brother, the bishop of Jerusalem. It might therefore be reasonably concluded that this James is here meant. And this view is confirmed by an extant fragment of the Gospel according to the Hebrews, the most important of all the Apocryphal Gospels, which seems to have preserved more than one true tradition, and which expressly relates the appearance of our Lord to His brother James after His ascension."[1] If Bishop Lightfoot's inference be accepted there are nine recorded appearances of the Lord after His resurrection, if that to James be placed before His ascension there are ten.

Tradition preserves a beautiful memory of an appearance to His mother. It is difficult to suppose that the inspired historian of the Magnificat, who does not either forget to mention her presence with the apostles, with the women, and with His brethren in the upper chamber (Acts i 14), should have omitted, or been ignorant of such a record. But " le cœur a ses raisons,"[2] and upon such heart reasons we dare not contradict, though we may not affirm, such a greeting between mother and Son as would have been a foretaste of the first in heaven.

The Lord might also have made an unrecorded appearance to His "brethren," i.e, Joseph's sons by a former wife,[3] His foster-brethren Certainly we find them gathered together with the apostolic company after the Resurrection, "all" of whom "continued with one accord in prayer and supplication" (Acts i. 14). Yet shortly before His passion they did not believe in Him (John vii. 5). How did this happy change come about? Bishop Lightfoot suggests that the Lord's appearance after the Ascension, as he places it, to James was the turning point in his religious life and that of his brethren. This is open, however, to the serious objection mentioned above of James being in the company of the faith before the Ascension. Nor have we any records of our Lord's appearing to unbelievers in order to win their faith, for Thomas had been no unbeliever before the passion. It would seem, then, the more natural sup-

---

[1] Bp Lightfoot, "Galatians," p. 265. [2] Pascal.
[3] According to the Epiphanian view.

position that James and His brethren were among the fruits of the Passion-travail of His soul, whom the Resurrection brought out of the tremors and hesitations of imperfect conviction. The influence of the Lord's mother, and His kinsmen after the flesh, such as the sons of Zebedee, would have told in this direction. And the appearance to James, if it really took place after, not before, the Ascension, would have been the reward of faith, its effect, not its cause.

Such changes of conviction are suggestive of others like them. The inward histories of faith are not hewn after the same fashion, but vary with the infinite diversities of human character. Among the "more than five hundred," some of whom still "doubted," but probably ended in full conviction, at least when the Holy Spirit came down and convicted thousands of the sin and sinfulness of unbelief (John xvi. 9); among the thousands of the Pentecostal day of conversion; among the "great company of the priests" (Acts vi. 7) who became obedient unto the faith; among the number of the disciples who within so short a time as that preceding the preaching of St. Stephen "multiplied in Jerusalem greatly;" among the many, in short, of the apostolic first-fruits there cannot fail to have been some in various stages of progress towards the faith, who had witnessed or heard of the crucifixion, who if among the recognized five hundred brethren had witnessed, if outside the inner circle had not witnessed, but heard the report of witnesses. Certainly the statistics of the faith would have been very different on Good Friday, on Ascension Day, and a week after Pentecost.

The great Forty Days must be regarded as an organic whole. The moral education of the disciples had been completed. The discipline of character had received its finishing touches. The shafts had been polished (Isa. xlix. 2), they had been kept close in the quiver: now they must fly abroad. The Church had centred in Christ's own Person. The Church had been integrating. The little community who followed Him constituted the faithful. The Divine society had been in the nursery stage. Childish things must now be put away, as when a young man leaves a godly father's roof, enriched by hallowed examples and speaking memories, to do battle in the struggle for existence. The example of Christ had done its work. Memory was filled to the full. A fund of energy could be drawn from the past. New resources must be opened up. New powers furnished. A new impetus derived from the present.

The great Forty Days is the period of organization. The differentiating movement had begun in the separation of the Twelve, it continued in the separation of the Seventy, it was now made constant. The simple unclassified collection of believers formed a little Messianic knot and nidus.

The new society was organized upon a definite basis, with a definite formula of initiation and bond of cohesion. It was gifted with the promise and potency of self-government, self-development, self-propagation, "a plant, like those of the first creation, having seed in itself upon the earth."[1] The family of God was promised indestructibility and spiritual fertility. The unexplained title, Son of Man, cast its light forward. The Son of Man was the ideal Man, and the King of men. His kingdom found satisfaction for all the wants of humanity in all relations Godward and manward. Every development of truth and righteousness in every direction is a ray from the Kingdom of light. The Light in the world must now diffuse itself into the world. The mind of Christ is the ideal human mind. The soul of Christ is the glorified human soul. The Body of Christ is the glorified spiritualized human body. Christward march all the forces in heaven and earth, good to their consummation and coronation, evil to their destruction,

> "On to the distant
> Star of existent
> Rapture and love."[2]

As there was development in the sphere of order, so there was development in the sphere of faith. The germ of the Catholic faith lay in the confession of the leading apostle, "Thou art the Christ, the Son of the living God," at a crucial moment. The baptismal formula embodies and completes the definition. Whatever legitimate development there has been in the formulation of Christian truth has rendered explicit what was implicit. There have been parasitic growths which have cumbered the ground, and embarrassed the freedom of natural progress and soiled its many-hued bloom. As all true develop-

[1] Bp. Cotterill, "Genesis of the Church."
[2] Goethe, "Faust," translated by Bayard Taylor.

ment tends to repair to its original source, and to conform to its proper type, so all excrescences tend to fall away. As the different sections of Christendom, which stand self-condemned by the very fact of being sections, gravitate nearer to their Centre and source they must draw nearer to one another. In the end the centripetal tendency must fuse all together who obey it. As there are three Persons in one indivisible God, as Jesus Christ eternally unites divinity and humanity in Himself, so through and in Him humanity moves on to its deification. The nearer humanity approaches Christ, ideally and actually, the nearer it approaches unity, Divine and human. For such Christian unification, inward and outward, all Christians should work and pray. And the day of days must come when Christ's unfulfilled words are fulfilled, and Christ's unanswered prayer is answered.

The permanence, the identity, of the Lord's Body was as real as the permanence, the identity of His soul. He had submitted His risen Body to the touch of Thomas and the others ; He had allowed Mary to cling to His feet, if but for a moment ; He had in the preceding meal taken and eaten before them. His Body then was under new conditions, but the same. It was a spiritual Body, yet it had not put off material relations. It consisted then of spiritualized matter. That all the bodies of the faithful Christians will be so spiritualized, St. Paul has expressly taught under the figure of the seed. That all matter will undergo spiritual transformation seems a further inference necessitated by the view of the Son of Man as the Head and Archetype of Creation. So, too, early Christian thinkers taught. "The Lord," says St. Cyril of Jerusalem, "will roll up the heavens, not in order to destroy them, but in order to raise them up better."[1] Such a conception follows upon the consideration of the view of Creation opened up by St. Paul in the eighth chapter of the Romans. As Irenæus long ago discovered, "The Creation, therefore, itself must be renewed to its old condition, and without hindrance serve the righteous."[2] And it is needless to dwell, for it would take us too far away from our subject, upon the sidelights flashed in by such physical doctrines as those of the conservation of energy.

The permanence, the identity, of the Lord's human soul was

[1] Quoted by Rev. P. G. Medd, Bampton Lectures, p. 566.
[2] Irenæus, v. xxxii. 1.

also proved by His human feelings. He took a human interest in the places and the persons He knew before. There was no break in the continuity of His affection. Whatever scenes He witnessed in the bodiless world, He had not forgotten any of His earthly life or any of His earthly friends. St. Peter's denial is recalled to the apostle His little flock are His brethren. The Cross had not stamped out, but stamped in, all that had gone before. The Resurrection had brought new life, had not abolished the old, but preserved it. The permanence, the identity, of human affections in the risen state is surely here indicated beyond any possibility of doubt. All that has gone to form the Christ-life and the Christ-love, and to contribute thereto, will remain under revived glory and resurgent blessedness. All the sweet affections and friendships, all the heaven-born recollections, whereby hearts have been bound in the strongest, tenderest bands, sundered awhile by death, shall here find their fullest consecration, their highest development, their perfected resurrection. All that is Christian in every possible development of the Christ-energy, from the highest glories of the greatest saint to the lowest and least stone in the Temple, rose in Him. The thoughts raised thereby are boundless, they burst the limitations of the human mind, enlarged and illuminated by the radiant revelations of the inspired prophets of the new Covenant, of the Apocalypses of the Divine character and working.

The four distinct records of the resurrection life of Christ shed differing, but converging, lights upon that life. Briefly, it may be said that St. Matthew views Jesus from his Jewish point of belief as the risen Messiah, victorious and triumphant, "establishing an external polity upon the basis of the Old Covenant;"[1] and "over all is the light of a glorious majesty, abiding even unto the end."[2] And "he alone notices the humble adoration of the risen Lord before His ascension, and, as if with jealous care, traces to its origin the calumny currently reported among the Jews to this day."[3] St. Mark's account is complicated by the question of the original source of the last verses. That question is still an open one, for weighty names are ranged upon both sides.[4] But even those who reject the verses as a

---

[1] Bp John Wordsworth, "Un   ity Sermons," p. 22.
[2] Westcott, "Study of the Gospels," p 332   [3] Ibid.
[4] Lachmann, Griesbach, Tregelles, Tischendorf, Weiss, Westcott and

THE RESURRECTION AND THE FORTY DAYS.

part of the original Mark accept their canonicity, and so, for our purpose, as trustworthy documentary evidence they may be provisionally admitted. St. Mark is then seen to be filled with the personal energy of the strong Son of God. And the strongest argument on internal grounds for retaining the last section, or regarding it, at all events, as the later work of the same hand, springs from the "moral connection" and unity of tone "between the body of the Gospel and the last and crowning section."[1] St. Luke, according to the uniform drift of his Gospel, depicts the risen Lord as the incarnate Saviour, and connecting the Resurrection with the Passion "unfolds the spiritual necessity by which suffering and victory were united."[2] St. John, on the other hand, great organizer of the Church [3] as he was before and at the time he wrote, dwells upon the Lord in His individual and inner relations with disciples in the interlacings of faith within the communion of saints.

Yet the fourfold picture in itself was inadequate. Outlines of the risen, as of the whole earthly, life, are all that have reached us. For "even the world itself," said the last and greatest witness, "would not contain the books that should be written," if all were told.

Hort reject , Bleek, Lange, Hilgenfeld, Broadus, McLellan, Scrivener, Morison, Cook, Bishops Wordsworth of Lincoln and Salisbury, and Dr. Salmon retain See especially Salmon, p 190 foll , and Schaff, "Companion," p 189

[1] Bishop John Wordsworth, of Salisbury, l. c p., p 23, in an eloquent defence of the retention of the section in the original body of the Gospel.

[2] Westcott, l. c.   [3] In Asia Minor.

CHAPTER XXI.

THE ASCENSION AND AFTER.

> "When fire is kindled on the earth it glows
> In highest heaven, none run uncall'd, none love
> Unloved, below, above,
> Thy works are many, but Thy Name is One."
>
> DORA GREENWELL, "Carmina Crucis."

THE scene fitly closes at Jerusalem. May it not re-open there in the fulness of time? He leads out the witnesses, not to, but towards, Bethany. "To three only had the first Transfiguration been granted. All the apostles are to behold the second, and yet greater, Transfiguration."[1] The traditional scene must be rejected, for it is only half a mile from the city. One of the eastern slopes of Olivet, overhanging Bethany, satisfies the requirements of the narratives. Somewhere here He visibly ascended, accompanied by a choir of prayer, and escorted by a guard of angels. The Blessed One was last seen blessing. Some have supposed that "the nine days of the ascent refer to the nine orders of angels through whom He passed to reign." Let only Dante eyes look into the clouds of glory which roll between the upper and under Church.

> "Ascendit in cœlos, sedet ad dextram Patris."

The glad tidings of the kingdom of God end with the music of uplifted hearts and voices in the Temple, like a far-off ringing of heavenly bells about the feet of the great High Priest. *Sursum corda.*

[1] Archdeacon J. P. Norris.

THE ASCENSION AND AFTER.

The Ascension was an act as strictly necessary as the Resurrection. The ’Αυτοζωή, the very Life could not but return to its own level. And for the disciples it was necessary as supplying the last link in the chain of faith. If Christ came in a supernatural way it was meet that He should leave in a supernatural way. " How could His resurrection have formed, for the disciples, the basis for belief in an eternal life, if it had been subsequently followed by death?"[1] Even if the account had never been given the conviction of the Lord's ascension and continuous life above is the constant presupposition of the disciples' life and worship and work. The evidence of the fact and the evidence of their conviction of the fact are interdependent. And the result of their convictions in themselves and others ends to proof independently the validity of the same.

St. Luke, upon whose mind the before-mentioned allusion to the Ascension,[2] shows how vivid an impression that event made upon his mind, gives a brief summary in the Acts of the great Forty Days in the light of the Ascension and its Pentecostal sequel.

The question of the future developments of Christ's kingdom upon earth is too wide an one for brief treatment. We can only note one or two headings. First, that past progress, inward and outward, past development, inward and outward, is the pledge and the earnest of future. Parallel development of force seems suggested on the side of evil, and foreshadowed upon whole lines of Scripture. The accumulations, the organizations of spiritual activity, motive or latent, both in the realms of the seen and the unseen, increase with the increase of every unit to the one side or the other.

Upon a merely arithmetical basis, the conversion[3] of India at the present rate of Christian increase in comparison with the rate of increase of population is within measurable distance. And if of India, of China and the great races of Central Africa. In both these barely opened doors the signs of future submission to Christ are not wanting.

---

[1] Neander.   [2] Chap ix 51.

[3] The data upon which these views are based are too lengthy to insert, and lead to conclusions quite at variance with Canon Taylor's. Special reference may be made to Sir R. Temple's evidence, "Oriental Experien e ' pp. 134, 135, 142, 143, 161, 162, "India in 1880," and Sir W Hunt r . statistics.

The most difficult problem before the Christian is the conversion of Israel. But even in this peculiar field there is the promise and potency of life from the dead. The Jewish sabbath hymn may be applied in a wholly Christian sense,

> "Thou city of our King! Thou royal shrine!
> Rise from thy ruins! rise once more and shine!
> Soon shall thy tears in the sad vale be o'er!
> Soon shall His mercy bid thee weep no more!"[1]

The language of the Old Testament in regard to the return of the chosen people not only to God, but to their own country also, is read by some in a purely spiritual light in reference to spiritual blessing, but the present writer agrees with a living scholar that "the general tenour of the Old Testament prophetic language with regard to God's treatment of purposes towards the Jews does point to a recovery and a restoration to His favour and to their own country;"[2] and echoes his question with regard to St. Paul's language in the eleventh chapter of the Romans, may the apostle "mean that in the predicted and now visibly incipient decay of faith among Gentile Churches, a movement towards faith in Christ on the part of the Jews, or some considerable portion of them, may revive Christianity in the world; and that, coincidently with the return of the Jews in large numbers, whether with Christward tendencies or otherwise, to their own land, Jerusalem, when the times of the Gentiles shall have been fulfilled, may become once more, through the faith of Christian Jews, the centre of Christian life in the world?" Such would be a Messianic age fulfilling under Christian conditions many of the most sublime previsions of Jewish seers, and the most patriotic aspirations of the higher Rabbinism.

Christian thought cannot stop at the Ascension. Christian revelation itself beckons it further. Christian science rigorously demands a continuity of life and energy. Such life and energy might conceivably be a vanished force. It might upon such ground be held that Christ's relation to the earth had ceased with His departure. But the same record which hands down

---

[1] A Bernstein, "The City of David," p 25
[2] Canon Medd, for a long list of texts *vide* Medd's Bampton Lecture, p. 553, note xvi.

THE ASCENSION AND AFTER.

His departure contains His promises of return by the Spirit, and of His permanent continuance even unto the end of the world, and intimates a development, an increase in the exercise of His powers and functions. In whatever sense, and with whatever power, Jesus was Prophet, Priest, and Sovereign of His people below, initially, the same is He under glorified conditions now. The full and entire discharge of all corresponding and consequent offices and functions belong to Him still. His environment is changed infinitely for the higher. His powers must correspond. What is unchangeable in Him is His Divine Person and Character. What is unchanged in Him, though glorified, is His human Nature, indissolubly annexed to the Divine, which has gone from glory to glory. It is through His human Nature enthroned above that He is the causative force and primitive energy of all the energies of His kingdom.

The sketches of the Acts, the histories and experiences disclosed or implied in the Epistles, both of churches and individuals, supplement the Gospel memoirs They constitute "the Gospel of the Holy Spirit." They are brief typical examples of the heavenly life of Christ transmitting itself through and into earthly lives, characters, ministries, agencies. They are the uplifting of His hand, the stretching out of His arm, the breathing of His breath. He is the Thinker, the Worker, the Saviour, the Reformer, the Preacher, the Pastor, the Organizer, the Teacher, the Unifier.

He is either this or He is out of the world, and out of all relation to it. Here we find the truth which Pantheism distorts ; the Immanence of the Christ in the Church and in the world. Mankind will not be able to abide long in the half-way houses of Theism. Man will find God in Christ everywhere or nowhere. He will see the infinite radiations from the Light of light in all the scattered rays of light, or He will stand in blank blindness before the myriad dance of atoms, the fortuitous rush of impersonal forces, in a world unredeemed, bounded by the infinite dark of the unknowable, a Christless cosmic chaos, and chaotic cosmos. Between faith and faithlessness, hope and hopelessness, love and lovelessness, stands midway the form of a Cross, and the mystery-solving mystery of a Divine Sufferer with outstretched hands !

CHAPTER XXII.

THE CHARACTER OF CHRIST. CHRIST AS A MORAL AND SPIRITUAL WORKER.

"Jesus Christ the same yesterday, and to-day, and for ever" (HEBREWS xiii. 8).

Miracles morally conditioned—Jesus Christ a spiritual miracle—Strength of right will—His originality, negative and positive—Authoritativeness—Placed humanity upon the throne of the cosmos, and made moral and spiritual interests supreme—Gave a moral ideal, and a moral dynamic—Individualism—Universalism—Women—Children — Practical every-day morality—Consistency—New virtues and graces—Faith—Hope—Love—Humility—Truth—Religion of the Body—Unification of religion and morality—Prayerfulness—Self-assertion of sinlessness.

THE author of "Supernatural Religion" thinks that he has caught the Christian apologist in a vicious circle, when he says, "that the whole argument rests upon miracles which have nothing to rest upon themselves but the Revelation." But the statement is a begging of the question. Christianity rests as upon a foundation-stone upon the character of Jesus Christ. The character, the life of Jesus Christ appears to the honest seeker after truth to be a spiritual miracle, to be the spiritual miracle of history. Upon His character revealed in His life, and His life flowing out of His character the whole historic structure of the faith hangs. Physical miracles are but one expression of His character, and one of the many-sided exhibitions of His energy. They constitute, therefore, one line of evidence, and unquestionably they belong to the substance and texture of the revelation. But no candid thinker can impose upon them the whole weight of truth.

THE CHARACTER OF CHRIST.

Once admitting the supernaturalness of Christ as a personal spiritual force, the admission of supernatural in the physical region follows, as the less contained in the greater, the part in the whole, to any but the believer in the purely mechanical. When we further examine the miracles which disturb the phenomenal order of the world, as we understand it, we cannot escape the inference that they are spiritually conditioned. In no one single case can the mere manifestation of power for its own sake be detected. There is always a moral background. The currents of moral causation set those of physical effect. Moral conditions are annexed to the whole machinery of miracle, from the lesser ones of healing, which were, so to speak, the letting out of His own spiritual and physical health into the diseased spiritual and physical organisms of His patients, to the supreme miracle of His own Resurrection, which vindicated the truth of His claims to be the Lord of life and death, and the Master of an eternal life which no physical dissolution touched.

We further notice a strict principle of economy in the working of His miracles. Granting Him the power, how rarely He used it! How many needs were left unsatisfied, how many sufferers unhealed, how many evidential forces held back, even during His official life, and during His private life, the silence of self-control, the majestic, unhasting calm of those—

"Who only stand and wait,"

till a higher Power bids them wait no more, but work!

No one who harbours critical doubts of the verifiable testimony of the Gospels disputes the fact of Christ's life. If the character depicted in the Gospels was not His historical character, the miracle of conceiving and exhibiting His character must be transferred to the four Evangelists, and to the writers of the Epistles. This is to reject a smaller miracle in order to accept a much greater one. It has been reserved for Bruno Bauer to exemplify such a *reductio*, not *ad absurdum*, but *ad absurdissimum*, when he put forth in the year 1879 a book in which Seneca and Philo of Alexandria are averred to be the real founders of Christianity! Such criticism is its own refutation, and damages both moral and intellectual respect for the ultra-critical school all along the line, just as a bad professing Christian often does more harm than an open opponent.

We see in Jesus Christ more than in any one who ever lived the majestic strength of a self-determining will, perfectly bent on perfect ends. He was right Will incarnate. His personal causality was independent of His surroundings. He did not adapt Himself, except under the physical limitations of His real human Nature, to circumstances; He adapted circumstances to Hill will. He commanded them as their lawful Lord, subject in all times and places to the Will above. He lifted, He transformed the good; the evil He put down, He destroyed. Even His enemies never accused Him of being the tool of any party or person. His independence was acknowledged while it was condemned. In His life conscience sat upon a throne, threatened by a host of claimants, unshaken for a moment. In the court of His conscience the absolute rule of duty reigned—for duty was synonymous with the dear Will of His Father.

The moral creativeness of Jesus is admitted by unbelievers. But the absolute contrariety of His moral spirit, His authoritativeness, His temper, and His very words fairly taken in their context, to all the moral environment of the time, Pharisaic, Sadducaic, Essene, or Gentile, is fatal to any theory of its human derivation. The only moral teacher who approached the outer edge of His conceptions was the Baptist. But the Baptist never rose above the level of the prophets, and every word he spake sprang from legal roots. And the Baptist towered morally above his fellows, for he occupied the moral platform of the prophets while the Judaism of the day had sunk to the Rabbinical levels, both negatively and positively. The negative ideal was "to keep one's self from sin, not a positive one, to do good upon the earth."[1] While the positive ideal of devotion to the Law resulted in traditionalism and externalism, and the narrowest national and individual selfishness. "The Creator of heaven and earth becomes the manager of a petty scheme of salvation; the living God descends from His throne to make way for the Law. The Law thrusts itself in everywhere; it commands and blocks up the access to heaven; it regulates and sets limits to the under-

---

[1] Wellhausen, "History of Israel," p. 509.

THE CHARACTER OF CHRIST.

standing of the Divine working on earth. As far as it can, it takes the soul out of religion and spoils morality.[1]

Jesus showed indisputable originality as a moral Teacher, both negatively and positively. Negatively by rejecting the most approved teachers and rulers of thought of the time, by His polemics again externalism, by His reversing the moral positions of Pharisee and publican or sinner, and His opposition to mere traditionalism. Positively His originality consisted both in what must have seemed to His enemies a reactionary return to the primitive fountains of inspiration and revelation, an insistance upon the eternal validity of the moral law, and by superadding to it not a crust of overriding tradition, but a new height and breadth and depth, new sanctions, new promises, new penalties. There was no break with the old Law; there was expansion; there was development. Such expansion and development were not natural. The natural development had been downwards towards decay and deterioration. Rabbinism is the proof result; Hillel the finest flower. It was entirely supernatural, as the expression of a superhuman mind under the impetus of superhuman force. "Out of the covenant God of Israel grew the Father; out of the dignity of Israel, the dignity of man; out of the national fellowship, human love; out of the theocracy, the universal kingdom of God; out of the law of the two tables, with an omission of the sacrificial statutes, the service of the moral act of the heart."[2] This advance in ideas is tremendous measured from the highest height and purest purity of the old Covenant teaching; from the debased, adulterated teaching of a generation in Israel perverse and adulterous, and outside Israel corruption itself, the leap was infinite. It was a revolution, or rather a new creation. And as the teaching towered above contemporaneous teaching, so did the Life much more than ower above contemporaneous lives. The Lawgiver outdid His own law. The highest non-Christian ethical teaching, on the other hand, found and finds no adequate expression in the life. Ethical ideals are not lived, is the uniform complaint both of preacher and of disciple. *Video meliora proboque deteriora sequor.* Oh wretched man that I am, who can deliver me? without the unsaying answer ere the question has left the lips;

[1] Wellhausen. [2] Keim, vi. 429

I thank God—and how thank I God?—through Jesus Christ our Lord.

Another aspect of His originality was His authoritativeness. There had been strong authoritativeness in the illustrious line of the prophets. One after another had claimed to be the accredited organ of God's revelation. One to another had handed on the sure word of prophecy. One from another had received, confirmed, and transmitted to spiritual successors, the awful heritage of benediction and cursing, of promise and of threatening. Yet all had pointed on with hand uplifted to Him who was to come, and would fulfil and sum up, and complete all the preliminaries of prophecy. John the Baptist spake with the same authoritativeness. Yet he and they claimed only the place at the footstool; they were not the Light; they were but lights reflected, derivative. Christ spake with all the authoritativeness of all the prophets, and much more than all. For their authority was impersonal and derivative. His authority was native, personal, primary. They affirmed, *as saith the Lord*. Jesus affirmed, *I say unto you*.

As He transcended the Baptist and the prophets, much more, then, He transcended contemporary teachers. Their highest conception was faithfulness to tradition. They might draw out of their treasure things old, but things new never. The Rabbi was "'a well-plastered pit,' 'filled with the water of knowledge,' 'out of which not a drop could escape.'" The only room for spontaneity was in the manipulation and adaptation of precedents and the infinite subdivision of applications. Memory was the supreme intellectual virtue.

The moral and intellectual authoritativeness of Christ was original and self-dependent. It sprang from His Divine certitude. Christ had spiritual and intellectual certitude. Truth was to Him unclouded. It flowed from Him as from a pure perennial fountain fed from the Divine deeps. He had no wrestle with doubts, no hesitations, for His mind was perfectly poised. No fallacies could ever mislead Him, for they are spun of the Spirit of error which could find nothing in Him. But for His immediate contact with absolute truth He could never have apprehended the true Messianic ideal at a time when it was lost and had to be recovered. Perfectly humble, perfectly simple, perfectly sincere, He uniformly asserted, and uniformly acted upon the assertion, that He knew the truth, that indeed

He was the Truth. All the expansions and developments of truth through the ages in all departments of the knowable are the workings of His mind, the continuous outpourings from the treasures of wisdom and knowledge hidden in Him, and progressively disclosed through the minds He enlightens and leads on to all the truth. While He had immediate native communion with truth He did not slight, but honoured previous teachers. He drew from them words and thoughts. He appealed to historical, to prophetic evidence and instruction. "This day is this Scripture fulfilled in your ears." "Moses and the prophets," "What read ye in the Law?" are phrases constantly on His lips. Often instead of opening some new fountain of truth He turns a questioner to the old flow, the old familiar current coin.

Christ shifted the whole centre of interest in the world. The leading interest in the world became for the first time moral and human, and upon a definite basis. Human nature sprang into a supremacy of position and authority in the cosmos. Man is the explanation of Nature, the crown of its development, the god of its unconscious worship. In the hierarchy of forces he occupies the throne. Such a position was drawn out in the Epistle to the Romans in the great chapter which sees the enfranchisement of Nature implied in the glorious liberty of the children of God, and by a bold personification attributes to Nature a travail rainbowed with hope, and a hope issuing in fruition. Not only was human nature re-established in the dominion over Nature enjoyed before the Fall, but it was brought as a whole, and potentially in all its parts, to the throne of heaven.[1] And the whole process of redemption and glorification was transacted in the moral and spiritual region, upon moral and spiritual ground. "All the relations between it (human nature) and God became immediate and direct, not incident to it merely as part of the universal organism, but due to its own special state and essence ; so completely that they would remain the same were the visible frame of things to vanish and leave us alone in the infinite Presence."[2] If by "immediate and direct" be understood in and through Christ, the above statement is absolutely true for the Christian. Human

---

[1] Conf. Aristotle's splendid aspiration ἀλλ', ἐφ ὅσον ἐνδέχεται (sc. χρή) ἀθανατίζειν, N. Eth. x. 7.

[2] Prof. Martineau, "Types of Ethical Theory," i. p. 14 foll.

nature was elevated at every point, at every interest, pre-eminently in all its moral relations. In fact, under Christianity moral and spiritual relations penetrate and pervade all other, and measure their importance.

Christ elevated human nature in itself. He also armed it with powers of self-development. In the first place, He set before humanity a supreme and absolute ideal. This ideal is final, and absorbs and concentres all minor and incidental ideals. It is the ideal of His own character and life Divine seen under human conditions. This ideal was His own conception and His own creation.

More than this. It is one thing to exhibit an ideal, a very different thing to reach it. An art student may admire Michael Angelo, but does not dream of rivalling him. An ideal becomes a stimulus to the gifted, but the despair of the many. The Law had erected an ideal, and ended in repelling instead of attracting.

Christ then gave a new power. It was not enough to set an example for imitation, not indeed outward, as some rare spirits have understood it, and rightly it may be for themselves, for what Christian would have spared a Francis of Assisi to the Church?—but universally applicable as to its spirit and relation, Godward and manward. That power is Christ Himself, and the Spirit of Christ as an inward energy and life. "The powers of the God-united humanity are made available for us men through the Spirit. The life of the Incarnate has not vanished from the earth; it is perpetuated through spiritual channels in the race of the redeemed. The 'new Man,' like the 'old man,' exhibits Himself as a self-propagating type, self-propagating by its own laws, 'having its seed in itself, like every lower form or stage of life which had yet appeared."[1] The moral and spiritual self-developments of mankind hinge wholly upon the incorporation of the Christ self in each self, and the appropriation of His nature according to His prescribed and certified media of grace.

Christ gave a new sanction and meaning to the individual. The individual was the individual of God's love and care, and of the Son of man's, and consequently of man's. The individual was not lost in a crowd. Primitive society was a collection of families. Individual rights beyond the privileged classes were unknown outside the Jewish world. Aristotle regarded the

[1] *Church Quarterly Review*, July, 1883, pp. 292, 293.

slave as a human tool. Half the Roman Empire at least were at this time, it has been computed, in slavery. Even in Israel the ignorant Am-ha-aretz in Rabbinical eyes were accursed. Christ both declared the principle and acted upon the principle, of the sacredness of each separate individual in the eyes of the All-Father. Much of His time was given to the teaching of individuals. He did not deal only with masses. Rather His chief care was the individual training of the apostles.

Nor was the individual elevated as an isolated individual, but organically, in his relation to the race. Racial differences and national prejudices were ignored. Jew and Samaritan, Syro-Phenician and Greek and Peræan, were all welcomed into the kingdom of God. The Son of David was the Son of man. Nations and kingdoms were to enter into a new nation, a spiritual Israel, a catholic society. With the Zealots, who were the representatives of extreme nationalism politically, as the Pharisees were religiously, we do not find any trace of sympathy. The *de facto* Roman Government was recognized as *de jure*. The threefold inscription of scorn upon the Cross was one of the unconscious prophecies of hate. The Gentiles were uniformly regarded as unclean by all Jews, just as Englishmen by Brahmans. Christ opened the door to the Gentiles during His life, and commanded all nations to be baptized. All " hedges " and disabilities He broke down.

The attitude of Jesus Christ towards women was the germ of their whole after enfranchisement. ' The Mishna deliberately and constantly places women on a lower level than men, both legally and socially."[1] Jesus Christ treated the outcast Samaritaness with respect, was ministered to in life by women of their substance, and suffered His Body to be ministered to by women in death. He was the personal friend and guest of Mary and Martha. He had mercy and gentle words for the penitent harlot. Above all, He was born of a woman. And to His mother He rendered filial obedience for thirty years. His dealing with women has already been touched upon and contrasted with non-Christian practice.

Christ had sweet and gracious dealings with children. No children found place, or have left any record if they did, in the society of John the Baptist. Jesus loved them. He gave them

[1] Bennett, p 67

the Rabbi's blessing and touch. He observed their games, and drew illustrations of teaching from children playing in the market-place. They followed Him to the greenswards of the wilderness, and a little boy supplied the food of the five thousand. The children cried, "Hosanna," in the Temple. One child, unique in her history, He raised from the dead. Tenderness to children was no new thing even for fallen human nature. We see it in animals' affection for the young. Christ transfigured and renewed all natural affection. His intense desire for the spiritual regeneration and education of children breathes in His burning words against any who should offend one of these little ones; and in His sweet revelation of their angels.

Just as in His lowliness He raised women and children to new possibilities of honour in the future, and showed His reverence and honour to the weak, so His life and character revealed an every-day homeliness. His teaching was a living thing for every day, a living spirit which would pour oil and wine into the wounds of an injured man, which would forgive a brother his trespasses, which would pray for daily bread, which declared war with selfishness and covetousness in all shapes.

Consistency is another mark of Jesus' character and view of life. We entirely fail to see any contradictions, or discords, or any gradation of ideas, such as Renan has asserted but not proved. There was progress in revelation of ideas according to maturity of receptiveness, but no change in His own attitude or purpose. The Father; the Cross. These were the keywords from first to last. Wherever He was, He was always the same—in different places, societies, ethical sceneries, "the same soul, the same doctrine, the same faith in God the Father, the same religion of the love of God, of purity of heart, of renunciation of the earth, of heavenly hopes." [1]

In the sphere of His spiritual creativeness Jesus added new virtues, both in example and precept. Faith was the one word which summed up the virtue of psalmists and prophets. But faith received newer and higher meanings and applications, and was submitted to severer strains. Jesus Himself showed an uniform temper of faith in God; from first to last He trusted absolutely in His Father. When He committed His soul into

[1] E. Caro, "L'Idée de Dieu," chapitre iii.

His hands, it was the last act in the whole life of surrender. What He did He required, faith in God, faith in Himself. This was a necessary presupposition. Faith entered upon a new field. It formed the basis of all Christian life, the foundation of all morals. With faith, hope and love entered upon a new history. But this subject would require a treatise to itself. Let this remark suffice, faith, hope, and love, for Him and His bare both Godward and manward. He trusted in God, He knew man best of all, man's weakness, falseness, treachery, yet trusted too in man. To man He committed His work, His cause. He hoped in God, He hoped in man. He loved God, He loved man. The so-called service of man began with His life, His teaching, His death. He gave man a new interest in his brother. Neighbour was but one example of a word baptized into new meanings.

Humility, as has often been observed, was a newly created virtue, born in Christ's example, and bred in His teaching. " The characteristic of humility and submission," as Lotze [1] has observed, " that is lacking even in the most mournful expressions of this sense of finiteness in antiquity, was brought for the first time by Christianity into the heart of men, and with it hope came too. It was a redemption for men to be able to tell themselves that human strength is not sufficient for the accomplishment of its own ideals." Truthfulness, in life and speech, was certainly enforced by Christ with new sanctions and guarantees. " I am the Truth," He certified, and Christendom has not yet got to the bottom of that statement. The Spirit of Truth He promised to send to lead into all the truth.

A world of new religion began for the human body. Christ had supreme respect for matter, and for the human body, as the " roof and crown " of the material world. He showed it by His healings, generally by bodily touch. He showed by His bodily suffering and reverent burial. Above all, He showed it by His bodily resurrection. He showed it by His stress upon purity. This stands in the sharpest contrast to ultra-asceticism which treats the body as wholly evil, an idea so prevalent in Oriental religions. The death-bed of the eminent Buddhist pilgrim, Huian-Thsang, gives a striking example. " His friends are all invited to assemble round his couch and take a joyous leave of his 'impure and despicable body,' which, after having played its

[1] " Microcosmus," Eng transl , ii. p 270.

part, is lost to him for ever."[1] Hinduism, through all its opposing forms of thought, agrees in one desire, the deliverance from the body.[2] Christ came to purify and redeem body as well as soul, and to set both in an eternity of inseparable glory, where His own body reigns. His body, He taught, was the Temple, which destroyed in "three days would rise again." Such teaching bore its fruit in St. Paul's dicta about the bodies of the redeemed Christians being the temple of the Holy Spirit.

As in the redemption of the body, so in all ways, Jesus Christ effected an alliance and a permanent reconciliation between religion and morality. Contemporary religion consisted for the most part in ceremonialism. Jesus purified the Temple of traffic. The act was typical of His purification of all religion towards God. He found a moral factor in all religion. He enshrined forgiveness and brotherly love in the prayer of prayers. It is needless to contrast here Hinduism with its immoral divinities, its faith without works, its worshipper, who by offering up "an animal duly consecrated by Agni, and by Soma, is therewith able to buy off all deities at once;"[3] as needless to contrast Mohammedanism. Whether modern moral systems in declared antagonism to Christianity, such as Comtism, non-Christian forms of Socialism and the Service of Man, are more than eclectic fragments, borrowing without acknowledgment from Christianity, as when Comte, "finally getting his Positive doctrine 'free of theological oppression and metaphysical dryness, and condensing it into a maxim that shall hold it all, alights, unconscious of their source, upon the words of Jesus, 'It is more blessed to give than to receive,'"[4] whether such systems are capable of transcending Christianity and superseding it in the struggle for existence, is for the disciples of such systems to prove.

The very intellectual enfranchisement which is enjoyed by Christian and anti-Christian thinkers is a debt to Him who offered stimulus to thought as well as to feeling, who redeemed the intellect as well as the heart, whose after-course through the world, so far as it is traceable in the workings of Christians, has been a constant, steady progress towards

[1] Hardwick, "Christ and other Masters," Religions of China, p. 344.
[2] Cf Rev. E G Punchard, "Hinduism," *Mission Life*, Feb., 1880.
[3] Hardwick, "Christ and other Masters," p. 228.
[4] Prof Martineau, "Types of Ethical Theory," 1. p. 475.

CHRIST AS A MORAL AND SPIRITUAL WORKER. 225

the enfranchisement of all right thinking, right speaking, right doing, and the gradual overthrow of the legions of error. The Christian who works from a basis of belief in the guidance of the Spirit of truth, in individuals in less degree, in collective Christianity in a greater degree, has a sure intellectual as well as moral standing ground; whereas the non-Christian has only some man or system of thought to fall back upon, who, or which, must, in the invariable experience of the past, give way to new men and new systems.

Jesus would not have been true man if He had not shown a spirit of prayer. Prayer is the life breath of the Christian, and cannot have been less to the Son of man. The Divine indwelling did not exempt Him from the natural language of man conscious of God. Times of especial prayer were times of especial human need and signal work, times also of extraordinary Divine manifestation. It was while He prayed at the Baptism that the Holy Spirit descended; after a night of prayer that the Twelve Apostles were chosen; in prayer that He was transfigured; in the Gethsemane prayer that an angel comforted Him. It was the sight apparently of Jesus in prayer that prompted the prayer to be taught a form of prayer. At times He would give thanks before what He asked for to human eyes came to pass. "His prayer was the middle point of His activity, the holy altar upon which He ever consecrates and offers anew His humanity to God, and this is always in turn penetrated and illumined by the Divine."[1]

The most remarkable of all Christ's moral characteristics was His absence of any sense of sin, or moral shortcoming. Unlike any other moral teacher, He never expressed any moral regrets. He never, like the best of Israel's sons, a Moses, a David, a Nehemiah, a Daniel, bowed Himself in penitential confession. He not only knew His own sinlessness, but He asserted it; asserted it as a necessary factor in His self-revelation, self-vindication, self-evidence, challenging His enemies to convince Him of sin. And the question still rings from His lips. And the adoring hearts and bowed heads, and triumphant hopes of millions of Christians, past and present, in life, and in death, in prayer and in working, whether they eat or drink, whether they sleep or wake, or whatever they

[1] Dorner, "System of Christian Doctrine," iii p. 370.

do, bend before Him in His moral innocence, His spiritual strength, His inexhaustible love, His omnipresent energy, as still and for ever true Son of man and Son of God, as the centre and spring of their life in this world and their hope in the world to come.

THE END.

www.ingramcontent.com/pod-product-compliance
Lightning Source LLC
Chambersburg PA
CBHW071943160426
43198CB00011B/1524